ARCO
CLERICAL EXAMS HANDBOOK

E. P. Steinberg

Macmillan • USA

Second Edition

Macmillan General Reference
A Simon & Schuster Macmillan Company
1633 Broadway
New York, NY 10019

Copyright © 1996, 1994 by Arco Publishing,
a division of Simon & Schuster, Inc.
All rights reserved
including the right of reproduction
in whole or in part in any form

An Arco Book

MACMILLAN is a registered trademark of Macmillan, Inc.
ARCO is a registered trademark of Prentice-Hall, Inc.

ISBN: 0-02-861056-3

Manufactured in the United States of America

1 2 3 4 5 6 7 8 9 10

CONTENTS

Introduction to Clerical Careers 1

Part One
About the Jobs and How to Qualify for Them

Federal Clerical Jobs 7
Postal Clerks 19
Clerical Jobs with the State 40
County Clerical Employment 44
Clerical Employment in the Courts 46
Municipal Clerical Positions 48
Clerical Employment in the Private Sector 50
Test-Taking Techniques 52

Part Two
Sample Examinations for Practice

Federal Clerical Examination 59
U.S. Postal Service Clerk, Distribution Clerk (Machine)
   & Mark-up Clerk (Automated) Exam 93
U.S. Postal Service Clerk-Typist and Clerk-Stenographer Exam 129
The Typing Test 171
Senior Office Typist Exam (Court System) 175
Municipal Office Aide Exam 195
Typical Private Sector Clerical Examination 218

iii

INTRODUCTION TO CLERICAL CAREERS

Clerical work offers the proverbial "foot in the door" to thousands of occupations in government and in the private sector. Clerical work, in its own right, is clean and pleasant. Best of all, entry-level clerical work can open numerous different paths upwards to supervisory and administrative work or to other, totally nonclerical jobs within the organization.

Clerical work is an ideal entry point at which young people can begin their careers and mature adults can reenter the job market after years of absence. There also is opportunity for career change into less physically strenuous office work, for those whose earlier work demanded greater strength and stamina. Clerical work thus lends itself to those seeking semiretirement as well.

An alert clerical worker is in an ideal position to learn about the operations of the place in which he or she is employed. If the workplace is a government office, the clerical worker learns the functions of the office, the services delivered, the chain of command, the daily operations, and the ultimate mission of that office and the agency of which it is a unit. If the workplace is an office of an organization that provides a service to the public, the clerical worker's learning beyond the job at hand is similar to that of the government clerical worker. If the organization produces a product, then the clerical worker learns about the product itself, about the business of producing and distributing the product, and about advertising, marketing, and sales. Constant exposure to the business of the office, whatever it may be, allows the clerical worker to absorb knowledge while carrying out assigned duties. The job itself provides the education and background for moving ahead.

From a clerical job in government, a natural progression might be into higher-level, more complex clerical work with ever greater responsibility; or growth might be into different aspects of office work; or promotion might entail taking on supervisory duties with an eventual role in the ranks of administration.

A clerical job in the private sector opens even more avenues for growth and diversification of work. As the clerical worker grows more familiar with the firm, he or she may grow in any of the directions of the clerical worker in government, or may go into manufacturing itself, into the business aspects of the company, or out into the field as a member of the sales force. A clerical worker in one business tends to be exposed to many other businesses in the course of daily work. The clerical worker in one field may find that the business of a client or customer offers greater fulfillment and may move upward by moving to another company altogether.

Under the umbrella term "clerical work," there are hundreds of different jobs. There are filing jobs, typing jobs, stock-taking jobs, tabulating jobs, distribution jobs, bookkeeping jobs, data entry jobs, word processing jobs, statistical jobs, stenographic jobs—and the list goes on and on.

As varied as the types of jobs is the nature of employers. The Federal Government offers a wide range of clerical employment; so do state, county, and municipal governments. The U.S. Postal Service, an independent agency of the Federal Government, employs many clerical workers for processing and distributing mail. And jobs with private employers are too numerous to be categorized.

The U.S. Postal Service deserves an extra word. You may never have thought of the Postal Service in terms of a clerical career or any career. Indeed, your image of the Postal Service may be limited to your local letter carrier. However, the Postal Service is a good employer, and it affords excellent flexibility in terms of changing careers within the agency.

Employees of the Postal Service are Federal employees who enjoy the very generous benefits offered by the government. These benefits include an automatic raise at least once a year, regular cost-of-living adjustments, liberal paid vacation and sick leave, life insurance, hospitalization, and the opportunity to join a credit union. At the same time, the operation of the Postal Service is businesslike and independent of politics. A postal worker's job is secure even though administrations may change. An examination system is used to fill vacancies. The examination system provides opportunities for those who are able and motivated to enter the Postal Service and to advance within it.

Since postal employment is so popular, entry is very competitive. In some parts of the country certain exams are given as seldom as once every three years. The resulting list is used to fill vacancies as they occur during the next three years. An individual who has been employed by the Postal Service for at least a year may ask to take the exam for any position and, if properly qualified, may fill a vacancy ahead of a person whose name is on the regular list. (The supervisor does not need to grant the request to take a special exam to fill a vacancy, but such permission is usually given to employees with good performance records who have served an adequate period in their current positions.) It is even possible to change careers within the Postal Service. A distribution clerk might take an exam to enter personnel work; a mark-up clerk might aspire to and work up to a position as postal inspector. If the exam for the precise position that you want will not be administered for some time, it might be worthwhile to take the exam for another position in hopes of entering the Postal Service and then moving from within. There is never a fee for applying for a postal examination, so if you want to work for the Postal Service take every exam for which you are qualified.

Salaries, hours, and some other working conditions as well are subject to frequent change. The postal workers have a very effective union that bargains for them and gains increasingly better conditions. At the time of your employment, you should make your own inquiry as to salary, hours, and other conditions as they apply to you. Job descriptions and requirements are less subject to change.

This book offers you an overview of the world of clerical work, a brief introduction to some major employers and their hiring requirements, and in-depth description of and practice with a number of widely used clerical employment examinations. Some of the examinations in this book are real examinations or official sample examinations; others are model examinations closely patterned on the actual exams. Timing, level of difficulty, question styles, and scoring methods all conform closely to the examinations for which they are meant to prepare. And a special feature of this book is that all the correct answers are explained.

If you are career or job shopping at this time, you should start at the beginning and read through all of Part One very carefully. In Part One you will learn about many job opportunities. We hope you will be inspired and excited and will be motivated to apply for, study for, and land one of those jobs. If Part One helps you to narrow your area of interest, then concentrate on the Part Two exams that will help you prepare for the job you want. If you are still wide open, give equal attention to each exam. And even if you are clear as to which job you really want, it would be wise to try your hand at all of the exams in this book. Practice with the variety of test questions can only help when you must take one of these, or similar, examinations.

When you do take the sample exams, try to set aside the full measure of time to take the exam at one sitting. Time yourself accurately (a stop watch or a kitchen timer will work well) and stop working when the time is up. If you have not completed all of the questions when time expires, stop anyway. Check your answers against the provided correct answers and score your paper. Then continue with the remaining questions to get all the practice you can. Carefully study all the answer explanations, even those for questions that you answered correctly. By reading all of the explanations, you can gain greater insight into methods of answering questions and the reasoning behind the correct choices.

Part One

About the Jobs and How to Qualify for Them

FEDERAL CLERICAL JOBS

Jobs in over 60 different clerical fields are filled using the Federal Clerical Examination. These jobs, like many other jobs in the Federal Government, are in the General Schedule (or GS), which assigns different "grades" to jobs which have different levels of responsibility or require different levels of experience or education.

There are jobs at various grade levels in each clerical field. Generally, all you need to qualify for jobs at the entry grades is to have graduated from high school (or some previous job experience). Some of the occupations at the entry level also require specific skills, such as typing or shorthand.

As you gain experience, you become eligible for promotion to higher level, more specialized clerical and administrative jobs. You can also enter the Federal Government for the first time at these higher grade levels if you already have the specialized experience or additional education these jobs require.

Except for the clerk-stenographer, the entry level for clerical jobs is GS-2, and initial hires are usually made at either GS-2 or GS-3. The entry level for clerk-stenographers is GS-3, and initial hires are usually made at GS-3 or GS-4. Appointment at the higher grade levels is made for applicants who have appropriate experience or education above the high school level. Experience from summer jobs and part-time jobs is often appropriate. Therefore, many applicants are eligible for entry at the higher grades without additional education.

Following are descriptions of some of the jobs in the clerical field.

Clerk-Typist

Most hiring at the entry level in the clerical field is done for clerk-typist positions, which combine clerical work with typing duties. Thousands of these clerk-typist positions are filled each year, particularly in areas where a number of Federal agencies are located. Vacancies are constantly occurring in these positions as employees are promoted to higher-graded positions, transfer to other jobs, or leave for other reasons.

Clerk-Stenographer

Clerk-stenographer jobs combine clerical tasks with both dictation and typing duties. There are usually many job openings in areas where there are large concentrations of Federal employees, and many opportunities for movement into higher grades.

Office Automation Clerk

Office automation clerks and assistants operate personal computers to perform word processing tasks, desktop publishing, database management, financial spreadsheets, electronic bulletin boards, etc. This work can also be carried out on mainframe computers through telecommunications equipment. This occupation is new, and office automation clerks are taking the place of clerk-typists in many organizations.

Data Transcriber

The job title "data transcriber" covers positions which involve the input or recording of different types of data into data processing files. Several thousand entry-level data transcribers are usually hired each year, and the number of jobs in the field is increasing as more use is made of automated systems.

Clerk

The title "clerk" covers many specific positions in which typing, stenographic, or data entry skills either are not required or are not an important part of the job. (In a few cases, one of these skills is important, in which case it is included in the job title.) Opportunities at the entry level in these fields are more limited than for typist, stenographer, and data transcriber jobs because more of these positions require specialized experience or training. However, entry-level opportunities do exist in some fields, as described below.

There are thousands of general clerks, such as mail and file clerks and miscellaneous clerks, who perform a variety of typical office and record-keeping tasks. Most of these jobs are filled at the lower entry levels. There are also many entry-level openings for sales store checkers. These clerks work in a variety of store-like situations, usually on military bases or in agency supply stores.

There are a variety of clerical jobs, such as the calculating machine operator, which involve the use of some type of office machine. Many of these jobs are filled at the entry level, although they often require special skills and training and have additional selection requirements specific to each job. There are several hundred of these office machine operator types of jobs.

Jobs in the following fields are usually above the entry level. However, some entry-level jobs are available. There are many jobs in the personnel field, supporting the professional personnel staff. There are good opportunities for advancement to technical and administrative jobs in this field. There are opportunities in the fields of supply, transportation, and stock control. Most of these positions exist in military and supply agencies. Finally, there are clerical positions in accounting, payroll, and fiscal work. For example, payroll clerks keep records and do other work related to issuing paychecks, and cash processing clerks handle and track cash disbursements.

JOB BENEFITS

Salaries for Federal employees under the General Schedule are set to reflect non-Federal pay levels in similar occupations. Periodic pay increases are made for competent employees. Promotions, which are based on increases in responsibility and demonstration of increased experience and skill, result in more significant salary increases.

Paydays occur every two weeks. Deductions are made for Federal, state, and local taxes as required, as well as a percentage of salary for retirement purposes. (New Federal employees are covered under a combined Social Security and supplemental retirement program. This retirement system gives workers flexibility to move between private industry and Federal employment without losing basic retirement benefits.)

Group health insurance and life insurance are available at reduced rates since the Government pays part of the cost. Vacation benefits begin at 13 working days a year for most new employees who are working full time, and increase as length of experience increases. Most full-time employees also earn 13 days of sick leave with pay each year, regardless of their length of service.

Training for increased responsibility is often provided on the job, and employees are encouraged to continue their own training activities. In addition, the Government sponsors some formal training courses and sometimes pays for outside training which is directly related to improving job performance.

Selection Procedures

How and Where To Apply

Examinations for clerical jobs are given directly by the individual Federal agencies whenever they are ready to hire. Sometimes examinations will be announced and given for all clerical occupations at one time, and sometimes separate examinations for specific jobs are announced. Clerical examinations are given frequently because of the large number of available jobs.

Information about applying for these and other Federal jobs is provided by Federal Job Information Centers throughout the country. These centers are listed in local telephone directories under "U.S. Government." You may also directly contact the personnel offices of Federal agencies located in your area to find out if they are in the process of hiring and where they suggest you take the examination.

Selection Requirements

Selection requirements for the clerical occupations in the Federal Government are based on studies of the training, experience, and skills required for successful job performance at the different grade levels. Job applicants must meet the education or experience requirements, show evidence of having the required skills, and, for entry at GS-2 through 4 (GS-3 through 5 for clerk-stenographers), pass a job-related written test.

Ratings

Applicants who meet the minimum experience and education requirements and skill levels are given numerical ratings based on their written test scores. Applicants must pass the written test in order to receive a rating. Qualified veterans of the military service have additional points added to their qualifying ratings.

Written Tests

The written tests for clerical occupations measure the verbal and clerical skills needed for success in these jobs. In general, the same written test battery is used for all clerical jobs except data transcriber and sales store checker. This battery consists of two tests: a Verbal Tasks Test and a Clerical Tasks Test. Data transcriber and sales store checker applicants take only the Clerical Tasks Test. (There are other situations with other test requirements. These generally occur when a particular agency is testing applicants for clerical jobs located only in its offices, or for seasonal rather than permanent positions. For example, the Internal Revenue Service hires many seasonal clerical employees and uses a modified test for those positions.)

Because of these possible differences in requirements, you should check the specific examination announcement for each position in which you are interested to confirm the test battery you will have to take.

As long as a modified examination was not used, once you have passed the written test you do not have to take it again to apply for other clerical jobs. Nor do you have to reestablish that you meet the minimum experience or education requirements or have the required skills. (However, your rating can expire after a certain period of time; this will be shown on the rating form.)

Any questions you have about the tests you need to take, how your rating can be used, and whether it has expired can be answered by the Federal Job Information Center serving your area.

SKILL REQUIREMENTS

When a job requires typing skill, you must be able to type accurately at 40 words per minute. When dictation skill is required, you must be able to transcribe dictation accurately at 80 words per minute. GS-2 data transcribers must be able to type accurately at 20 words per minute, and GS-3 and 4 data transcribers must be able to type accurately at 25 words per minute. Stenographer applicants may use any system of taking and transcribing dictation they wish.

Skill requirements may be measured in several different ways. The most frequently used method is the proficiency certificate. These certificates may be issued by schools and other authorized training organizations and by some state employment services. If this method is used, applicants are told where they can obtain a certificate if they do not already have one. Applicants with proficiency certificates usually do not have to take further tests to demonstrate their skill levels.

Another method which is sometimes used is self-certification by applicants. In this process, an applicant signs a statement that he or she meets the skill requirements for the job. Agencies usually require applicants who have self-certified their skills to take a performance test before they are hired.

APPLICANTS WITH DISABILITIES

Persons with disabilities are encouraged to apply for positions in the Federal Government. There are Selective Placement Specialists in OPM offices and in the agencies in your area who are responsible for helping applicants with disabilities to take advantage of the available employment opportunities.

Applicants must be physically and mentally able to perform the essential functions of the job for which they apply. Federal agencies must make reasonable accommodation to the known physical and mental limitations of a qualified applicant, including during the test process. Many test batteries have been modified for visually disabled, motor disabled, deaf, and learning disabled applicants. If you have one or more disabilities, you should state the nature of your disability on your test application card so that special testing arrangements can be made.

The Federal Clerical Examination consists of two separately timed sections, a Verbal Tasks Test and a Clerical Tasks Test.

The Verbal Tasks Test

WHAT THE TEST IS ABOUT

The Verbal Tasks Test includes questions in such areas as spelling, meaning, and relationship of words; recognition of sentences which are grammatically correct; and reading, understanding, and using written material.

These test tasks relate to a variety of job tasks, such as proofreading and correcting typed copy, using instruction manuals, organizing new files of related materials, and carrying out written instructions.

There are 85 questions—25 on word meaning, 20 on word relationships, 20 on spelling, 10 on grammar, and 10 on reading. There are a few questions of each type on each page of the test. For each question, you will select the best answer from among a set of suggested answers.

How the Test Is Administered

Each applicant is given a copy of the test booklet with sample questions and an answer sheet. Three minutes are allowed to study the directions and answer the sample questions. The separate answer sheet is then used for recording answers to the test. Exactly 35 minutes are allowed for the test.

Here are the official directions and sample questions. You may allow yourself more than three minutes to study these now since you are not actually in a testing situation.

Directions: Study the sample questions carefully. Each question has four suggested answers. Decide which one is the best answer. Find the question number on the Sample Answer Sheet. Show your answer to the question by darkening completely the space corresponding to the letter that is the same as the letter of your answer. Keep your mark within the space. If you have to erase a mark, be sure to erase it completely. Mark only one answer for each question. Do NOT mark space E for any question.

1. *Previous* means most nearly

   (A) abandoned   (B) former   (C) timely   (D) younger

2. Just as the procedure of a collection department must be clear-cut and definite, the steps being taken with the sureness of a skilled chess player, so the various paragraphs of a collection letter must show clear organization, giving evidence of a mind that, from the beginning, has had a specific end in view.

   The paragraph best supports the statement that a collection letter should always

   (A) show a spirit of sportsmanship
   (B) be divided into several paragraphs
   (C) be brief, but courteous
   (D) be carefully planned

   Decide which sentence is preferable with respect to grammar and usage suitable for a formal letter or report.

3. (A) They do not ordinarily present these kind of reports in detail like this.
   (B) A report of this kind is not hardly ever given in such detail as this one.
   (C) This report is more detailed than what such reports ordinarily are.
   (D) A report of this kind is not ordinarily presented in this much detail.

   Find the correct spelling of the word and darken the proper answer space. If no suggested spelling is correct, darken space D.

4. (A) athalete   (B) athelete   (C) athlete   (D) none of these

5. SPEEDOMETER is related to POINTER as WATCH is related to

(A) case   (B) hands   (C) dial   (D) numerals

Sample Answer Sheet

1. Ⓐ Ⓑ Ⓒ Ⓓ Ⓔ   4. Ⓐ Ⓑ Ⓒ Ⓓ Ⓔ
2. Ⓐ Ⓑ Ⓒ Ⓓ Ⓔ   5. Ⓐ Ⓑ Ⓒ Ⓓ Ⓔ
3. Ⓐ Ⓑ Ⓒ Ⓓ Ⓔ

The correct answers for questions 1–5 are:

1. **B**   2. **D**   3. **D**   4. **C**   5. **B**

EXPLANATIONS

Sample Question 1. Word meaning questions consist of one given word followed by four different words labeled A, B, C, and D. You are to select the word which has the closest meaning to the word given in the question. It may help if you remember you are looking for the best match among the choices given, but not necessarily a perfect match.

Answering these questions depends upon your knowledge of vocabulary, but there are some steps you can take if you do not recognize the correct answer immediately.

- If you have a general idea about what the given word means, but are having trouble choosing an answer, try using the word in a short sentence. Then, substitute each of the answer choices in the same sentence to see which one seems best to fit the sentence.
- Try to break the given word into parts to see if the suffix (ending) or the prefix (beginning) of the word gives a clue about its meaning.

You could have used the above procedure to answer sample question 1. The correct answer to this question is choice **B**, "former." If you did not know the meaning of "previous," but you remembered that the prefix "pre" usually means "before," you could have used that clue to help you to select choice **B** as the correct answer.

Sample Question 2. The reading questions consist of a paragraph followed by four statements. You read the paragraph first and then select the one statement which is based on information given in the paragraph.

- Do not worry if you are unfamiliar with the subject discussed in the paragraph. You do not need to have any knowledge about the subject of the paragraph since the answer to the question is always given in the paragraph itself.
- Do not worry about whether the correct statement, or any of the incorrect statements, are true. The important thing is that the correct answer is the *only* statement which says the same thing as is said in the paragraph. Some of the other statements may be true, but they are not based on the content of the paragraph.
- To select the correct statement, first eliminate choices which clearly conflict with the paragraph. Then, if you still have two or more choices, look for the specific section of the paragraph which covers the information given in each one of the choices.

- Compare the facts given carefully, until you can eliminate the remaining incorrect choices.

For sample question 2, choice **D** is correct because it is the only choice which states the basic point made in the paragraph. Choice A is meant to draw attention if you did not read the paragraph carefully and remembered only that chess, which is similar to a sport, was mentioned. Choice B would draw attention because the word "paragraphs" was mentioned, but the reading paragraph did not specify that a collection letter should have any particular number of paragraphs. Similarly, the reading paragraph did not say anything about being brief or courteous, so choice C is incorrect.

Sample Question 3. Grammar questions give four versions of a single sentence. Each sentence tries to express the same thought, but only one of them is *grammatically* correct.

- Most of the incorrect sentences are obviously poorly constructed.
- Others have such errors as using singular verbs with plural nouns.
- In the more difficult questions, you must pay attention to smaller details, like the misuse of punctuation, which can make a sentence very difficult to understand.

To answer these questions, first eliminate the sentences you are sure are incorrect. Then compare the remaining ones until you can choose one as being more correct than the others.

- It is possible that one sentence will seem to be correct because it uses the same informal grammar that people often use when talking. However, this type of sentence structure is not suitable for writing.

In sample question 3, choice **D** is correct. The major errors in the other choices are: choice A uses the plurals "these" and "reports" with the singular "kind"; choice B uses "not hardly ever" instead of the preferable "never"; and choice C inappropriately inserts "what" into the sentence.

Sample Question 4. Spelling questions give three spellings of a common word, labeled A, B, and C. Each question also offers the option of "none of these" as choice D. You must decide which one of the three given spellings is correct, or that none of them is correct.

- Sometimes it helps to answer these questions by looking away from the given choices and writing the word yourself on the margin of your test booklet. Then check to see if the spelling you believe is correct is given as one of the choices.

In sample question 4, choice **C** is correct.

Sample Question 5. Word relationship questions give two words which are related in some way, and then give the first word of a second word relationship which you are to complete. You are given four choices of words to complete that relationship. The correct choice is the word which completes that relationship in the way most similar to the relationship in the first pair of words.

To answer these questions, look at the first pair of words and decide what the relationship between the words is. Then choose the answer that best completes that relationship for the second pair of words.

- Remember that the correct answer is chosen because it completes an analogous relationship, not because it is on the same subject as the first pair of words.

Sample question 5 would be answered this way. Consider what a pointer is used for on a speedometer. It is used to indicate speed at a particular moment. A watch uses hands (choice **B**) for the same general function, that is, to indicate something at a particular moment. In this case, the indication is of time. Choice A is incorrect because the watch case has nothing to do with this function. Choices C and D are wrong because although the dial and the numerals have to do with indicating the time, they do not perform the specific function of indicating something at any one particular moment.

The Clerical Tasks Test

WHAT THE TEST IS ABOUT

The Clerical Tasks Test is a test of speed and accuracy on four clerical tasks. There are 120 questions given with a short time limit. The test contains 30 questions on name and number checking, 30 on arranging names in correct alphabetical order, 30 on simple arithmetic, and 30 on inspecting groups of letters and numbers. The questions are arranged in groups or cycles of five questions of each type.

HOW THE TEST IS ADMINISTERED

Each applicant is given a copy of the test booklet with sample questions and an answer sheet. Ten minutes are allowed to study the directions and answer the sample questions printed on the two pages.

The separate answer sheet is then used for recording answers to the test. Exactly 15 minutes are allowed for this test.

HOW TO ANSWER THE TEST QUESTIONS

Directions for answering all four of the types of questions on the Clerical Tasks Test are given with the sample questions. Additional specific information on how to answer each type of question is given below. Look first at the sample questions on the test and then study the information here until you can understand how to answer the questions. (Do not limit yourself to the ten minutes allowed in the actual test situation.)

The Clerical Tasks Test is planned as a test of speed in carrying out these relatively simple clerical tasks. This means you should work quickly through the test. However, the test is also planned to measure accuracy, and there is a penalty for wrong answers in the total test score. This means you need to be careful as you work and that wild guessing is not a good idea. However, do not be so concerned about accuracy that you do the test more slowly than you should. Remember that both speed and accuracy are important to achieve a good score.

The different question types in this test appear on each page of the test. You may find it easier to answer all questions of one type that appear in the test rather than switching from one question type to another. This is perfectly acceptable, but extra caution should be taken to mark your answers in the right place on the answer sheet.

Directions: This test contains four kinds of questions. There are some of each kind of question on each page in the booklet. The time limit for the test will be announced by the examiner.

Study the sample questions carefully. Each question has five suggested answers. Decide which one is the best answer. Find the question number on the Sample Answer Sheet. Show your answer to the question by darkening com-

Federal Clerical Jobs / 15

pletely the space that is lettered the same as the letter of your answer. Keep your mark within the space. If you have to erase a mark, be sure to erase it completely. Mark only one answer for each question.

In each line across the page there are three names or numbers that are very similar. Compare the three names or numbers and decide which ones are exactly alike. On the Sample Answer Sheet at the right, mark the answer:

A   if ALL THREE names or numbers are exactly ALIKE
B   if only the FIRST and SECOND names or numbers are exactly ALIKE
C   if only the FIRST and THIRD names or numbers are exactly ALIKE
D   if only the SECOND and THIRD names or numbers are exactly ALIKE
E   if ALL THREE names or numbers are DIFFERENT

1. Davis Hazen   David Hozen   David Hazen
2. Lois Appel   Lois Appel   Lois Apfel
3. June Allan   Jane Allan   Jane Allan
4. 10235   10235   10235
5. 32614   32164   32614

If you finish the sample questions before you are told to turn to the test, it will be to your advantage to study the code given above for A, B, C, D, and E. This code is repeated on every page.

In the next group of sample questions, there is a name in a box at the left, and four other names in alphabetical order at the right. Find the correct location for the boxed name so that it will be in alphabetical order with the others, and mark the letter of that location as your answer.

6. | Jones, Jane |

(A) →
   Goodyear, G. L.
(B) →
   Haddon, Harry
(C) →
   Jackson, Mary
(D) →
   Jenkins, William
(E) →

7. | Kessler, Neilson |

(A) →
   Kessel, Carl
(B) →
   Kessinger, D. J.
(C) →
   Kessler, Karl
(D) →
   Kessner, Lewis
(E) →

Sample Answer Sheet

1. Ⓐ Ⓑ Ⓒ Ⓓ Ⓔ   5. Ⓐ Ⓑ Ⓒ Ⓓ Ⓔ
2. Ⓐ Ⓑ Ⓒ Ⓓ Ⓔ   6. Ⓐ Ⓑ Ⓒ Ⓓ Ⓔ
3. Ⓐ Ⓑ Ⓒ Ⓓ Ⓔ   7. Ⓐ Ⓑ Ⓒ Ⓓ Ⓔ
4. Ⓐ Ⓑ Ⓒ Ⓓ Ⓔ

16 / *Clerical Exams Handbook*

The correct answers for questions 1–7 are:

1. **E** 3. **D** 5. **C** 7. **D**
2. **B** 4. **A** 6. **E**

In the following questions, solve each problem and find your answer among the list of suggested answers for that question. Mark the Sample Answer Sheet A, B, C, or D for the answer you obtained; or if your answer is not among these, mark E for that question.

Answers

8. Add: 22
       + 33

(A) 44
(B) 45
(C) 54
(D) 55
(E) none of these

9. Subtract: 24
            − 3

(A) 20
(B) 21
(C) 27
(D) 29
(E) none of these

10. Multiply: 25
             × 5

(A) 100
(B) 115
(C) 125
(D) 135
(E) none of these

11. Divide: 6/126

(A) 20
(B) 22
(C) 24
(D) 26
(E) none of these

There is one set of suggested answers for the next group of sample questions. Do not try to memorize these answers, because there will be a different set on each page in the test.

To find the answer to a question, find which suggested answer contains numbers and letters all of which appear in the question. If no suggested answer fits, mark E for that question.

12.	8	N	K	9	G	T	4	6	
13.	T	9	7	Z	6	L	3	K	Suggested
14.	Z	7	G	K	3	9	8	N	Answers
15.	3	K	9	4	6	G	Z	L	
16.	Z	N	7	3	8	K	T	9	

A = 7, 9, G, K
B = 8, 9, T, Z
C = 6, 7, K, Z
D = 6, 8, G, T
E = none of these

Sample Answer Sheet

8. Ⓐ Ⓑ Ⓒ Ⓓ Ⓔ   13. Ⓐ Ⓑ Ⓒ Ⓓ Ⓔ
9. Ⓐ Ⓑ Ⓒ Ⓓ Ⓔ   14. Ⓐ Ⓑ Ⓒ Ⓓ Ⓔ
10. Ⓐ Ⓑ Ⓒ Ⓓ Ⓔ   15. Ⓐ Ⓑ Ⓒ Ⓓ Ⓔ
11. Ⓐ Ⓑ Ⓒ Ⓓ Ⓔ   16. Ⓐ Ⓑ Ⓒ Ⓓ Ⓔ
12. Ⓐ Ⓑ Ⓒ Ⓓ Ⓔ

Federal Clerical Jobs / 17

The correct answers for questions 8–16 are:

8. D	10. C	12. D	14. A	16. B
9. B	11. E	13. C	15. E	

EXPLANATIONS

Sample Questions 1–5. Memorizing the answer choices for this question type may be helpful in increasing your speed. In these questions, you are to compare three names or numbers and decide which ones are exactly alike. You then select your answer from a set of choices which describe whether all of them, some of them, or none of them are alike. These choices are labeled A, B, C, D, and E and are given at the top of the first page of the Sample Questions for the Clerical Tasks Test and are repeated on each page of the test booklet.

- These choices remain the same for all questions of this type in the test so if you memorize these choices you will not have to refer constantly back to them before choosing your answers.

Sample Questions 6–7. For the alphabetizing questions, remember that the most important rule for putting the names in order is to consider each letter in the complete last name in strict alphabetical order, exactly as it appears.

- This is true even when the name includes more than one capital letter (as in DeLong), or involves prefixes which are often spelled differently in different names (as in McDuff and MacDuff).
- Ignore punctuation, such as apostrophes and hyphens, that appear in a name (as in O'Hara).

When two last names are identical in every way, then alphabetize according to the first and second names given, following the same rules.

Sample Questions 8–11. The key to the arithmetic questions is to avoid careless errors. Remember that the correct answer may not be included as one of the given alternatives. In this case you mark choice E on the answer sheet.

- Answers will always be exact (no decimal places), so if the answer you get is not exact, work the problem again.

Sample Questions 12–16. There are several different ways of approaching the letter and number inspection questions. You should use the method that works best for you.

One method is to work from the answer choices to the questions. Look at each answer choice and, one at a time, compare each letter or number it contains with the question until you can accept or reject it. Here is how you would use this method to answer Sample Question 12:

- Start by looking at the first number given in choice A, which is a 7.
- Quickly scan question 12 for this number. Since it does not include a 7, choice A can be rejected.
- Next consider the first letter in choice B, which is an 8. Scanning question 12 confirms that an 8 is present. Moving on to the next number in choice B (a 9), scanning of the question confirms its presence also, as well as the next letter in choice B (a T). There is no Z, however, so choice B is then rejected.

- Using the same process of elimination for choice C, no number 7 is found, and this choice is rejected.

- One by one, all of the letters and numbers in choice D are found, so choice D is marked as correct on the separate answer sheet.

- If all the letters and numbers in choice D had not been found in question 12, then choice E, "none of these," would have been marked as the correct answer.

You may be able to save time using this method by scanning for two of the letters or numbers given at one time.

Another method is to look at the particular question and quickly and lightly memorize all the numbers and letters it contains. Then, glance at each choice to select one which is a good possibility based on your memory.

- Carefully double-check this choice with each of the numbers and letters given in the question.

- If you use this method, be sure to spend only a few seconds memorizing the numbers and letters in the question, or you will waste too much time on one question.

Whichever method you choose, remember that any of the answer choices given may be used to answer more than one of the five questions included in the set on each page. Also, note that the letters and numbers given in the answer choices and questions do not have to be in the same order. Finally, unlike the situation with the answer choices given for the first five sample questions on the Clerical Tasks Test, the answer choices for these questions do not remain the same throughout the test. Therefore, it will not help you to memorize any of the answer choices given with these sample questions.

POSTAL CLERKS

Even within the Postal Service, the title "clerk" is used to designate a number of different functions. One group of clerks comprises window clerks, distribution clerks, machine-operating distribution clerks, and mark-up clerks. These clerks, all of whom directly handle mail in one way or another, are all chosen by virtue of their scores on Postal Examination 470, the Postal Clerk and Carrier Exam. Mark-up clerk candidates must also qualify on a computer-administered alpha-numeric typing test designated as Examination 715. The other group of clerks in the postal service perform more traditional clerical functions. These are the clerk-typists and clerk-stenographers. All candidates for these clerical positions must compete on Examination 710, which is a test of clerical aptitude and verbal abilities. In addition, they must qualify on Examination 712, a typing test which is administered on a computer. Candidates for the position of clerk-stenographer must also earn competitive scores on Examination 711, the stenography test.

POSTAL CLERK—DUTIES OF THE JOB

People are most familiar with the window clerk who sits behind the counter in post office lobbies selling stamps or accepting parcel post. However, the majority of postal clerks are distribution clerks who sort incoming and outgoing mail in workrooms. Only in a small post office does a clerk do both kinds of work.

When mail arrives at the post office, it is dumped on long tables where distribution clerks and mail handlers separate it into groups of letters, parcel post, and magazines and newspapers. Clerks feed letters into stamp-canceling machines and cancel the rest by hand. The mail is then taken to other sections of the post office to be sorted by destination. Clerks first separate the mail into primary destination categories: mail for the local area, for each nearby state, for groups of distant states, and for some of the largest cities. This primary distribution is followed by one or more secondary distributions. For example, local mail is combined with mail coming in from other cities and is sorted according to street and number. In post offices with electronic mail-sorting machines, clerks simply push a button corresponding to the letter's destination, and the letter drops into the proper slot.

The clerks at post office windows provide a variety of services in addition to selling stamps and money orders. They weigh packages to determine postage and check to see if their size, shape, and condition are satisfactory for mailing. Clerks also register and insure mail and answer questions about postage rates, mailing restrictions, and other postal matters. Occasionally they may help a customer file a claim for a damaged package. In large post offices a window clerk may provide only one or two of these services and be called a registry, stamp, or money order clerk.

Working conditions of clerks differ according to the specific work assignments and the amount and kind of labor-saving machinery in the post office. In small post offices, clerks must carry heavy mail sacks from one part of the building to another and sort the mail by hand. In large post offices, chutes and conveyors move the mail, and much of the sorting is done by machine. In either case, clerks are on their feet most of the time, reaching for sacks of mail, placing packages and bundles into sacks while sorting, and walking around the workroom.

Distribution clerks may become bored with the routine of sorting mail unless they enjoy trying to improve their speed and accuracy. They also may have to work at night, because most large post offices process mail around the clock.

A window clerk, on the other hand, has a greater variety of duties, has frequent contact with the public, generally has a less strenuous job, and never has to work a night shift.

New clerks are trained on the job. Most clerks begin with simple tasks to learn regional groupings of states, cities, and ZIP codes. To help clerks learn these groupings, many post offices offer classroom instruction. A good memory, good coordination, and the ability to read rapidly and accurately are important. These traits are measured by performance on Exam 470.

Distribution clerks work closely with other clerks, frequently under the tension and strain of meeting deadlines. Window clerks must be tactful when dealing with the public, especially when answering questions or receiving complaints.

DISTRIBUTION CLERK, MACHINE—DUTIES OF THE JOB

Distribution clerks work indoors. Often clerks must handle sacks of mail weighing as much as 70 pounds. They sort mail and distribute it by using a complicated scheme that must be memorized. Machine distribution clerks must learn computer codes for the automatic routing of mail. Clerks may be on their feet all day. They also have to stretch, reach, and throw mail. The work of the distribution clerk is more routine than that of other postal clerks; however, the starting salary is higher. Distribution clerks begin at postal pay level six while other clerks and carriers begin at level five. Increasing automation within the postal service has made the job of the distribution clerk quite secure.

Although the amount of mail post offices handle is expected to grow as both the population and the number of businesses grow, modernization of post offices and installation of new equipment will increase the amount of mail each clerk can handle. For example, machines that semiautomatically mark destination codes on envelopes are now being introduced. These codes can be read by computer-controlled letter-sorting machines, which automatically drop each letter into the proper slot for its destination. With this system, clerks read addresses only once, at the time they are coded, instead of several times, as they do now. Eventually this equipment will be installed in all large post offices.

Applicants must be physically able to perform the duties described. Any physical condition that causes the applicant to be a hazard to him/herself or to others will be a disqualification for appointment.

The distant vision for clerk positions must test at least 20/30 (Snellen) in one eye (glasses are permitted). Some distribution clerk positions may be filled by the deaf.

A physical examination, drug test, and psychological interview are required before appointment.

Letter-sorting machine operator applicants must take Exam 470.

MARK-UP CLERK, AUTOMATED—DUTIES OF THE JOB

The mark-up clerk, automated, operates an electro-mechanical machine to process mail that is classified as "undeliverable as addressed." In doing this, the mark-up clerk operates the keyboard of a computer terminal to enter data into and extract it from several databases including change of address, mailer's database, and address-correction file. The mark-up clerk must select the correct program and operating mode for each application, must affix labels to mail either manually or with mechanical devices, and must prepare forms for address-correction services. Other duties may include distribution of processed mark-ups to appropriate separations for further handling, operation of a photocopy machine, and other job-related tasks in support of primary duties.

QUALIFICATION REQUIREMENTS

An applicant for a mark-up clerk position must have had either six months of clerical or office-machine-operating experience or have completed high school or have had a full academic year (36 weeks) of business school. The record of experience and training must show ability to use reference materials and manuals; ability to perform effectively under pressure; ability to operate any office equipment appropriate to the position; ability to work with others; and ability to read, understand, and apply certain regulations and procedures commonly used in processing mail that is undeliverable as addressed.

For appointment, a mark-up clerk must be 18 years old, or 16 years old if a high school graduate. An applicant who will reach his or her eighteenth birthday within two years from the date of the exam may participate. A mark-up clerk must be able to read, without strain, printed material the size of typewritten characters and must have 20/40 (Snellen) vision in one eye. Glasses are permitted. In addition, the applicant must pass a computer-administered alpha-numeric typing test. Candidates with high scores on the competitive exam, Exam 470, and with the requisite experience are called to the alpha-numeric typing test, Exam 715, individually as openings occur and hiring is likely. The exam is administered on a personal computer with its numeric keyboard disabled so that the candidate must use only the main keyboard. The Postal Service does not distribute sample questions for Exam 715, but the instructions at the test site are very clear and ample time is allowed for preparation. The alpha-numeric typing test is not a competitive test. The candidate need only pass to qualify.

OFFICIAL SAMPLE QUESTIONS FOR EXAMINATION 470

Test Instructions

During the test session, it will be your responsibility to pay close attention to what the examiner has to say and to follow all instructions. One of the purposes of the test is to see how quickly and accurately you can work. Therefore, each part of the test will be carefully timed. You will not START until you are told to do so. Also, when you are told to STOP, you must immediately STOP answering the questions. When you are told to work on a particular part of the examination, regardless of which part, you are to work on that part ONLY. If you finish a part before time is called, you may review your answers for that part, but you will not go on or back to any other part. Failure to follow ANY directions given to you by the examiner may be grounds for disqualification. Instructions read by the examiner are intended to ensure that each applicant has the same fair and objective opportunity to compete in the examination.

Sample Questions

Study carefully before the examination.
The following questions are like the ones that will be on the test. Study these carefully. This will give you practice with the different kinds of questions and show you how to mark your answers.

Part A: Address Checking

In this part of the test, you will have to decide whether two addresses are alike or different. If the two addresses are exactly *Alike* in every way, darken circle A for the question. If the two addresses are *Different* in any way, darken circle D for the question.

22 / Clerical Exams Handbook

Mark your answers to these sample questions on the Sample Answer Sheet below.

1. 2134 S 20th St   2134 S 20th St

Since the two addresses are exactly alike, mark A for question 1 on the Sample Answer Sheet.

2. 4608 N Warnock St   4806 N Warnock St
3. 1202 W Girard Dr   1202 W Girard Rd
4. Chappaqua NY 10514   Chappaqua NY 10514
5. 2207 Markland Ave   2207 Markham Ave

Sample Answer Sheet

1. Ⓐ Ⓓ   4. Ⓐ Ⓓ
2. Ⓐ Ⓓ   5. Ⓐ Ⓓ
3. Ⓐ Ⓓ

The correct answers to questions 2 to 5 are: 2D, 3D, 4A, and 5D.

Your score on Part A of the actual test will be based on the number of wrong answers as well as on the number of right answers. Part A is scored right answers minus wrong answers. Random guessing should not help your score. For the Part A test, you will have six minutes to answer as many of the 95 questions as you can. It will be to your advantage to work as quickly and as accurately as possible. You will not be expected to be able to answer all the questions in the time allowed.

Part B: Memory for Addresses

In this part of the test, you will have to memorize the locations (A, B, C, D, or E) of 25 addresses shown in five boxes, like those below. For example, "Sardis" is in Box C, "6800-6999 Table" is in Box B, and so forth. (The addresses in the actual test will be different.)

A	B	C	D	E
4700-5599 Table Lismore 5600-6499 West Hesper 4400-4699 Blake	6800-6999 Table Kelford 6500-6799 West Musella 5600-6499 Blake	5600-6499 Table Joel 6800-6999 West Sardis 6500-6799 Blake	6500-6799 Table Tatum 4400-4699 West Porter 4700-5599 Blake	4400-4699 Table Ruskin 4700-5599 West Nathan 6800-6999 Blake

Study the locations of the addresses for five minutes. As you study, silently repeat these to yourself. Then cover the boxes and try to answer the questions below. Mark your answers for each question by darkening the circle as was done for questions 1 and 2

1. Musella   **5.** 4400-4699 Blake   **9.** 6500-6799 Blake   **13.** Porter
2. 4700-5599 Blake   **6.** Hesper   **10.** Joel   **14.** 6800-6999 Blake
3. 4700-5599 Table   **7.** Kelford   **11.** 4400-4699 Blake
4. Tatum   **8.** Nathan   **12.** 6500-6799 West

Sample Answer Sheet

1. Ⓐ ● Ⓒ Ⓓ Ⓔ   6. Ⓐ Ⓑ Ⓒ Ⓓ Ⓔ   11. Ⓐ Ⓑ Ⓒ Ⓓ Ⓔ
2. Ⓐ Ⓑ Ⓒ ● Ⓔ   7. Ⓐ Ⓑ Ⓒ Ⓓ Ⓔ   12. Ⓐ Ⓑ Ⓒ Ⓓ Ⓔ
3. Ⓐ Ⓑ Ⓒ Ⓓ Ⓔ   8. Ⓐ Ⓑ Ⓒ Ⓓ Ⓔ   13. Ⓐ Ⓑ Ⓒ Ⓓ Ⓔ
4. Ⓐ Ⓑ Ⓒ Ⓓ Ⓔ   9. Ⓐ Ⓑ Ⓒ Ⓓ Ⓔ   14. Ⓐ Ⓑ Ⓒ Ⓓ Ⓔ
5. Ⓐ Ⓑ Ⓒ Ⓓ Ⓔ   10. Ⓐ Ⓑ Ⓒ Ⓓ Ⓔ

The correct answers for questions 3 to 14 are: 3A, 4D, 5A, 6A, 7B, 8E, 9C, 10C, 11A, 12B, 13D, and 14E.

During the examination, you will have three practice exercises to help you memorize the location of addresses shown in the five boxes. After the practice exercises, the actual test will be given. Part B is scored right answers minus one-fourth of the wrong answers. Random guessing should not help your score, but if you can eliminate one or more alternatives, it is to your advantage to guess. For the Part B test, you will have five minutes to answer as many of the 88 questions as you can. It will be to your advantage to work as quickly and as accurately as you can. You will not be expected to be able to answer all the questions in the time allowed.

Part C: Number Series

For each *Number Series* question there is at the left a series of numbers that follow some definite order and at the right five sets of two numbers each. You are to look at the numbers in the series at the left and find out what order they follow. Then decide what the next two numbers in that series would be if the same order were continued. Mark your answers on the Sample Answer Sheet.

1. 1 2 3 4 5 6 7 . . . .   (A) 1 2   (B) 5 6   (C) 8 9   (D) 4 5   (E) 7 8

The numbers in this series are increasing by 1. If the series were continued for two more numbers, it would read: 1 2 3 4 5 6 7 8 9. Therefore the correct answer is 8 and 9 and you should have darkened C for question 1.

2. 15 14 13 12 11 10 9 . . . . . .   (A) 2 1   (B) 17 16   (C) 8 9   (D) 8 7   (E) 9 8

The numbers in this series are decreasing by 1. If the series were continued for two more numbers, it would read: 15 14 13 12 11 10 9 8 7. Therefore the correct answer is 8 and 7 and you should have darkened D for question 2.

3. 20 20 21 21 22 22 23 . . . . .   (A) 23 23   (B) 23 24   (C) 19 19   (D) 22 23   (E) 21 22

Each number in this series is repeated and then increased by 1. If the series were continued for two more numbers, it would read: 20 20 21 21 22 22 23 23 24. Therefore the correct answer is 23 and 24 and you should have darkened B for question 3.

4. 17 3 17 4 17 5 17 . . . .   (A) 6 17   (B) 6 7   (C) 17 6   (D) 5 6   (E) 17 7

This series is the number 17 separated by numbers increasing by 1, beginning with the number 3. If the series were continued for two more numbers, it would read: 17 3 17 4 17 5 17 6 17. Therefore the correct answer is 6 and 17 and you should have darkened A for question 4.

5. 1 2 4 5 7 8 10 . . . .   (A) 11 12   (B) 12 14   (C) 10 13   (D) 12 13   (E) 11 13

> **Sample Answer Sheet**
>
> 1. Ⓐ Ⓑ Ⓒ Ⓓ Ⓔ   4. Ⓐ Ⓑ Ⓒ Ⓓ Ⓔ
> 2. Ⓐ Ⓑ Ⓒ Ⓓ Ⓔ   5. Ⓐ Ⓑ Ⓒ Ⓓ Ⓔ
> 3. Ⓐ Ⓑ Ⓒ Ⓓ Ⓔ

The numbers in this series are increasing first by 1 (plus 1) and then by 2 (plus 2). If the series were continued for two more numbers, it would read: 1 2 4 5 7 8 10 (plus 1) 11 and (plus 2) 13. Therefore the correct answer is 11 and 13 and you should have darkened E for question 5.

Now read and work sample questions 6 through 10 and mark your answers on the Sample Answer Sheet.

6. 21 21 20 20 19 19 18 . . . .   (A) 18 18   (B) 18 17   (C) 17 18   (D) 17 17   (E) 18 19

7. 1 22 1 23 1 24 1 . . . .   (A) 26 1   (B) 25 26   (C) 25 1   (D) 1 26   (E) 1 25

8. 1 20 3 19 5 18 7 . . . .   (A) 8 9   (B) 8 17   (C) 17 10   (D) 17 9   (E) 9 18

9. 4 7 10 13 16 19 22 . . . . . .   (A) 23 26   (B) 25 27   (C) 25 26   (D) 25 28   (E) 24 27

10. 30 2 28 4 26 6 24 . . . . . .   (A) 23 9   (B) 26 8   (C) 8 9   (D) 26 22   (E) 8 22

> **Sample Answer Sheet**
>
> 6. Ⓐ Ⓑ Ⓒ Ⓓ Ⓔ   9. Ⓐ Ⓑ Ⓒ Ⓓ Ⓔ
> 7. Ⓐ Ⓑ Ⓒ Ⓓ Ⓔ   10. Ⓐ Ⓑ Ⓒ Ⓓ Ⓔ
> 8. Ⓐ Ⓑ Ⓒ Ⓓ Ⓔ

The correct answers to sample questions 6 to 10 are: 6B, 7C, 8D, 9D and 10E. Explanations follow.

6. Each number in the series repeats itself and then decreases by 1 or minus 1; 21 (repeat) 21 (minus 1) 20 (repeat) 20 (minus 1) 19 (repeat) 19 (minus 1) 18 (repeat) ? (minus 1) ?

7. The number 1 is separated by numbers that begin with 22 and increase by 1; 1 22 1 (increase 22 by 1) 23 1 (increase 23 by 1) 24 1 (increase 24 by 1)?

8. This is best explained by two alternating series—one series starts with 1 and increases by 2 or plus 2; the other series starts with 20 and decreases by 1 or minus 1.

    ```
    1     3     5     7     ?
       20    19    18    ?
    ```

9. This series of numbers increases by 3 (plus 3) beginning with the first number—4 7 10 13 16 19 22 ? ?

10. Look for two alternating series—one series starts with 30 and decreases by 2 (minus 2): the other series starts with 2 and increases by 2 (plus 2).

Now try questions 11 to 15.

11. 5 6 20 7 8 19 9 .... (A) 10 18 (B) 18 17 (C) 10 17 (D) 18 19 (E) 10 11
12. 4 6 9 11 14 16 19 ...... (A) 21 24 (B) 22 25 (C) 20 22 (D) 21 23 (E) 22 24
13. 8 8 1 10 10 3 12 .... (A) 13 13 (B) 12 5 (C) 12 4 (D) 13 5 (E) 4 12
14. 10 12 50 15 17 50 20 .... (A) 50 21 (B) 21 50 (C) 50 22 (D) 22 50 (E) 22 24
15. 20 21 23 24 27 28 32 33 38 39
     .... (A) 45 46 (B) 45 52 (C) 44 45 (D) 44 49 (E) 40 46

Sample Answer Sheet

11. Ⓐ Ⓑ Ⓒ Ⓓ Ⓔ   14. Ⓐ Ⓑ Ⓒ Ⓓ Ⓔ
12. Ⓐ Ⓑ Ⓒ Ⓓ Ⓔ   15. Ⓐ Ⓑ Ⓒ Ⓓ Ⓔ
13. Ⓐ Ⓑ Ⓒ Ⓓ Ⓔ

The correct answers to the sample questions above are: 11A, 12A, 13B, 14D and 15A.

It will be to your advantage to answer every question in Part C that you can, since your score on this part of the test will be based on the number of questions that you answer correctly. Answer first those questions that are easiest for you. For the Part C test, you will have 20 minutes to answer as many of the 24 questions as you can.

Part D: Following Oral Directions

In this part of the test, you will be told to follow directions by writing in a test booklet and then on an answer sheet. The test booklet will have lines of material like the following five samples:

SAMPLE 1.   5 ___

SAMPLE 2.   1   6   4   3   7

SAMPLE 3.   D   B   A   E   C

SAMPLE 4.   (8 __) (5 __) (2 __) (9 __) (10 __)

SAMPLE 5.   (7 __) [6 __] (1 __) [12 __]

To practice this part of the test, tear out the page of instructions to be read. Then have somebody read the instructions to you while you follow them. When he or she tells you to darken the space on the Sample Answer Sheet, use the one on this page.

Your score for Part D will be based on the number of questions that you answer correctly. Therefore, if you are not sure of an answer, it will be to your advantage to guess. Part D will take about 25 minutes.

Sample Answer Sheet

1. Ⓐ Ⓑ Ⓒ Ⓓ Ⓔ   5. Ⓐ Ⓑ Ⓒ Ⓓ Ⓔ   9. Ⓐ Ⓑ Ⓒ Ⓓ Ⓔ
2. Ⓐ Ⓑ Ⓒ Ⓓ Ⓔ   6. Ⓐ Ⓑ Ⓒ Ⓓ Ⓔ   10. Ⓐ Ⓑ Ⓒ Ⓓ Ⓔ
3. Ⓐ Ⓑ Ⓒ Ⓓ Ⓔ   7. Ⓐ Ⓑ Ⓒ Ⓓ Ⓔ   11. Ⓐ Ⓑ Ⓒ Ⓓ Ⓔ
4. Ⓐ Ⓑ Ⓒ Ⓓ Ⓔ   8. Ⓐ Ⓑ Ⓒ Ⓓ Ⓔ   12. Ⓐ Ⓑ Ⓒ Ⓓ Ⓔ

Postal Clerks / 27

Instructions to be read for Part D. (The words in parentheses should NOT be read aloud.)

You are to follow the instructions that I shall read to you. I cannot repeat them.

Look at the samples. Sample 1 has a number and a line beside it. On the line write A as in ace. **(Pause 2 seconds.)** Now, on the Sample Answer Sheet, find number 5 **(pause 2 seconds)** and darken the letter you just wrote on the line. **(Pause 2 seconds.)**

Look at Sample 2. (Pause slightly.) Draw a line under the third number. **(Pause 2 seconds.)** Now, on the Sample Answer Sheet, find the number under which you just drew a line and darken B as in boy. **(Pause 5 seconds.)**

Look at the letters in Sample 3. (Pause slightly.) Draw a line under the third letter in the line. **(Pause 2 seconds.)** Now, on your Sample Answer Sheet, find number 9 **(pause 2 seconds)** and darken the letter under which you drew a line. **(Pause 5 seconds.)**

Look at the five circles in Sample 4. (Pause slightly.) Each circle has a number and a line in it. Write D as in dog on the line in the last circle. **(Pause 2 seconds.)** Now, on the Sample Answer Sheet, darken the number-letter combination that is in the circle you just wrote in. **(Pause 5 seconds.)**

Look at Sample 5. (Pause slightly.) There are two circles and two boxes of different sizes with numbers in them. **(Pause slightly.)** If 4 is more than 2 and if 5 is less than 3, write A as in ace in the smaller circle. **(Pause slightly.)** Otherwise write C as in car in the larger box. **(Pause 2 seconds.)** Now, on the Sample Answer Sheet, darken the number-letter combination in the box or circle in which you just wrote. **(Pause 5 seconds.)**

Now look at the Sample Answer Sheet. (Pause slightly.) You should have darkened 4B, 5A, 9A, 10D, and 12C on the Sample Answer Sheet. **(If the person preparing to take the examination made any mistakes, try to help him or her see why he or she made wrong marks.)**

EXAM 715—ALPHA-NUMERIC TYPING TEST FOR MARK-UP CLERK, AUTOMATED

The Postal Service does not issue official sample questions for Exam 715.

Exam 715, the typing test for Mark-up Clerk applicants, is quite different from an ordinary typing test. You will take this test by private appointment, and all interaction will be between you and a computer. Do not be frightened. Even if you have had no experience whatsoever with computers, this is not an intimidating test. The computer is user-friendly and is very specific in spelling out directions. And, unless you are a typing whiz, the typing test itself is probably easier than a plain paper copying test.

As Exam 715 begins, the computer screen explains to you which buttons you will be using and what each does. You need to use very few buttons—letters, numbers, "return," "delete," and "lock caps." You will get a chance to use these and to become familiar with their operation as you fill in basic name and social security number types of information. A test administrator remains in the room to answer questions.

The computer then explains the typing task of the exam itself. A letter-number code appears on the upper right screen; you are to copy it, then press the return button to bring the next code to the screen. That's it. The codes all consist of four letters and three numbers, such as TYHO346 or BZIP801. The faster you type, the more codes you have an opportunity to copy. In the explanation phase of the exam, you will have 15 seconds in which to copy five codes. The computer will tell you how many you copied correctly.

After the explanation phase comes a practice session. You will be allowed five minutes to copy as many codes as you can correctly, again one at a time. The five-minute practice session does not count. This is your chance to experiment with looking at your fingers or at the screen; with memorizing each code to be typed, or with staring at the code while typing; with typing as fast as you can, not even looking at the screen to see if you are typing correctly; or with checking to make sure you are copying correctly and repairing errors before continuing.

Be aware than an error that has been corrected on the computer is not counted as an error. Since accuracy is so important and since correction is so easy on the computer, it is worthwhile to correct errors. Unless you are extremely inaccurate, you will not lose much time correcting errors and will gain valuable points through accuracy.

Here is a suggested approach:

1. Look at the code and quickly memorize it; four letters and three numbers should pose no problem for such a short-term task.
2. Type in the code, looking at the center of the screen where the letters and numbers that you are typing appear.
3. Delete and retype if you spot an error.
4. Hit the return button and do the same for the next code.

The five-minute practice period should allow you to establish a rhythm for this process. When the five minutes are up, your score will flash on the screen. A score of 14 is required for passing. If you have scored 14 or higher, approach the actual test with confidence. If your score is lower than 14, be reassured that it will not be counted. Remember that you used the first few minutes of the practice period to perfect your system. You now have five minutes to use the system with which you have become comfortable. Your second score, the score that does count, will be higher.

The actual test session is exactly like the practice session, with different codes of course. At the end of the five-minute test, your final score will appear on the screen. You will know instantly whether you have passed or failed; whether you are eligible or ineligible. If you are eligible, you can expect to be called for an employment interview sometime in the near future.

Clerk-Typist—Duties of the Job

A clerk-typist types records, letters, memorandums, reports, and other materials from handwritten and other drafts or from a dictating machine; he or she sets up the material typed in accordance with prescribed format and assembles it for initialing, signing, routing, and dispatch. The clerk-typist also cuts mimeograph stencils and masters for duplication by other processes. The miscellaneous office clerical duties of the position include: making up file folders, keeping them in the prescribed order, and filing in them; making and keeping routine office records; composing routine memorandums and letters relating to the business of the office, such as acknowledgments and transmittals; examining incoming and outgoing mail of the office, routing it to the appropriate persons, and controlling the time allowed for preparation of replies to incoming correspondence; receipting and delivering salary checks and filling out various personnel forms; acting as receptionist and furnishing routine information over the telephone; relieving other office personnel in their absence; operating office machines such as the mimeograph, comptometer, and adding machine.

The applicant for a position as clerk-typist must have had one year of office experience or four years of high school business courses or 36 weeks of business or secretarial school. The applicant must also show that he or she has enough of the skills, abilities, and knowledge to read and understand instructions; perform basic arithmetic computations; maintain accurate records; prepare reports and correspondence if required; and operate office machines such as calculators, adding machines, duplicators, and the like. The applicant for a clerk-typist position must pass a test of clerical abilities, Exam 710, and a "plain copy" typing test, Exam 712, administered on a personal computer, with a speed of 45 wpm and good accuracy.

Clerk-Stenographer—Duties of the Job

The clerk-stenographer performs all of the functions of the clerk-typist. In addition, the clerk-stenographer takes dictation, in shorthand or on a shorthand writing machine, of letters, memorandums, reports, and other materials given by the supervisor of the office and other employees. He or she then transcribes it on the typewriter, or word processor, setting up the material transcribed in accordance with prescribed format and assembling it for required initialing, signing, routing, and dispatch. In consideration of the extra training and skill required in the taking of dictation, the clerk-stenographer is rated at salary level five, rather than at the salary level four of the clerk-typist.

The applicant for the position of clerk-stenographer must meet all the requirements of the applicant for clerk-typist in terms of education or experience and in terms of skills, abilities, and knowledge. In addition to passing the test of clerical ability, Exam 710, and the computer-administered plain-copy typing test, Exam 712, the clerk-stenographer applicant must also pass the stenography test, Exam 711.

Official Sample Questions for Examination 710

This section discusses the exam of clerical abilities for clerk-typist and clerk-stenographer.

The following questions are samples of the types of questions that will be used on Examination 710. Study these questions carefully. Each question has several suggested answers. You are to decide which one is the **best answer.** Next, on the Sample Answer Sheet below, find the answer space that is numbered the same number as the question, then darken the space that is lettered the same as the answer you have selected. After you have answered all the questions, compare your answers with the ones given in the Correct Answers to Sample Questions.

Sample Questions 1 through 14—Clerical Aptitude

In Sample Questions 1 through 3, there is a name, number, or code in a box at the left and four other names, numbers, or codes in alphabetical or numerical order at the right. Find the correct space for the boxed name or number so that it will be in alphabetical and/or numerical order with the others and mark the letter of that space on your Sample Answer Sheet below.

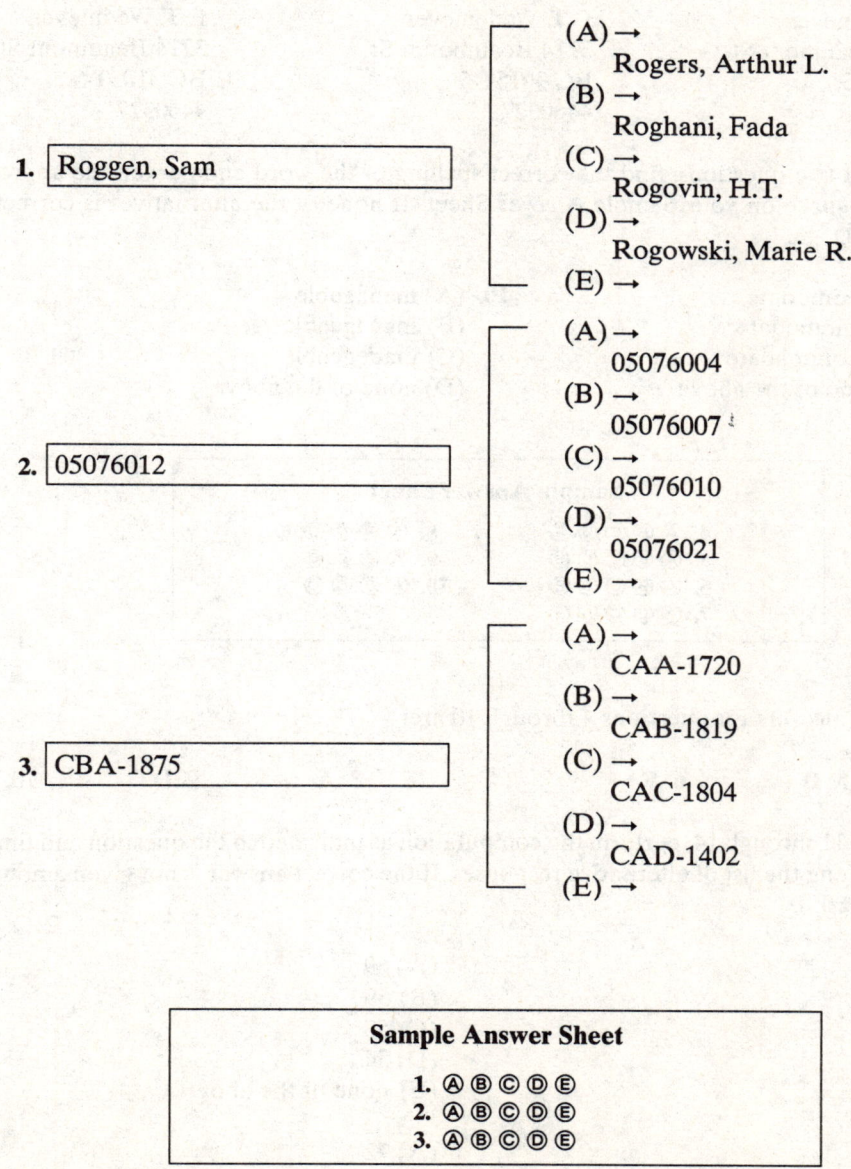

The correct answers for questions 1 through 3 are: 1. B, 2. D and 3. E

Sample Questions 4 through 8 require you to compare names, addresses, or codes. In each line across the page there are three names, addresses, or codes that are very much alike. Compare the three and decide which ones are EXACTLY alike. On the Sample Answer Sheet, mark:

A if **ALL THREE** names, addresses, or codes are exactly **ALIKE**
B if only the **FIRST** and **SECOND** names, addresses, or codes are exactly **ALIKE**
C if only the **FIRST** and **THIRD** names, addresses, or codes are exactly **ALIKE**
D if only the **SECOND** and **THIRD** names, addresses, or codes are exactly **ALIKE**
E if **ALL THREE** names, addresses, or codes are **DIFFERENT**

4. Helene Bedell	Helene Beddell	Helene Beddell
5. F. T. Wedemeyer	F. T. Wedemeyer	F. T. Wedmeyer
6. 3214 W. Beaumont St.	3214 Beaumount St.	3214 Beaumont St.
7. BC 3105T-5	BC 3015T-5	BC 3105T-5
8. 4460327	4460327	4460327

For the next two questions, find the correct spelling of the word and darken the appropriate answer space on your Sample Answer Sheet. If none of the alternatives is correct, darken space D.

9. (A) accomodate
   (B) acommodate
   (C) accommadate
   (D) none of the above

10. (A) manageble
    (B) manageable
    (C) manegeable
    (D) none of the above

Sample Answer Sheet

4. Ⓐ Ⓑ Ⓒ Ⓓ Ⓔ   8. Ⓐ Ⓑ Ⓒ Ⓓ Ⓔ
5. Ⓐ Ⓑ Ⓒ Ⓓ Ⓔ   9. Ⓐ Ⓑ Ⓒ Ⓓ
6. Ⓐ Ⓑ Ⓒ Ⓓ Ⓔ   10. Ⓐ Ⓑ Ⓒ Ⓓ
7. Ⓐ Ⓑ Ⓒ Ⓓ Ⓔ

The correct answers for questions 4 through 10 are:

4. **D**   5. **B**   6. **E**   7. **C**   8. **A**   9. **D**   10. **B**

For Questions 11 through 14, perform the computation as indicated in the question and find the answer among the list of alternative responses. If the correct answer is not given among the choices, mark E.

11. 32 + 26 =
    (A) 69
    (B) 59
    (C) 58
    (D) 54
    (E) none of the above

12. 57 − 15 =
    (A) 72
    (B) 62
    (C) 54
    (D) 44
    (E) none of the above

13. 23 × 7 = (A) 164
 (B) 161
 (C) 154
 (D) 141
 (E) none of the above

14. 160 / 5 = (A) 32
 (B) 30
 (C) 25
 (D) 21
 (E) none of the above

Sample Answer Sheet

11. Ⓐ Ⓑ Ⓒ Ⓓ Ⓔ   13. Ⓐ Ⓑ Ⓒ Ⓓ Ⓔ
12. Ⓐ Ⓑ Ⓒ Ⓓ Ⓔ   14. Ⓐ Ⓑ Ⓒ Ⓓ Ⓔ

The correct answers for questions 11 through 14 are:

11. **C**   12. **E**   13. **B**   14. **A**

Sample Questions 15 through 22—Verbal Abilities

Sample Questions 15 through 17 test your ability to follow instructions. Each question directs you to mark a specific number and letter combination on your Sample Answer Sheet. The questions require your total concentration because the answers that you are instructed to mark are, for the most part, NOT in numerical sequence (i.e., you would not use Number 1 on your answer sheet to answer Question 1; Number 2 for Question 2; etc.). Instead, you must mark the number and space specifically designated in each test question.

15. Look at the letters below. Draw a circle around the middle letter. Now, on your Sample Answer Sheet, find Number 16 and darken the space for the letter you just circled.

     R   C   H

16. Draw a line under the number shown below that is more than 10 but less than 20. Find that number on your Sample Answer Sheet, and darken Space A.

     5   9   17   22

17. Add the numbers 11 and 4 and write your answer on the blank line below. Now find this number on your Sample Answer Sheet and darken the space for the second letter in the alphabet.

     _____

Sample Answer Sheet

15. Ⓐ Ⓑ Ⓒ Ⓓ Ⓔ
16. Ⓐ Ⓑ Ⓒ Ⓓ Ⓔ
17. Ⓐ Ⓑ Ⓒ Ⓓ Ⓔ

The correct answers for questions 14 through 17 are:

15. **B**   16. **C**   17. **A**

Answer the remaining Sample Test Questions on the Sample Answer Sheet in numerical sequence (i.e., Number 18 on the Sample Answer Sheet for Question 18; Number 19 for Question 19, etc.).

Choose the sentence below that is most appropriate with respect to grammar, usage, and punctuation, so as to be suitable for a business letter or report and darken its letter on the Sample Answer Sheet.

18. (A) He should of responded to the letter by now.
    (B) A response to the letter by the end of the week.
    (C) The letter required his immediate response.
    (D) A response by him to the letter is necessary.

Questions 19 and 20 consist of a sentence containing a word in **boldface** type. Choose the best meaning for the word in **boldface** type and darken its letter on the Sample Answer Sheet.

19. The payment was **authorized** yesterday. **Authorized** most nearly means
    (A) expected
    (B) approved
    (C) refunded
    (D) received

20. Please **delete** the second paragraph. **Delete** most nearly means
    (A) type
    (B) read
    (C) edit
    (D) omit

Sample Answer Sheet

18. Ⓐ Ⓑ Ⓒ Ⓓ
19. Ⓐ Ⓑ Ⓒ Ⓓ
20. Ⓐ Ⓑ Ⓒ Ⓓ

The correct answers for questions 18 through 20 are:

18. **C**   19. **B**   20. **D**

In questions 21 and 22 below, read each paragraph and answer the question that follows it by darkening the letter of the correct answer on the Sample Answer Sheet.

21. Window Clerks working for the Postal Service have direct financial responsibility for the selling of postage. In addition, they are expected to have a thorough knowledge concerning the acceptability of all material offered by customers for mailing. Any information provided to the public by these employees must be completely accurate.

The paragraph best supports the statement that Window Clerks

(A) must account for the stamps issued to them for sale
(B) have had long training in other Postal Service jobs
(C) must help sort mail to be delivered by carriers
(D) inspect the contents of all packages offered for mailing

22. The most efficient method for performing a task is not always easily determined. That which is economical in terms of time must be carefully distinguished from that which is economical in terms of expended energy. In short, the quickest method may require a degree of physical effort that may be neither essential nor desirable.

The paragraph best supports the statement that

(A) it is more efficient to perform a task slowly than rapidly
(B) skill in performing a task should not be acquired at the expense of time
(C) the most efficient execution of a task is not always the one done in the shortest time
(D) energy and time cannot both be considered in the performance of a single task

Sample Answer Sheet
21. Ⓐ Ⓑ Ⓒ Ⓓ
22. Ⓐ Ⓑ Ⓒ Ⓓ

The correct answers for questions 21 and 22 are:

21. **A**   22. **C**

OFFICIAL SAMPLE QUESTIONS FOR EXAMINATION 712

This section discusses the plain copy typing test for clerk-typist, clerk-stenographer, and other positions requiring typing of text.

The plain copy typing test is administered on a personal computer, not on a typewriter. A qualifying speed is 45 words per minute, because, since corrections on the computer are quick and clean, the attitude toward errors is more relaxed than with a typing test on a typewriter. Nonetheless, accuracy is a consideration along with the 45-wpm speed required.

All stenographer and typist competitors will take this typing test (plain copy). The sample given below shows the kind of material that competitors must copy. See whether you can copy it twice in five minutes and how many errors your copy contains. Competitors will be required to meet a certain minimum in accuracy as well as in speed.

Space, paragraph, spell, punctuate, capitalize, and begin and end each line precisely as shown in the exercise.

36 / Clerical Exams Handbook

In the examination you will have five minutes in which to make copies of the test exercise, keeping in mind that your eligibility will depend on accuracy as well as speed. When you complete the exercise, simply double space and begin again.

This is an example of the type of material which will
be presented to you as the actual typewriting examination.
Each competitor will be required to typewrite the practice
material exactly as it appears on the copy. You are to space,
capitalize, punctuate, spell, and begin and end each line
exactly as it is presented in the copy. Each time you reach
the end of the paragraph you should begin again and continue
to practice typing the practice paragraph on scratch paper
until the examiner tells you to stop. You are advised that
it is more important to type accurately than to type rapidly.

OFFICIAL SAMPLE QUESTIONS FOR EXAMINATION 711

This section discusses the stenography test for clerk-stenographer.

Only stenographer competitors take a stenography test. The sample below shows the length of material dictated. Sit down with your pencil and notebook, and hand this book to a friend. Have that person dictate the passage to you so that you can see how well prepared you are to take dictation at the rate of 80 words a minute. Each pair of lines is dictated in 10 seconds. Your friend should dictate periods, but not commas, and should read the exercise with the expression that the punctuation indicates.

Exactly on a minute start dictating. Finish reading each line at the number of seconds indicated below.

I realize that this practice dictation	
is not a part of the examination	10 sec.
proper and is not to be scored. (Period)	
When making a study of the private	20 sec.
pension structure and its influence on	
turnover, the most striking feature is its	30 sec.
youth. (Period) As has been shown, the time	
of greatest growth began just a few years	40 sec.
ago. (Period) The influence that this	
growth has had on the labor market and	50 sec.
worker attitudes is hard to assess,	
partly because the effects have not yet fully	1 min.
evolved and many are still in the	
growing stage. (Period) Even so, most pension	10 sec.
plans began with much more limited gains	
than they give now. (Period) For example,	20 sec.
as private plans mature they grant	
a larger profit and a greater range of gains to	30 sec.
more workers and thereby become more	
important. (Period) Plans that protect accrued pension	40 sec.
credits are rather new and are being	
revised in the light of past trends. (Period)	50 sec.
As informal and formal information on pension	
plans spreads, the workers become more	2 min.
aware of the plans and their provisions	
increase. (Period) Their impact on employee attitudes	10 sec.
and decisions will no doubt become	
stronger. (Period) Each year, more and more workers	20 sec.
will be retiring with a private pension,	
and their firsthand knowledge of the benefits to	30 sec.
be gained from private pensions will spread	
to still active workers. (Period) Thus, workers	40 sec.
may less often view pensions as just	
another part of the security package	50 sec.
based on service and more often	
see them as unique benefits. (Period)	3 min.

38 / Clerical Exams Handbook

This transcript and word list for part of the above dictation are similar to those each competitor will receive for the dictation test. Many words have been omitted from the transcript. Compare your notes with it. When you come to a blank space in the transcript, decide what word (or words) belongs there. Look for the missing word in the word list. Notice what letter (A, B, C, or D) is printed beside the word. Write that letter in the blank. B is written in blank 1 to show how you are to record your choice. Write E if the exact answer is not in the word list. You may also write the word (or words) or the shorthand for it, if you wish. The same choice may belong in more than one blank.

ALPHABETIC WORD LIST

Write E if the answer is **not** listed.

a — D	make — A
attitudes — C	making — B
be — B	market — B
been — C	markets — D
began — D	marking — D
being — A	never — B
completely — A	not — D
examination — A	over — C
examine — B	part — C
examining — D	partly — D
feat — A	pension — C
feature — C	practical — C
full — B	practice — B
fully — D	private — D
greater — D	proper — C
grow — B	section — D
growing — C	so — B
had — D	still — A
has — C	structure — D
has been — B	structured — B
has had — A	to — D
has made — A	to be — C
in — C	trial — A
in part — B	turn — D
influence — A	turnover — B
labor — C	values — A
main — B	yet — C

TRANSCRIPT

I realize that this $\underset{1}{\text{B}}$ dictation is $\underset{2}{\underline{}}$ a $\underset{3}{\underline{}}$ of the $\underset{4}{\underline{}}$ $\underset{5}{\underline{}}$ and is $\underset{6}{\underline{}}$ $\underset{7}{\underline{}}$ scored.

When $\underset{8}{\underline{}}$ a $\underset{9}{\underline{}}$ of the $\underset{10}{\underline{}}$ $\underset{11}{\underline{}}$ $\underset{12}{\underline{}}$ and its $\underset{13}{\underline{}}$ on $\underset{14}{\underline{}}$, the most striking $\underset{15}{\underline{}}$ is its youth. As $\underset{16}{\underline{}}$ shown, the time of $\underset{17}{\underline{}}$ growth began just a few years ago. The $\underset{18}{\underline{}}$ that this growth $\underset{19}{\underline{}}$ on the labor $\underset{20}{\underline{}}$ and worker $\underset{21}{\underline{}}$ is hard to assess, $\underset{22}{\underline{}}$ because the effects have not yet $\underset{23}{\underline{}}$ evolved and many are $\underset{24}{\underline{}}$ in the $\underset{25}{\underline{}}$ stage....

(For the next sentences there would be another word list, if the entire sample dictation were transcribed.)

You will be given an answer sheet like the sample that follows, on which your answers can be scored by machine. Each number on the answer sheet stands for the blank with the same number in the transcript. Darken the space for the letter that is the same as the letter you wrote in the transcript. If you have not finished writing letters in the blanks in the transcript, or if you wish to make sure you have lettered them correctly, you may continue to use your notes after you begin marking the answer sheet.

Answer Sheet for Sample Transcript

1. Ⓐ Ⓑ Ⓒ Ⓓ Ⓔ   8. Ⓐ Ⓑ Ⓒ Ⓓ Ⓔ   15. Ⓐ Ⓑ Ⓒ Ⓓ Ⓔ   22. Ⓐ Ⓑ Ⓒ Ⓓ Ⓔ
2. Ⓐ Ⓑ Ⓒ Ⓓ Ⓔ   9. Ⓐ Ⓑ Ⓒ Ⓓ Ⓔ   16. Ⓐ Ⓑ Ⓒ Ⓓ Ⓔ   23. Ⓐ Ⓑ Ⓒ Ⓓ Ⓔ
3. Ⓐ Ⓑ Ⓒ Ⓓ Ⓔ   10. Ⓐ Ⓑ Ⓒ Ⓓ Ⓔ   17. Ⓐ Ⓑ Ⓒ Ⓓ Ⓔ   24. Ⓐ Ⓑ Ⓒ Ⓓ Ⓔ
4. Ⓐ Ⓑ Ⓒ Ⓓ Ⓔ   11. Ⓐ Ⓑ Ⓒ Ⓓ Ⓔ   18. Ⓐ Ⓑ Ⓒ Ⓓ Ⓔ   25. Ⓐ Ⓑ Ⓒ Ⓓ Ⓔ
5. Ⓐ Ⓑ Ⓒ Ⓓ Ⓔ   12. Ⓐ Ⓑ Ⓒ Ⓓ Ⓔ   19. Ⓐ Ⓑ Ⓒ Ⓓ Ⓔ
6. Ⓐ Ⓑ Ⓒ Ⓓ Ⓔ   13. Ⓐ Ⓑ Ⓒ Ⓓ Ⓔ   20. Ⓐ Ⓑ Ⓒ Ⓓ Ⓔ
7. Ⓐ Ⓑ Ⓒ Ⓓ Ⓔ   14. Ⓐ Ⓑ Ⓒ Ⓓ Ⓔ   21. Ⓐ Ⓑ Ⓒ Ⓓ Ⓔ

The correct answers for questions 1 to 25 are:

1. **B**   6. **D**   11. **C**   16. **B**   21. **C**
2. **D**   7. **C**   12. **D**   17. **E**   22. **D**
3. **C**   8. **B**   13. **A**   18. **A**   23. **D**
4. **A**   9. **E**   14. **B**   19. **A**   24. **A**
5. **C**   10. **D**   15. **C**   20. **B**   25. **C**

CLERICAL JOBS WITH THE STATE

Following the lead of the Federal Government, every state has instituted some form of civil service or merit-based hiring procedure. In matters of internal hiring, each state has complete autonomy; no higher authority tells a state which positions must be filled by examination or which examination to use. However, in the interests of efficiency and fairness in hiring, nearly all states fill clerical positions through civil service examinations.

In addition to administering examinations to fill job vacancies in state government, many states offer their testing services to counties and municipalities as well. Thus a person qualifying on a state-administered clerical examination may, if he or she wishes, have name and ranking listed on any number of eligibility rosters in counties or towns in which the person might be willing to work. In other states, state testing is only for state positions, and counties and municipalities have their own individual arrangements or independent systems.

As testing arrangements may vary from state to state, so procedures and the tests themselves may also vary. In general, state-administered clerical tests will test the skills and abilities needed for specific jobs or families of jobs. Where applicable, typing and stenographic tests are part of the testing package. Since budgetary restraints limit available state personnel, most state examinations are of the multiple-choice variety for easy scoring.

Because of the variety in state examinations, we cannot give you the precise information you need for *your* exam in *your* state. However, the following excerpts from a Pennsylvania announcement are illustrative.

COMMONWEALTH OF PENNSYLVANIA STATE CIVIL SERVICE COMMISSION

Announces Examinations for

CLERICAL AND SECRETARIAL POSITIONS IN STATE AND LOCAL GOVERNMENT

Exam No.	Job Title	Job Code	Pay Schedule and Range
	State Government		
1.	Clerk Typist 1	00210	S 2
2.	Clerk Typist 2	00220	S 3
3.	Clerk Stenographer 1	00410	S 2
4.	Clerk Stenographer 2	00420	S 3

		Local Government		
5.		Clerk Typist 1	L0031	*
6.		Clerk Typist 2	L0032	*
7.		Clerk Stenographer 1	L0021	*
8.		Clerk Stenographer 2	L0022	*

*Local government salaries vary. Contact the Personnel Office of the local government program where you are interested in working for specific information.

APPLICATIONS WILL BE ACCEPTED UNTIL FURTHER NOTICE.

<u>IN ITEM 2 OF YOUR "APPLICATION FOR EMPLOYMENT/PROMOTION," LIST THE SPECIFIC STATE AND/OR LOCAL JOB TITLES FOR WHICH YOU ARE WILLING TO ACCEPT EMPLOYMENT.</u>

SPECIAL NOTE

In Harrisburg, Philadelphia and Pittsburgh you may take the typing test on either a typewriter or an IBM personal computer. You <u>do not</u> need any previous computer experience to take the computer version of the test. If you want to take the test on a personal computer, write "PC" on you application in Item 2.

NATURE OF WORK

<u>Typists</u> compose and type documents, letters and memoranda. They also sort, file, check material and provide information. Duties vary in complexity from limited (Clerk Typist 1) to moderate (Clerk Typist 2).

<u>Stenographers</u> take dictation and transcribe the notes. They also compose and type letters and memoranda, provide information and sort and file materials.

JOB REQUIREMENTS

You must be a Pennsylvania resident, of good moral character and capable of performing the physical activities of the job.

Minimum Requirements: If you pass the tests you will be considered to have met the minimum requirements.

JOB OPPORTUNITIES

Opportunities for appointment depend on normal turnover due to retirements, promotions, transfers, resignations and so forth.

STATE GOVERNMENT POSITIONS
These positions are located throughout Pennsylvania. The majority of jobs are in the metropolitan areas of Harrisburg, Philadelphia, and Pittsburgh. It will be to your advantage to make yourself available for locations where clerical positions are concentrated. You may choose as many as 10 counties or as few as one. PLEASE DO NOT MAKE YOURSELF AVAILABLE FOR LOCATIONS IN WHICH YOU ARE NOT WILLING TO WORK. ENTRY HIRES ARE MADE AT BOTH THE CLERK TYPIST 1 AND CLERK TYPIST 2 LEVELS. THEREFORE, YOU ARE ENCOURAGED TO APPLY FOR BOTH JOB TITLES.

There is a continuing need for bilingual (English and Spanish) typists and stenographers in the Philadelphia area. Individuals hired for these positions provide information and assistance to Spanish-speaking clients. Individuals possessing the required bilingual skills are encouraged to apply.

For the most recent information on job opportunities in State Government, contact either the personnel office of the state facility in your area or the agency personnel office located in Harrisburg.

Summer Positions
The Department of Environmental Resources will have approximately ten (10) seasonal Clerk Typist 1 positions available at State Parks throughout Pennsylvania. These jobs last from either the beginning of April or June to Labor Day or the beginning of October. Individuals hired for these jobs will be placed on leave without pay status during the winter months and have the right to return to the job the following year without retaking the clerical test. They also will have the opportunity to be considered for permanent employment if it becomes available.

LOCAL GOVERNMENT POSITIONS
Agencies using these classes include: City and County Housing Authorities, Job Training Partnership Act Sponsors, Pennsylvania Emergency Management Agency Offices, Area Agency on Aging Offices, County Mental Health/Mental Retardation Offices, County Children and Youth Offices and County Drug and Alcohol Abuse Centers. For most recent information on job opportunities, contact the personnel office where you are interested in working.

TESTING

The Clerical examination is made up of 3 parts: a written test, typing test and a stenographic test. All applicants must take a written and a typing test. The written test will be weighted 50% and the typing test will be weighted 50%. Applicants for Clerk Stenographer 1 and 2 must also pass a stenographic test. The stenographic test will not be weighted as part of the final score.

You must pass all parts of the test to be considered for employment.

Any part of the test may be cancelled by the Commission, and the weight added to the remaining part.

The written test will consist of a 12-minute Name and Number Checking speed test, and a 1 1/2-hour clerical abilities test which will cover the subject areas below.

Subject Matter Areas	Number of Questions
Name and Number Checking	65
Sorting File Material	10
Alphabetizing	15
Taking Telephone Messages	15
Capitalization/Punctuation/Grammar	15
Effective Expression	10
Spelling	25
Arithmetic Operations	15
Total	170

Typing Test
The typing performance test will consist of a 5-minute practice exercise followed by the actual test, which will have a 5-minute time limit. A score of 40 words per minute, after deduction for errors, must be achieved in order to pass the typing performance test. Applicants may provide their own typewriters for the typing test.

Stenographic Test
The stenographic test will consist of a practice exercise followed by the actual test. Dictation will be given at the rate of 80 words per minute. Applicants will have time to transcribe their notes. Applicants for Clerk Stenographer 1 must not have more than 10% errors on the stenographic test. Applicants for Clerk Stenographer 2 must not have more than 5% errors on the test. Any stenographic system including the use of a shorthand machine is acceptable. Applicants who wish to use shorthand machines must provide their own.

TEST RESULTS

Employment and promotion lists will be established. You will be notified in writing of your test results.

If you take the test and want to take it again, you may be retested 6 months after the date of your last examination. You must retake all parts of the examination. A new application is required for a retest.

COUNTY CLERICAL EMPLOYMENT

In some states, county subdivisions serve as convenient geographical and political units but have relatively little operational governmental function. In such states, county clerical testing is limited to selection of personnel to staff county offices, most often health departments and court systems. In those states the bulk of nonmunicipal government services are distributed between the state itself and townships, towns, or boroughs. Where the state is the main coordinating body, the state may test and compile eligibility lists for its constituent local governments.

Other states have vested a great deal of power and autonomy in their counties. The counties operate and administer their own highway systems, police divisions, hospitals, educational units, prisons, and recreational areas. Where the counties deliver so many services, they also tend to offer support and assistance to local governments within their borders. Thus, strong counties tend to assume the testing function for county-wide employment at various levels. A single clerical exam administered by a county might be used to establish eligibility lists for towns, incorporated villages, school districts, and library districts within that county. Applicants taking county exams can specify which local entities they would like to be considered for and can have their names placed on a number of lists on the basis of one exam score.

Counties also have a great deal of discretion in test development and in choosing which tests to administer. Any given county may decide at any time to purchase an examination from a commercial test developer, to utilize a state-developed exam, or to join a consortium of neighboring counties and have an examination specially developed according to the specifications of the cooperating counties. The county may also change its examination from administration to administration, searching out the best vehicle for choosing the most productive employees.

Variations of exam subjects and formats are greatest among law enforcement and correctional examinations. Subjects of clerical examinations are more limited by the nature of clerical work itself. There are just so many dimensions along which to test, just so many relevant predictors of clerical success. Even so, there are differences in approach according to job descriptions and from county to county.

For example, Westchester County in New York administers an examination for the entry-level job title "jr. typist." This is a two-part examination testing only typing speed and accuracy and spelling. Rank-order certification is made on the basis of this 90-question, 10-minute spelling test and five-minute plain-paper-copy typing test. With this certification, applicants may seek employment with local governments, school districts, and libraries throughout the county. The hiring bodies may, of course, require candidates to demonstrate other skills and abilities as well.

For a somewhat higher-level job title, that of "senior clerk-typist," Suffolk County of New York administers a much more comprehensive exam. The job description reads:

> **DUTIES:** Performs a wide variety of difficult and responsible clerical and typing functions requiring the application of independent judgment and clerical knowledge. Checks the accuracy and completeness of documents, applications, legal instruments, payment claims of vendors and contract claims. Composes routine letters and transcribes from dictating machine or types from rough copy of such items as reports, letters, statements, tabulations, vouchers and legal documents. Keeps perpetual in-

County Clerical Employment / 45

ventory and consumption records. May supervise a small number of clerical personnel engaged in routine clerical duties. Does related work as required.

Description of the examination is as follows:

SCOPE OF THE EXAMINATION

The examination for this title will consist of two parts: (I) a written test; and (II) a qualifying typing performance test.

I. The *Written test* will cover knowledge, skills, and/or abilities in such areas as:
   1. Office practices;
   2. English usage;
   3. Reading comprehension;
   4. Arithmetic reasoning;
   5. Record keeping.

II. *TYPING TEST* — Straight-copy typing test rated for speed and accuracy at 35 words per minute on a personal computer. (Candidates will not be permitted to bring their own typewriters.)

There is so much variation in county clerical examinations that a sample exam might prove misleading. The best preparation for a county clerical examination, and indeed for any clerical examination, is thorough grounding in basic clerical skills and practice with many different kinds of exams.

Straight-copy typing tests, on the other hand, are all alike. Only the speed and error standards and requirements may vary. The chapter entitled "The Typing Test" specifically addresses the typing test for the Postal Clerk-Typist Exam. However, your own exam, for whatever typing-inclusive clerical position, will be very similar to it.

CLERICAL EMPLOYMENT IN THE COURTS

The job title "court clerk" is generally not a title filled by entry-level clerical workers. The court clerk is usually a senior employee of the court with a number of years of service as a court officer and considerable legal knowledge. The court clerk does, indeed, perform many clerical duties, but these duties are only secondary to administrative and even paralegal responsibilities. Where the court clerk position is a promotional one, the clerical-type exams will have been passed at earlier stages of employment testing. The court clerk exam will be a test of legal knowledge.

In those areas where "court clerk" is the title applied to any clerical worker in the court system, the court clerk exam will, of course, be more typical of clerical examinations. More often, clerical workers in the courts fill job titles like "file clerk," "office clerk," and "clerk-typist." In the Unified Court System of New York, which staffs state and municipal courts, a typical job designation is "senior office typist." In announcing opening of this job title, the Unified Court System of New York published the following job description:

> Senior Office Typists work with a limited degree of independence on a variety of office clerical and keyboarding tasks, as supervisors of small clerical sub-units, at public counters as information clerks, and perform other related duties.

The same announcement supplied the following test description.

The written examination will be multiple-choice and will assess the following:

1. Spelling
   These questions are designed to test a candidate's ability to spell words that office clerical employees encounter in their daily work.

2. Knowledge of English Grammar and Usage, Punctuation and Sentence Structure
   These questions are designed to test a candidate's knowledge of the basic rules of English grammar, usage, punctuation, and sentence structure.

3. Clerical Checking
   These questions are designed to test a candidate's ability to identify differences among sets of written materials which are almost alike. Candidates are presented with sets of information containing names, numbers, codes, etc., and must determine how the sets may differ.

4. Office Record Keeping
   These questions are designed to test a candidate's ability to read, combine, and manipulate written information organized from several different sources. Candidates are presented with different types of tables which contain names, numbers, codes, etc., and must combine and reorganize the information to answer questions. All of the information required to answer the questions is provided in the tables; candidates are not required to have any special knowledge relating to the information provided.

5. Reading, Understanding and Interpreting Written Material
   These questions are designed to test how well candidates can understand what they have read. Candidates are provided with short written passages from which some words have been removed. Candidates are required to select from four alternatives the word that best fits in each of the spaces.

Keyboarding Test

Candidates will be notified when to appear for the performance examination. Only candidates who obtain a passing score on the written examination will be invited to participate in the performance examination(s).

All candidates who are successful on the above written exam will be called to take a qualifying performance test in keyboarding (typing) which will be held after the written examination date. Candidates will be required to type an exact copy of a selection at the rate of <u>45 words per minute</u>. This is a five-minute test of accuracy and speed of keyboarding from straight copy.

Electric in-place typewriters and paper are available at all test sites. You may bring your own typewriter, whether electric or manual. If you bring an electric typewriter, you must bring an extension cord at least 10 feet long.

The sample examination for senior office typist, New York Unified Court System, in Part Two of this book is based upon the most recent administration of this exam. In some ways it is similar to many other clerical examinations; in some ways it is unique and intriguing. This exam introduces some new question styles and formats. It will be very much worth your time to try your hand at these questions. You want to prepare yourself for whatever type of question may appear on *your* exam. In a field of competent applicants, familiarity with question styles can give you the competitive edge, a higher score, and an offer of employment.

MUNICIPAL CLERICAL POSITIONS

If you were not aware of this fact before, you most certainly now are convinced that clerical positions appear at every governmental level and in every locality. Big cities are no exception. Most big cities operate their own civil service systems, develop and administer their own examinations, and maintain their own eligibility lists. The job titles can be simple and all-inclusive, or they can be highly specialized, as in New York City. The following list comprises *some* of the clerical positions filled through the tests of the Personnel Department in the city of New York.

Account Clerk
Cashier
Chief Clerk
Chief Office Assistant
Clerical Aide
Clerk
Clerk, Community Action Activities
Clerk, Income Maintenance
Clerk to the Board
College Aide
College Assistant
College Office Assistant
College Secretarial Assistant
Committee Clerk
Communications Clerk
Computer Aide
Computer Operator
Deputy Chief Clerk
Deputy City Clerk
Document Clerk
Legislative Clerical Assistant
Legislative Clerk
Legislative Stenographer
Legislative Typist
Medical Clerk
Office Aide
Office Aide (Typing Positions)
Office Appliance Operator
Office Assistant
Office Associate
Office Machine Associate
Police Administrative Aide
Property Clerk
Public Records Aide
Railroad Clerk
Secretary
Senior Clerk
Senior Legislative Clerical Assistant
Senior Legislative Clerk
Senior Office Appliance Operator
Senior Satisfaction Clerk

The city of New York tends to administer a separate exam for each job title as the list of eligibles for that title is exhausted or expires. But the exams used to test for similar positions are very similar to each other. Numbers of questions, timing, subjects tested, and proportion of questions on each subject vary little from exam to exam. Only the words and figures change.

The office aide exam in the second part of this book is an actual office aide examination given by the city of New York some years ago. Some question styles have changed over the years. Some new styles have been introduced; old, discredited question styles have been discarded. If you are taking a New York City exam, it will be similar, but not exactly the same as this. If your exam is for a city other than New York, you can expect less similarity.

Municipal Clerical Positions / 49

Another city's exam may look more like a Federal or state exam. Whatever the format, however, clerical skills are clerical skills, and much of the subject matter will be the same. Emphasis and question form may differ, but the ability you must demonstrate is the ability to perform clerical duties.

Do not ignore the municipal office aide exam in the second part of the book just because you are not taking a New York City exam. This exam will give you good practice in taking a varied exam that is not divided into discrete segments. Any test-taking practice will help in preparation for the exam you will take.

CLERICAL EMPLOYMENT IN THE PRIVATE SECTOR

Civil service testing, that is, testing for positions in the public sector, is standardized and uniform within each governmental jurisdiction. Testing in the private sector, by contrast, is highly individualized. A private employer has the option to test or not to test, to devise tailor-made tests for positions within the company, or to purchase ready-made exams from a commercial test publisher.

Most often a small, private employer will rely on school records, recommendations, personal interview, and, if relevant, typing and stenography tests. Large corporations often screen applicants with clerical tests of their own devising so as to avoid the time and effort of checking references and interviewing applicants who are unqualified in terms of skills and abilities.

Within the private sector, most clerical exams are administered by employment agencies—both temporary agencies and agencies that specialize in placing permanent employees. The agencies gain and maintain their reputations by sending qualified prospects to their clients. One way for an agency to verify the competence of people seeking employment is by testing their skills.

Since private sector testing is not organized or regulated, there is no one battery of tests and no one format that can be described. However, common sense dictates that prospective clerical workers are likely to be tested for ability in some of the following areas:

> Reading Comprehension
> Spelling
> Ability to Follow Directions
> Clerical Speed and Accuracy
> Proofreading
> Typing
>
> Vocabulary
> Simple Arithmetic Calculations
> Grammar and English Usage
> Interpreting Tables and Charts
> Stenography
> Computer Literacy

As the subjects for examination may vary, so the means for testing may vary as well. Some employers may administer tests entirely by computer. The applicant demonstrates subject matter mastery and competence at the computer at the same time. Since use of the computer is so central to so much clerical work—data entry, word processing, information retrieval, etc.—testing by computer is highly appropriate and is becoming more and more prevalent.

Most often the testing assumes some sort of combination form. Part of the exam is paper and pencil, either multiple choice or short answer, and part is typewriter or computer based.

The most significant difference between public and private sector testing is the nature of the competition. In a public sector civil service test, you compete against the entire population taking that test and strive for a high competitive rating. In a private sector testing situation, you are proving your own skills as an individual. While you may well be competing against other applicants for the same opening, your test performance only proves your competence for the work at hand. The competition is based on many personal factors of which clerical skill is only one aspect. Obviously you must have the skills and be able to prove yourself, but you do not face the same pressure to earn a high score on a private sector exam.

Clerical Employment in the Private Sector / 51

The best preparation for a private sector exam, as for a civil service exam, is competence in the subject areas and practice in the skills areas. If you can gain experience on a number of different typewriter models and with a number of computer programs you are more likely to find yourself being tested on a familiar machine. Familiarity leads to self-confidence and better performance.

The private sector clerical examination in the second part of this book is typical of that given by a number of large employment agencies that specialize in placement of clerical workers on both temporary and permanent bases. It is not an actual exam. Your exam may be quite different. Practice with this exam, however, will give you exposure to the non-multiple-choice exam style often favored by private sector employers.

TEST-TAKING TECHNIQUES

Many factors enter into a test score. The most important factor should be ability to answer the questions, which in turn indicates ability to learn and perform the duties of the job. Assuming that you have this ability, knowing what to expect on the exam and familiarity with techniques of effective test taking should give you the confidence you need to do your best on the exam.

There is no quick substitute for long-term study and development of your skills and abilities to prepare you for doing well on tests. However, there are some steps you can take to help you do the very best that you are prepared to do.

Some of these steps are done before the test, and some are followed when you are taking the test. Knowing these steps is often called being "test-wise." Following these steps may help you feel more confident as you take the actual test.

"Test-wiseness" is a general term which simply means being familiar with some good procedures to follow when getting ready for and taking a test. The procedures fall into four major areas: (1) being prepared, (2) avoiding careless errors, (3) managing your time, and (4) guessing.

Be prepared! Don't make the test harder than it has to be by not preparing yourself. You are taking a very important step in preparation by reading this book and taking the sample tests which are included. This will help you to become familiar with the tests and the kinds of questions you will have to answer.

As you use this book, read the sample questions and directions for taking the test carefully. Then, when you take the sample tests, time yourself as you will be timed in the real test.

As you are doing the sample questions, don't look at the correct answers before you try to answer them on your own. This can fool you into thinking you understand a question when you really don't. Try it on your own first, and then compare your answer with the one given. Remember, in a sample test, you are your own grader; you don't gain anything by pretending to understand something you really don't.

On the examination day assigned to you, allow the test itself to be the main attraction of the day. Do not squeeze it in between other activities. Be sure to bring admission card, identification, and pencils, as instructed. Prepare these the night before so that you are not flustered by a last-minute search. Arrive rested, relaxed, and on time. In fact, plan to arrive a little bit early. Leave plenty of time for traffic tie-ups or other complications that might upset you and interfere with your test performance.

In the test room, the examiner will hand out forms for you to fill out. He or she will give you the instructions that you must follow in taking the examination. The examiner will tell you how to fill in the grids on the forms. Time limits and timing signals will be explained. If you do not understand any of the examiner's instructions, ASK QUESTIONS. It would be ridiculous to score less than your best because of poor communication.

At the examination, you must follow instructions exactly. Fill in the grids on the forms carefully and accurately. Misgridding may lead to loss of veteran's credits to which you may be entitled to or misaddressing of your test results. Do not begin until you are told to begin. Stop as soon as the examiner tells you to stop. Do not turn pages until you are told to do so. Do not go back to parts you have already completed. Any infraction of the rules is considered cheating. If you cheat, your test paper will not be scored, and you will not be eligible for appointment.

The answer sheet for most multiple-choice exams is machine scored. You cannot give any explanations to the machine, so you must fill out the answer sheet clearly and correctly.

How to Mark Your Answer Sheet

1. Blacken your answer space firmly and completely. ● is the only correct way to mark the answer sheet. ◐, ⊗, ✓, and ∅ are all unacceptable. The machine might not read them at all.

2. Mark only one answer for each question. If you mark more than one answer you will be considered wrong even if one of the answers is correct.

3. If you change your mind, you must erase your mark. Attempting to cross out an incorrect answer like this ✗ will not work. You must erase any incorrect answer completely. An incomplete erasure might be read as a second answer.

4. All of your answering should be in the form of blackened spaces. The machine cannot read English. Do not write any notes in the margins.

5. MOST IMPORTANT: Answer each question in the right place. Question 1 must be answered in space 1; question 52 in space 52. If you should skip an answer space and mark a series of answers in the wrong places, you must erase all those answers and do the questions over, marking your answers in the proper places. You cannot afford to use the limited time in this way. Therefore, as you answer *each* question, look at its number and check that you are marking your answer in the space with the same number.

Avoid careless errors! Don't reduce your score by making careless mistakes. Always read the instructions for each test section carefully, even when you think you already know what the directions are.

What if you are wrong? You will have risked getting the answers wrong for a whole test section. As an example, vocabulary questions can sometimes test synonyms (words which have similar meanings), and sometimes test antonyms (words with opposite meanings). You can easily see how a mistake in understanding in this case could make a whole set of answers incorrect.

If you have time, reread any complicated instructions after you do the first few questions to check that you really do understand them. Of course, whenever you are allowed to, ask the examiner to clarify anything you don't understand.

Other careless mistakes affect only the response to particular questions. This often happens with arithmetic questions, but can happen with other questions as well. This type of error, called a "response error," usually stems from a momentary lapse of concentration.

Example: The question reads: "The capital of Massachusetts is ...." The answer is (D) Boston, and you mark (B) because "B" is the first letter of the word "Boston." Example: The question reads: "8 − 5 = ..." The answer is (A) 3, but you mark (C) thinking "third letter."

Manage your time! Before you begin, take a moment to plan your progress through the test. Although you are usually not expected to finish all of the questions given on a test, you should at least get an idea of how much time you should spend on each question in order to answer them all. For example, if there are 60 questions to answer and you have 30 minutes, you will have about one-half minute to spend on each question.

Keep track of the time on your watch or the room clock, but do not fixate on the time remaining. Your task is to answer questions. Do not spend too much time on any one question. If you find yourself stuck, do not take the puzzler as a personal challenge. Either guess and mark the question in the question booklet or skip the question entirely, marking the question as a skip and taking care to skip the answer space on the answer sheet. If there is time at the end of the exam or exam part, you can return and give marked questions another try.

Should You Guess?

You may be wondering whether or not it is wise to guess when you are not sure of an answer or whether it is better to skip the question when you are not certain. The wisdom of guessing depends on the scoring method for the particular examination part. If the scoring is "rights only," that is, one point for each correct answer and no subtraction for wrong answers, then by all means you should guess. Read the question and all of the answer choices carefully. Eliminate those answer choices that you are certain are wrong. Then guess from among the remaining choices. You cannot gain a point if you leave the answer space blank; you may gain a point with an educated guess or even with a lucky guess. In fact, it is foolish to leave any spaces blank on a test that counts "rights only." If it appears that you are about to run out of time before completing such an exam, mark all the remaining blanks with the same letter. According to the law of averages, you should get some portion of those questions right.

If the scoring method is rights minus wrongs, such as the address checking test found on Postal Clerk Exam 470, DO NOT GUESS. A wrong answer counts heavily against you. On this type of test, do not rush to fill answer spaces randomly at the end. Work as quickly as possible while concentrating on accuracy. Keep working carefully until time is called. Then stop and leave the remaining answer spaces blank.

In guessing the answers to multiple-choice questions, take a second to eliminate those answers that are obviously wrong, then quickly consider and guess from the remaining choices. The fewer choices from which you guess, the better the odds of guessing correctly. Once you have decided to make a guess, be it an educated guess or a wild stab, do it right away and move on; don't keep thinking about it and wasting time. You should always mark the test questions at which you guess so that you can return later.

For those questions which are scored by subtracting a fraction of a point for each wrong answer, the decision as to whether or not to guess is really up to you.

A correct answer gives you one point; a skipped space gives you nothing at all, but costs you nothing except the chance of getting the answer right; a wrong answer costs you ¼ point. If you are really uncomfortable with guessing, you may skip a question, BUT you must then remember to skip its answer space as well. The risk of losing your place if you skip questions is so great that we advise you to guess even if you are not sure of the answer. Our suggestion is that you answer every question in order, even if you have to guess. It is better to lose a few ¼ points for wrong guesses than to lose valuable seconds figuring where you started marking answers in the wrong place, erasing, and re-marking answers. On the other hand, do not mark random answers at the end. Work steadily until time is up.

One of the questions you should ask in the testing room is what scoring method will be used on your particular exam. You can then guide your guessing procedure accordingly.

Scoring

If your exam is a short-answer exam such as those often used by companies in the private sector, your answers will be graded by a personnel officer trained in grading test questions. If you blackened spaces on the separate answer sheet accompanying a multiple-choice exam, your answer sheet will be machine scanned or will be hand scored using a punched card stencil. Then a raw score will be calculated using the scoring formula that applies to that test or test portion—rights only, rights minus wrongs, or rights minus a fraction of wrongs. Raw scores on test parts are then added together for a total raw score.

A raw score is *not* a final score. The raw score is not the score that finds its way onto an eligibility list. The civil service testing authority, Postal Service, or other testing body converts raw scores to a scaled score according to an unpublicized formula of its own. The scaling formula allows for slight differences in difficulty of questions from one form of the exam to another and allows for equating the scores of all candidates. Regardless of the number of questions and possible different weights of different parts of the exam, most civil service clerical test scores are reported on a scale of 1 to 100. The entire process of conversion from raw to scaled score is confidential information. The score you receive is not your number right, is not your raw score, and, despite being on a scale of 1 to 100, is not a percentage. It is a scaled score. If you are entitled to veterans' service points, these are added to your passing scaled score to boost your rank on the eligibility list. Veterans' points are added only to passing scores. A failing score cannot be brought to passing level by adding veterans' points. The score earned plus veterans' service points, if any, is the score that finds its place on the rank order eligibility list. Highest scores go to the top of the list.

Test-Taking Tips

1. READ. Read every word of the instructions. Read every word of every question.

2. Mark your answers by completely blackening the answer space of your choice.

3. Mark only ONE answer for each question, even if you think that more than one answer is correct. You must choose only one. If you mark more than one answer, the scoring machine will consider you wrong.

4. If you change your mind, erase completely. Leave no doubt as to which answer you mean.

5. If your exam permits you to use scratch paper or the margins of the test booklet for figuring, don't forget to mark the answer on the answer sheet. Only the answer sheet is scored.

6. Check often to be sure that the question number matches the answer space, that you have not skipped a space by mistake.

7. Guess according to the guessing suggestions we have made.

8. Stay alert. Be careful not to mark a wrong answer just because you were not concentrating.

9. Do not panic. If you cannot finish any part before time is up, do not worry. If you are accurate, you can do well even without finishing. It is even possible to earn a scaled score of 100 without entirely finishing an exam part if you are very accurate. At any rate, do not let your performance on any one part affect your performance on any other part.

10. Check and recheck, time permitting. If you finish any part before time is up, use the remaining time to check that each question is answered in the right space and that there is only one answer for each question. Return to the difficult questions and rethink them.

Good luck!

Part Two

Sample Examinations for Practice

Answer Sheet for Federal Clerical Examination

Verbal Tasks Test

1. Ⓐ Ⓑ Ⓒ Ⓓ Ⓔ
2. Ⓐ Ⓑ Ⓒ Ⓓ Ⓔ
3. Ⓐ Ⓑ Ⓒ Ⓓ Ⓔ
4. Ⓐ Ⓑ Ⓒ Ⓓ Ⓔ
5. Ⓐ Ⓑ Ⓒ Ⓓ Ⓔ
6. Ⓐ Ⓑ Ⓒ Ⓓ Ⓔ
7. Ⓐ Ⓑ Ⓒ Ⓓ Ⓔ
8. Ⓐ Ⓑ Ⓒ Ⓓ Ⓔ
9. Ⓐ Ⓑ Ⓒ Ⓓ Ⓔ
10. Ⓐ Ⓑ Ⓒ Ⓓ Ⓔ
11. Ⓐ Ⓑ Ⓒ Ⓓ Ⓔ
12. Ⓐ Ⓑ Ⓒ Ⓓ Ⓔ
13. Ⓐ Ⓑ Ⓒ Ⓓ Ⓔ
14. Ⓐ Ⓑ Ⓒ Ⓓ Ⓔ
15. Ⓐ Ⓑ Ⓒ Ⓓ Ⓔ
16. Ⓐ Ⓑ Ⓒ Ⓓ Ⓔ
17. Ⓐ Ⓑ Ⓒ Ⓓ Ⓔ
18. Ⓐ Ⓑ Ⓒ Ⓓ Ⓔ
19. Ⓐ Ⓑ Ⓒ Ⓓ Ⓔ
20. Ⓐ Ⓑ Ⓒ Ⓓ Ⓔ
21. Ⓐ Ⓑ Ⓒ Ⓓ Ⓔ
22. Ⓐ Ⓑ Ⓒ Ⓓ Ⓔ
23. Ⓐ Ⓑ Ⓒ Ⓓ Ⓔ
24. Ⓐ Ⓑ Ⓒ Ⓓ Ⓔ
25. Ⓐ Ⓑ Ⓒ Ⓓ Ⓔ
26. Ⓐ Ⓑ Ⓒ Ⓓ Ⓔ
27. Ⓐ Ⓑ Ⓒ Ⓓ Ⓔ
28. Ⓐ Ⓑ Ⓒ Ⓓ Ⓔ
29. Ⓐ Ⓑ Ⓒ Ⓓ Ⓔ
30. Ⓐ Ⓑ Ⓒ Ⓓ Ⓔ
31. Ⓐ Ⓑ Ⓒ Ⓓ Ⓔ
32. Ⓐ Ⓑ Ⓒ Ⓓ Ⓔ
33. Ⓐ Ⓑ Ⓒ Ⓓ Ⓔ
34. Ⓐ Ⓑ Ⓒ Ⓓ Ⓔ
35. Ⓐ Ⓑ Ⓒ Ⓓ Ⓔ
36. Ⓐ Ⓑ Ⓒ Ⓓ Ⓔ
37. Ⓐ Ⓑ Ⓒ Ⓓ Ⓔ
38. Ⓐ Ⓑ Ⓒ Ⓓ Ⓔ
39. Ⓐ Ⓑ Ⓒ Ⓓ Ⓔ
40. Ⓐ Ⓑ Ⓒ Ⓓ Ⓔ
41. Ⓐ Ⓑ Ⓒ Ⓓ Ⓔ
42. Ⓐ Ⓑ Ⓒ Ⓓ Ⓔ
43. Ⓐ Ⓑ Ⓒ Ⓓ Ⓔ
44. Ⓐ Ⓑ Ⓒ Ⓓ Ⓔ
45. Ⓐ Ⓑ Ⓒ Ⓓ Ⓔ
46. Ⓐ Ⓑ Ⓒ Ⓓ Ⓔ
47. Ⓐ Ⓑ Ⓒ Ⓓ Ⓔ
48. Ⓐ Ⓑ Ⓒ Ⓓ Ⓔ
49. Ⓐ Ⓑ Ⓒ Ⓓ Ⓔ
50. Ⓐ Ⓑ Ⓒ Ⓓ Ⓔ
51. Ⓐ Ⓑ Ⓒ Ⓓ Ⓔ
52. Ⓐ Ⓑ Ⓒ Ⓓ Ⓔ
53. Ⓐ Ⓑ Ⓒ Ⓓ Ⓔ
54. Ⓐ Ⓑ Ⓒ Ⓓ Ⓔ
55. Ⓐ Ⓑ Ⓒ Ⓓ Ⓔ
56. Ⓐ Ⓑ Ⓒ Ⓓ Ⓔ
57. Ⓐ Ⓑ Ⓒ Ⓓ Ⓔ
58. Ⓐ Ⓑ Ⓒ Ⓓ Ⓔ
59. Ⓐ Ⓑ Ⓒ Ⓓ Ⓔ
60. Ⓐ Ⓑ Ⓒ Ⓓ Ⓔ
61. Ⓐ Ⓑ Ⓒ Ⓓ Ⓔ
62. Ⓐ Ⓑ Ⓒ Ⓓ Ⓔ
63. Ⓐ Ⓑ Ⓒ Ⓓ Ⓔ
64. Ⓐ Ⓑ Ⓒ Ⓓ Ⓔ
65. Ⓐ Ⓑ Ⓒ Ⓓ Ⓔ
66. Ⓐ Ⓑ Ⓒ Ⓓ Ⓔ
67. Ⓐ Ⓑ Ⓒ Ⓓ Ⓔ
68. Ⓐ Ⓑ Ⓒ Ⓓ Ⓔ
69. Ⓐ Ⓑ Ⓒ Ⓓ Ⓔ
70. Ⓐ Ⓑ Ⓒ Ⓓ Ⓔ
71. Ⓐ Ⓑ Ⓒ Ⓓ Ⓔ
72. Ⓐ Ⓑ Ⓒ Ⓓ Ⓔ
73. Ⓐ Ⓑ Ⓒ Ⓓ Ⓔ
74. Ⓐ Ⓑ Ⓒ Ⓓ Ⓔ
75. Ⓐ Ⓑ Ⓒ Ⓓ Ⓔ
76. Ⓐ Ⓑ Ⓒ Ⓓ Ⓔ
77. Ⓐ Ⓑ Ⓒ Ⓓ Ⓔ
78. Ⓐ Ⓑ Ⓒ Ⓓ Ⓔ
79. Ⓐ Ⓑ Ⓒ Ⓓ Ⓔ
80. Ⓐ Ⓑ Ⓒ Ⓓ Ⓔ
81. Ⓐ Ⓑ Ⓒ Ⓓ Ⓔ
82. Ⓐ Ⓑ Ⓒ Ⓓ Ⓔ
83. Ⓐ Ⓑ Ⓒ Ⓓ Ⓔ
84. Ⓐ Ⓑ Ⓒ Ⓓ Ⓔ
85. Ⓐ Ⓑ Ⓒ Ⓓ Ⓔ

TEAR HERE

The total raw score on this test consists of the total number of questions that are answered correctly. There is no penalty for wrong answers or correction made for guessing. However, no credit is given for any question with more than one answer marked.

My raw score _____

CLERICAL TASKS TEST

[Answer sheet grid with questions 1–120, each with bubbles A B C D E, arranged in four columns: 1–30, 31–60, 61–90, 91–120]

TEAR HERE

On this test there is a penalty for wrong answers. The total raw score on the test is the number of right answers minus one-fourth of the number of wrong answers. (Fractions of one-half or less are dropped.) First count the number of correct answers you have made. Do not count as correct any questions with more than one answer marked. Then count the number of incorrect answers. Omits are not counted as wrong answers, but double responses do count as wrong. Multiply the total number of incorrect answers by one-fourth. Subtract this number from the total number correct to get the test total score. For example, if you were to answer 89 questions correctly and 10 questions incorrectly, and you omitted 21 questions, your total score would be 87 (89 minus one-fourth of 10 equals 87).

Number Right	minus	Number Wrong (÷ 4)	equals	Raw Score
_____	−	_____	=	_____

FEDERAL CLERICAL EXAMINATION

Verbal Tasks Test

35 Minutes—85 Questions

Directions: Read each question carefully. Select the best answer and darken the proper space on the answer sheet. Correct answers are on p. 83.

1. *Flexible* means most nearly
   - (A) breakable
   - (B) flammable
   - (C) pliable
   - (D) weak

2. *Option* means most nearly
   - (A) use
   - (B) choice
   - (C) value
   - (D) blame

3. To *verify* means most nearly to
   - (A) examine
   - (B) explain
   - (C) confirm
   - (D) guarantee

4. *Indolent* means most nearly
   - (A) moderate
   - (B) hopeless
   - (C) selfish
   - (D) lazy

5. *Respiration* means most nearly
   - (A) recovery
   - (B) breathing
   - (C) pulsation
   - (D) sweating

6. PLUMBER is related to WRENCH as PAINTER is related to
   - (A) brush
   - (B) pipe
   - (C) shop
   - (D) hammer

7. LETTER is related to MESSAGE as PACKAGE is related to
   - (A) sender
   - (B) merchandise
   - (C) insurance
   - (D) business

8. FOOD is related to HUNGER as SLEEP is related to
   - (A) night
   - (B) dream
   - (C) weariness
   - (D) rest

9. KEY is related to TYPEWRITER as DIAL is related to
   - (A) sun
   - (B) number
   - (C) circle
   - (D) telephone

61

10. (A) I think that they will promote whoever has the best record.
(B) The firm would have liked to have promoted all employees with good records.
(C) Such of them that have the best records have excellent prospects of promotion.
(D) I feel sure they will give the promotion to whomever has the best record.

11. (A) The receptionist must answer courteously the questions of all them callers.
(B) The receptionist must answer courteously the questions what are asked by the callers.
(C) There would have been no trouble if the receptionist had have always answered courteously.
(D) The receptionist should answer courteously the questions of all callers.

12. (A) collapsible   (C) collapseble
(B) collapseable   (D) none of these

13. (A) ambigeuous   (C) ambiguous
(B) ambigeous   (D) none of these

14. (A) predesessor   (C) predecesser
(B) predecesar   (D) none of these

15. (A) sanctioned   (C) sanctionned
(B) sancktioned   (D) none of these

16. "Some fire-resistant buildings, although wholly constructed of materials that will not burn, may be completely gutted by the spread of fire through their contents by way of hallways and other openings. They may even suffer serious structural damage by the collapse of metal beams and columns."

The quotation best supports the statement that some fire-resistant buildings

(A) can be damaged seriously by fire
(B) have specially constructed halls and doors
(C) afford less protection to their contents than would ordinary buildings
(D) will burn readily

17. Civilization started to move ahead more rapidly when people freed themselves of the shackles that restricted their search for the truth.

The paragraph best supports the statement that the progress of civilization

(A) came as a result of people's dislike for obstacles
(B) did not begin until restrictions on learning were removed
(C) has been aided by people's efforts to find the truth
(D) is based on continually increasing efforts

18. *Vigilant* means most nearly
(A) sensible   (C) suspicious
(B) watchful   (D) restless

19. *Incidental* means most nearly
(A) independent   (C) infrequent
(B) needless   (D) casual

20. *Conciliatory* means most nearly
    (A) pacific   (C) obligatory
    (B) contentious   (D) offensive

21. *Altercation* means most nearly
    (A) defeat   (C) controversy
    (B) concurrence   (D) vexation

22. *Irresolute* means most nearly
    (A) wavering   (C) impudent
    (B) insubordinate   (D) unobservant

23. DARKNESS is related to SUNLIGHT as STILLNESS is related to
    (A) quiet   (C) sound
    (B) moonlight   (D) dark

24. DESIGNED is related to INTENTION as ACCIDENTAL is related to
    (A) purpose   (C) damage
    (B) caution   (D) chance

25. ERROR is related to PRACTICE as SOUND is related to
    (A) deafness   (C) muffler
    (B) noise   (D) horn

26. RESEARCH is related to FINDINGS as TRAINING is related to
    (A) skill   (C) supervision
    (B) tests   (D) teaching

27. (A) If properly addressed, the letter will reach my mother and I.
    (B) The letter had been addressed to myself and my mother.
    (C) I believe the letter was addressed to either my mother or I.
    (D) My mother's name, as well as mine, was on the letter.

28. (A) The supervisors reprimanded the typists, whom she believed had made careless errors.
    (B) The typists would have corrected the errors had they of known that the supervisor would see the report.
    (C) The errors in the typed reports were so numerous that they could hardly be overlooked.
    (D) Many errors were found in the reports which they typed and could not disregard them.

29. (A) minieture   (C) mineature
    (B) minneature   (D) none of these

30. (A) extemporaneous   (C) extemperaneous
    (B) extempuraneus   (D) none of these

31. (A) problemmatical   (C) problematicle
    (B) problematical   (D) none of these

32. (A) descendant   (C) desendant
    (B) decendant   (D) none of these

33. The likelihood of America's exhausting its natural resources seems to be growing less. All kinds of waste are being reworked and new uses are constantly being found for almost everything. We are getting more use out of our goods and are making many new byproducts out of what was formerly thrown away.

    The paragraph best supports the statement that we seem to be in less danger of exhausting our resources because

    (A) economy is found to lie in the use of substitutes
    (B) more service is obtained from a given amount of material
    (C) we are allowing time for nature to restore them
    (D) supply and demand are better controlled

34. Telegrams should be clear, concise, and brief. Omit all unnecessary words. The parts of speech most often used in telegrams are nouns, verbs, adjectives, and adverbs. If possible, do without pronouns, prepositions, articles, and copulative verbs. Use simple sentences, rather than complex or compound ones.

    The paragraph best supports the statement that in writing telegrams one should always use

    (A) common and simple words
    (B) only nouns, verbs, adjectives, and adverbs
    (C) incomplete sentences
    (D) only the words essential to the meaning

35. To *counteract* means most nearly to
    (A) undermine   (C) preserve
    (B) censure   (D) neutralize

36. *Deferred* means most nearly
    (A) reversed   (C) considered
    (B) delayed   (D) forbidden

37. *Feasible* means most nearly
    (A) capable   (C) practicable
    (B) justifiable   (D) beneficial

38. To *encounter* means most nearly to
    (A) meet   (C) overcome
    (B) recall   (D) retreat

39. *Innate* means most nearly
    (A) eternal   (C) native
    (B) well-developed   (D) prospective

40. STUDENT is related to TEACHER as DISCIPLE is related to
    (A) follower   (C) principal
    (B) master   (D) pupil

41. LECTURE is related to AUDITORIUM as EXPERIMENT is related to
    (A) scientist   (C) laboratory
    (B) chemistry   (D) discovery

42. BODY is related to FOOD as ENGINE is related to
    (A) wheels   (C) motion
    (B) fuel   (D) smoke

43. SCHOOL is related to EDUCATION as THEATER is related to
    (A) management   (C) recreation
    (B) stage   (D) preparation

44. (A) Most all these statements have been supported by persons who are reliable and can be depended upon.
    (B) The persons which have guaranteed these statements are reliable.
    (C) Reliable persons guarantee the facts with regards to the truth of these statements.
    (D) These statements can be depended on, for their truth has been guaranteed by reliable persons.

45. (A) The success of the book pleased both the publisher and authors.
    (B) Both the publisher and they was pleased with the success of the book.
    (C) Neither they or their publisher was disappointed with the success of the book.
    (D) Their publisher was as pleased as they with the success of the book.

46. (A) extercate   (C) extricate
    (B) extracate   (D) none of these

47. (A) hereditory   (C) hereditairy
    (B) hereditary   (D) none of these

48. (A) auspiceous   (C) auspicious
    (B) auspiseous   (D) none of these

49. (A) sequance   (C) sequense
    (B) sequence   (D) none of these

50. The prevention of accidents makes it necessary not only that safety devices be used to guard exposed machinery but also that mechanics be instructed in safety rules which they must follow for their own protection, and that the lighting in the plant be adequate.

    The paragraph best supports the statement that industrial accidents

    (A) may be due to ignorance
    (B) are always avoidable
    (C) usually result from inadequate machinery
    (D) cannot be entirely overcome

51. The English language is peculiarly rich in synonyms, and there is scarcely a language spoken that has not some representative in English speech. The spirit of the Anglo-Saxon race has subjugated these various elements to one idiom, making not a patchwork, but a composite language.

    The paragraph best supports the statement that the English language

    (A) has few idiomatic expressions
    (B) is difficult to translate
    (C) is used universally
    (D) has absorbed words from other languages

52. To *acquiesce* means most nearly to
(A) assent
(B) acquire
(C) complete
(D) participate

53. *Unanimity* means most nearly
(A) emphasis
(B) namelessness
(C) harmony
(D) impartiality

54. *Precedent* means most nearly
(A) example
(B) theory
(C) law
(D) conformity

55. *Versatile* means most nearly
(A) broad-minded
(B) well-known
(C) up-to-date
(D) many-sided

56. *Authentic* means most nearly
(A) detailed
(B) reliable
(C) valuable
(D) practical

57. BIOGRAPHY is related to FACT as NOVEL is related to
(A) fiction
(B) literature
(C) narration
(D) book

58. COPY is related to CARBON PAPER as MOTION PICTURE is related to
(A) theater
(B) film
(C) duplicate
(D) television

59. EFFICIENCY is related to REWARD as CARELESSNESS is related to
(A) improvement
(B) disobedience
(C) reprimand
(D) repetition

60. ABUNDANT is related to CHEAP as SCARCE is related to
(A) ample
(B) costly
(C) inexpensive
(D) unobtainable

61. (A) Brown's & Company employees have recently received increases in salary.
(B) Brown & Company recently increased the salaries of all its employees.
(C) Recently Brown & Company has increased their employees' salaries.
(D) Brown & Company have recently increased the salaries of all its employees.

62. (A) In reviewing the typists' work reports, the job analyst found records of unusual typing speeds.
(B) It says in the job analyst's report that some employees type with great speed.
(C) The job analyst found that, in reviewing the typists' work reports, that some unusual typing speeds had been made.
(D) In the reports of typists' speeds, the job analyst found some records that are kind of unusual.

63. (A) oblitorate   (C) obbliterate
    (B) oblitterat   (D) none of these

64. (A) diagnoesis   (C) diagnosis
    (B) diagnossis   (D) none of these

65. (A) contenance   (C) countinance
    (B) countenance   (D) none of these

66. (A) conceivably   (C) conceiveably
    (B) concieveably (D) none of these

67. Through advertising, manufacturers exercise a high degree of control over consumers' desires. However, the manufacturer assumes enormous risks in attempting to predict what consumers will want and in producing goods in quantity and distributing them in advance of final selection by the consumers.

    The paragraph best supports the statement that manufacturers

    (A) can eliminate the risk of overproduction by advertising
    (B) distribute goods directly to the consumers
    (C) must depend upon the final consumers for the success of their undertakings
    (D) can predict with great accuracy the success of any product they put on the market

68. In the relations of humans to nature, the procuring of food and shelter is fundamental. With the migration of humans to various climates, ever new adjustments to the food supply and to the climate became necessary.

    The paragraph best supports the statement that the means by which humans supply their material needs are

    (A) accidental
    (B) varied
    (C) limited
    (D) inadequate

69. *Strident* means most nearly
    (A) swaggering   (C) angry
    (B) domineering   (D) harsh

70. To *confine* means most nearly to
    (A) hide   (C) eliminate
    (B) restrict   (D) punish

71. To *accentuate* means most nearly to
    (A) modify   (C) sustain
    (B) hasten   (D) intensify

72. *Banal* means most nearly
    (A) commonplace   (C) tranquil
    (B) forceful   (D) indifferent

73. *Incorrigible* means most nearly
    (A) intolerable (C) irreformable
    (B) retarded (D) brazen

74. POLICEMAN is related to ORDER as DOCTOR is related to
    (A) physician (C) sickness
    (B) hospital (D) health

75. ARTIST is related to EASEL as WEAVER is related to
    (A) loom (C) threads
    (B) cloth (D) spinner

76. CROWD is related to PERSONS as FLEET is related to
    (A) expedition (C) navy
    (B) officers (D) ships

77. CALENDAR is related to DATE as MAP is related to
    (A) geography (C) mileage
    (B) trip (D) vacation

78. (A) Since the report lacked the needed information, it was of no use to them.
    (B) This report was useless to them because there were no needed information in it.
    (C) Since the report did not contain the needed information, it was not real useful to them.
    (D) Being that the report lacked the needed information, they could not use it.

79. (A) The company had hardly declared the dividend till the notices were prepared for mailing.
    (B) They had no sooner declared the dividend when they sent the notices to the stockholders.
    (C) No sooner had the dividend been declared than the notices were prepared for mailing.
    (D) Scarcely had the dividend been declared than the notices were sent out.

80. (A) compitition (C) competetion
    (B) competition (D) none of these

81. (A) occassion (C) ocassion
    (B) occasion (D) none of these

82. (A) knowlege (C) knowledge
    (B) knolledge (D) none of these

83. (A) deliborate (C) delibrate
    (B) deliberate (D) none of these

84. What constitutes skill in any line of work is not always easy to determine; economy of time must be carefully distinguished from economy of energy, as the quickest method may require the greatest expenditure of muscular effort, and may not be essential or at all desirable.

    The paragraph best supports the statement that

    (A) the most efficiently executed task is not always the one done in the shortest time
    (B) energy and time cannot both be conserved in performing a single task
    (C) a task is well done when it is performed in the shortest time
    (D) skill in performing a task should not be acquired at the expense of time

85. It is difficult to distinguish between bookkeeping and accounting. In attempts to do so, bookkeeping is called the art, and accounting the science, of recording business transactions. Bookkeeping gives the history of the business in a systematic manner; and accounting classifies, analyzes, and interprets the facts thus recorded.

The paragraph best supports the statement that

(A) accounting is less systematic than bookkeeping
(B) accounting and bookkeeping are closely related
(C) bookkeeping and accounting cannot be distinguished from one another
(D) bookkeeping has been superseded by accounting

END OF VERBAL TASKS TEST

If you finish before time is up, check your work on this part only. Do not turn to the next part until the signal is given.

Clerical Tasks Test

15 Minutes—120 Questions

Correct answers are on page 83.

In questions 1 through 5, compare the three names or numbers, and mark the answer:

A if ALL THREE names or numbers are exactly ALIKE
B if only the FIRST and SECOND names or numbers are exactly ALIKE
C if only the FIRST and THIRD names or numbers are exactly ALIKE
D if only the SECOND and THIRD names or numbers are exactly ALIKE
E if ALL THREE names or numbers are DIFFERENT

1. 5261383	5261383	5261338
2. 8125690	8126690	8125609
3. W. E. Johnston	W. E. Johnson	W. E. Johnson
4. Vergil L. Muller	Vergil L. Muller	Vergil L. Muller
5. Atherton R. Warde	Asheton R. Warde	Atherton P. Warde

In questions 6 through 10, find the correct place for the name in the box.

6. Hackett, Gerald

(A) →
Habert, James.
(B) →
Hachett, J. J.
(C) →
Hachetts, K. Larson
(D) →
Hachettson, Leroy
(E) →

7. Margenroth, Alvin

(A) →
Margeroth, Albert
(B) →
Margestein, Dan
(C) →
Margestein, David
(D) →
Margue, Edgar
(E) →

8. Bobbitt, Olivier E.

(A) →
Bobbitt, D. Olivier
(B) →
Bobbitt, Olive B.
(C) →
Bobbitt, Olivia H.
(D) →
Bobbitt, R. Olivia
(E) →

9. | Mosely, Werner |

(A) →
Mosely, Albert J.
(B) →
Mosley, Alvin
(C) →
Mosley, S. M.
(D) →
Mosley, Vinson, N.
(E) →

10. | Youmuns, Frank L. |

(A) →
Youmons, Frank G.
(B) →
Youmons, Frank H.
(C) →
Youmons, Frank K.
(D) →
Youmons, Frank M.
(E) →

11. Add: 43
        + 32

(A) 55
(B) 65
(C) 66
(D) 75
(E) none of these

12. Subtract: 83
             − 4

(A) 73
(B) 79
(C) 80
(D) 89
(E) none of these

13. Multiply: 41
             × 7

(A) 281
(B) 287
(C) 291
(D) 297
(E) none of these

14. Divide: 6/306

(A) 44
(B) 51
(C) 52
(D) 60
(E) none of these

15. Add: 37
        + 15

(A) 42
(B) 52
(C) 53
(D) 62
(E) none of these

For each question below, find which one of the suggested answers appears in that question.

16.	6	2	5	K	4	P	T	G	
17.	L	4	7	2	T	6	V	K	
18.	3	5	4	L	9	V	T	G	
19.	G	4	K	7	L	3	5	Z	
20.	4	K	2	9	N	5	T	G	

Suggested Answers
- A = 4, 5, K, T
- B = 4, 7, G, K
- C = 2, 5, G, L
- D = 2, 7, L, T
- E = none of these

In questions 21 through 25, compare the three names or numbers, and mark the answer:

A if ALL THREE names or numbers are exactly ALIKE
B if only the FIRST and SECOND names or numbers are exactly ALIKE
C if only the FIRST and THIRD names or numbers are exactly ALIKE
D if only the SECOND and THIRD names or numbers are exactly ALIKE
E if ALL THREE names or numbers are DIFFERENT

21.	2395890	2395890	2395890
22.	1926341	1926347	1926314
23.	E. Owens McVey	E. Owen McVey	E. Owen McVay
24.	Emily Neal Rouse	Emily Neal Rowse	Emily Neal Rowse
25.	H. Merritt Audubon	H. Merriott Audubon	H. Merritt Audubon

In questions 26 through 30, find the correct place for the name in the box.

26. Watters, N. O.

(A) →
Waters, Charles L.
(B) →
Waterson, Nina P.
(C) →
Watson, Nora J.
(D) →
Wattwood, Paul A.
(E) →

27. Johnston, Edward

(A) →
Johnston, Edgar R.
(B) →
Johnston, Edmond
(C) →
Johnston, Edmund
(D) →
Johnstone, Edmund A.
(E) →

28. Rensch, Adeline

(A) →
Ramsay, Amos
(B) →
Remschel, Augusta
(C) →
Renshaw, Austin
(D) →
Rentzel, Becky
(E) →

29. Schnyder, Maurice

(A) →
Schneider, Martin
(B) →
Schneider, Mertens
(C) →
Schnyder, Newman
(D) →
Schreibner, Norman
(E) →

30. Freedenburg, C. Erma

(A) →
Freedenberg, Emerson
(B) →
Freedenberg, Erma
(C) →
Freedenberg, Erma E.
(D) →
Freedinberg, Erma F.
(E) →

31. Subtract: 68
              −47

(A) 10
(B) 11
(C) 20
(D) 22
(E) none of these

32. Multiply: 50
              × 8

(A) 400
(B) 408
(C) 450
(D) 458
(E) none of these

33. Divide: 9)180

(A) 20
(B) 29
(C) 30
(D) 39
(E) none of these

34. Add: 78
         +63

(A) 131
(B) 140
(C) 141
(D) 151
(E) none of these

35. Subtract: 89
              −70

(A) 9
(B) 18
(C) 19
(D) 29
(E) none of these

For each question below, find which one of the suggested answers appears in that question.

36.	9	G	Z	3	L	4	6	N	
37.	L	5	N	K	4	3	9	V	
38.	8	2	V	P	9	L	Z	5	
39.	V	P	9	Z	5	L	8	7	
40.	5	T	8	N	2	9	V	L	

Suggested Answers
- A = 4, 9, L, V
- B = 4, 5, N, Z
- C = 5, 8, L, Z
- D = 8, 9, N, V
- E = none of these

In questions 41 through 45, compare the three names or numbers, and mark the answer:

A if ALL THREE names or numbers are exactly ALIKE
B if only the FIRST and SECOND names or numbers are exactly ALIKE
C if only the FIRST and THIRD names or numbers are exactly ALIKE
D if only the SECOND and THIRD names or numbers are exactly ALIKE
E if ALL THREE names or numbers are DIFFERENT

41.	6219354	6219354	6219354
42.	2312793	2312793	2312793
43.	1065407	1065407	1065047
44.	Francis Ransdell	Frances Ramsdell	Francis Ramsdell
45.	Cornelius Detwiler	Cornelius Detwiler	Cornelius Detwiler

In questions 46 through 50, find the correct place for the name in the box.

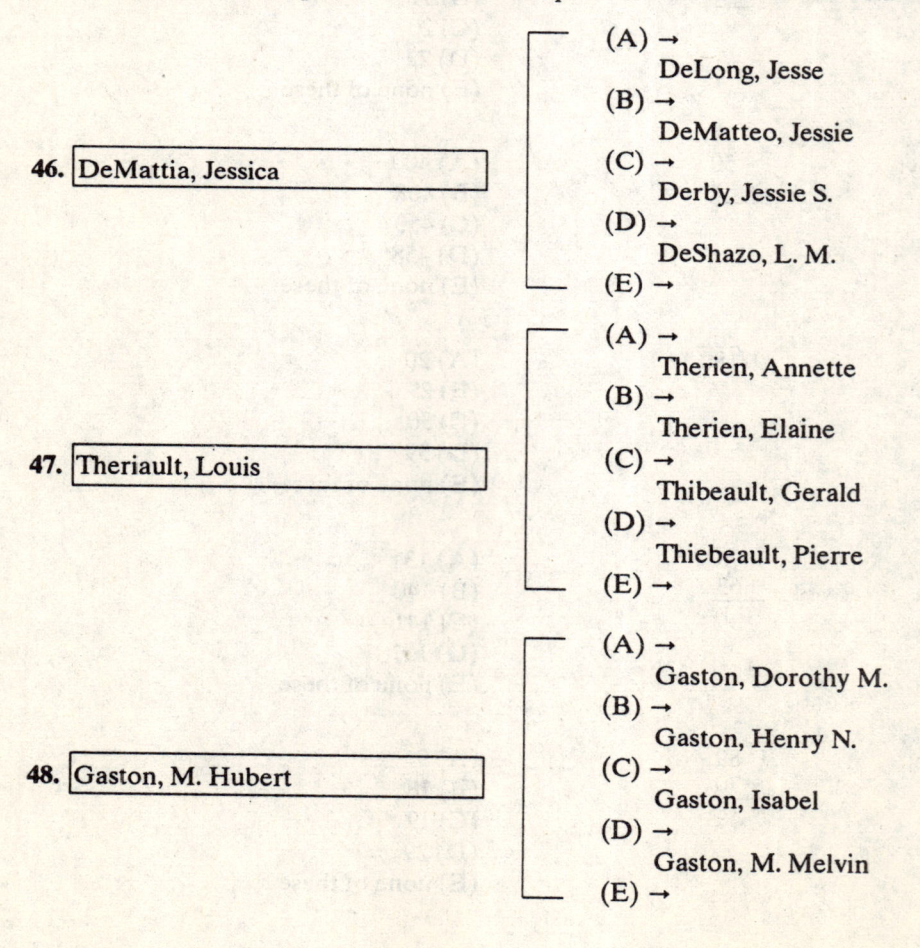

46. DeMattia, Jessica

(A) →
  DeLong, Jesse
(B) →
  DeMatteo, Jessie
(C) →
  Derby, Jessie S.
(D) →
  DeShazo, L. M.
(E) →

47. Theriault, Louis

(A) →
  Therien, Annette
(B) →
  Therien, Elaine
(C) →
  Thibeault, Gerald
(D) →
  Thiebeault, Pierre
(E) →

48. Gaston, M. Hubert

(A) →
  Gaston, Dorothy M.
(B) →
  Gaston, Henry N.
(C) →
  Gaston, Isabel
(D) →
  Gaston, M. Melvin
(E) →

(A) →

SanLuis, Juana

(B) →

Santilli, Laura

(C) →

Stinnett, Nellie

(D) →

Stoddard, Victor

49. SanMiguel, Carlos

(E) →

(A) →

Delargy, Harold

(B) →

DeLathouder, Hilda

(C) →

Lathrop, Hillary

(D) →

LaTour, Hulbert E.

50. DeLaTour, Hall F.

(E) →

51. Multiply: 62
             × 5

(A) 300
(B) 310
(C) 315
(D) 360
(E) none of these

52. Divide: 3√153

(A) 41
(B) 43
(C) 51
(D) 53
(E) none of these

53. Add: 47
         +21

(A) 58
(B) 59
(C) 67
(D) 68
(E) none of these

54. Subtract: 87
              −42

(A) 34
(B) 35
(C) 44
(D) 45
(E) none of these

55. Multiply: 37
              × 3

(A) 91
(B) 101
(C) 104
(D) 114
(E) none of these

Federal Clerical Examination / 75

76 / Clerical Exams Handbook

For each question below, find which one of the suggested answers appears in that question.

56.	N	5	4	7	T	K	3	Z
57.	8	5	3	V	L	2	Z	N
58.	7	2	5	N	9	K	L	V
59.	9	8	L	2	5	Z	K	V
60.	Z	6	5	V	9	3	P	N

Suggested Answers
- A = 3, 8, K, N
- B = 5, 8, N, V
- C = 3, 9, V, Z
- D = 5, 9, K, Z
- E = none of these

In questions 61 through 65, compare the three names or numbers, and mark the answer:

A if ALL THREE names or numbers are exactly ALIKE
B if only the FIRST and SECOND names or numbers are exactly ALIKE
C if only the FIRST and THIRD names or numbers are exactly ALIKE
D if only the SECOND and THIRD names or numbers are exactly ALIKE
E if ALL THREE names or numbers are DIFFERENT

61.	6452054	6452654	6452054
62.	8501268	8501268	8501286
63.	Ella Burk Newham	Ella Burk Newnham	Elena Burk Newnham
64.	Jno. K. Ravencroft	Jno. H. Ravencroft	Jno. H. Ravencroft
65.	Martin Wills Pullen	Martin Wills Pulen	Martin Wills Pullen

In questions 66 through 70, find the correct place for the name in the box.

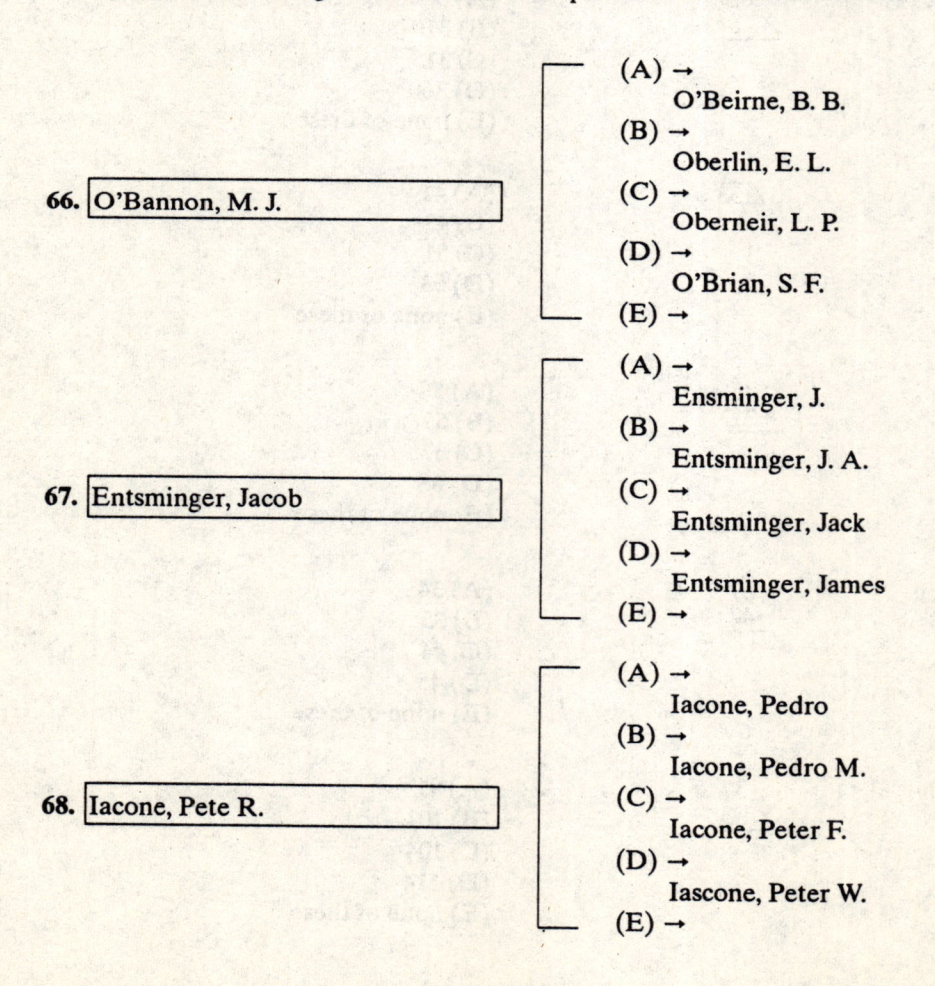

66. O'Bannon, M. J.
- (A) →
- O'Beirne, B. B.
- (B) →
- Oberlin, E. L.
- (C) →
- Oberneir, L. P.
- (D) →
- O'Brian, S. F.
- (E) →

67. Entsminger, Jacob
- (A) →
- Ensminger, J.
- (B) →
- Entsminger, J. A.
- (C) →
- Entsminger, Jack
- (D) →
- Entsminger, James
- (E) →

68. Iacone, Pete R.
- (A) →
- Iacone, Pedro
- (B) →
- Iacone, Pedro M.
- (C) →
- Iacone, Peter F.
- (D) →
- Iascone, Peter W.
- (E) →

Federal Clerical Examination / 77

69. Sheppard, Gladys

 (A) →
 Shepard, Dwight
 (B) →
 Shepard, F. H.
 (C) →
 Shephard, Louise
 (D) →
 Shepperd, Stella
 (E) →

70. Thackton, Melvin T.

 (A) →
 Thackston, Milton G.
 (B) →
 Thackston, Milton W.
 (C) →
 Thackston, Theodore
 (D) →
 Thackston, Thomas G.
 (E) →

71. Divide: 7/357

(A) 51
(B) 52
(C) 53
(D) 54
(E) none of these

72. Add: 58
    +27

(A) 75
(B) 84
(C) 85
(D) 95
(E) none of these

73. Subtract: 86
     −57

(A) 18
(B) 29
(C) 38
(D) 39
(E) none of these

74. Multiply: 68
     × 4

(A) 242
(B) 264
(C) 272
(D) 274
(E) none of these

75. Divide: 9/639

(A) 71
(B) 73
(C) 81
(D) 83
(E) none of these

For each question below, find which one of the suggested answers appears in that question.

76.	6	Z	T	N	8	7	4	V		
77.	V	7	8	6	N	5	P	L		
78.	N	7	P	V	8	4	2	L		
79.	7	8	G	4	3	V	L	T		
80.	4	8	G	2	T	N	6	L		

Suggested Answers

A = 2, 7, L, N
B = 2, 8, T, V
C = 6, 8, L, T
D = 6, 7, N, V
E = none of these

In questions 81 through 85, compare the three names or numbers, and mark the answer:

A if ALL THREE names or numbers are exactly ALIKE
B if only the FIRST and SECOND names or numbers are exactly ALIKE
C if only the FIRST and THIRD names or numbers are exactly ALIKE
D if only the SECOND and THIRD names or numbers are exactly ALIKE
E if ALL THREE names or numbers are DIFFERENT

81.	3457988	3457986	3457986
82.	4695682	4695862	4695682
83.	Stricklund Kanedy	Stricklund Kanedy	Stricklund Kanedy
84.	Joy Harlor Witner	Joy Harloe Witner	Joy Harloe Witner
85.	R. M. O. Uberroth	R. M. O. Uberroth	R. N. O. Uberroth

In questions 86 through 90, find the correct place for the name in the box.

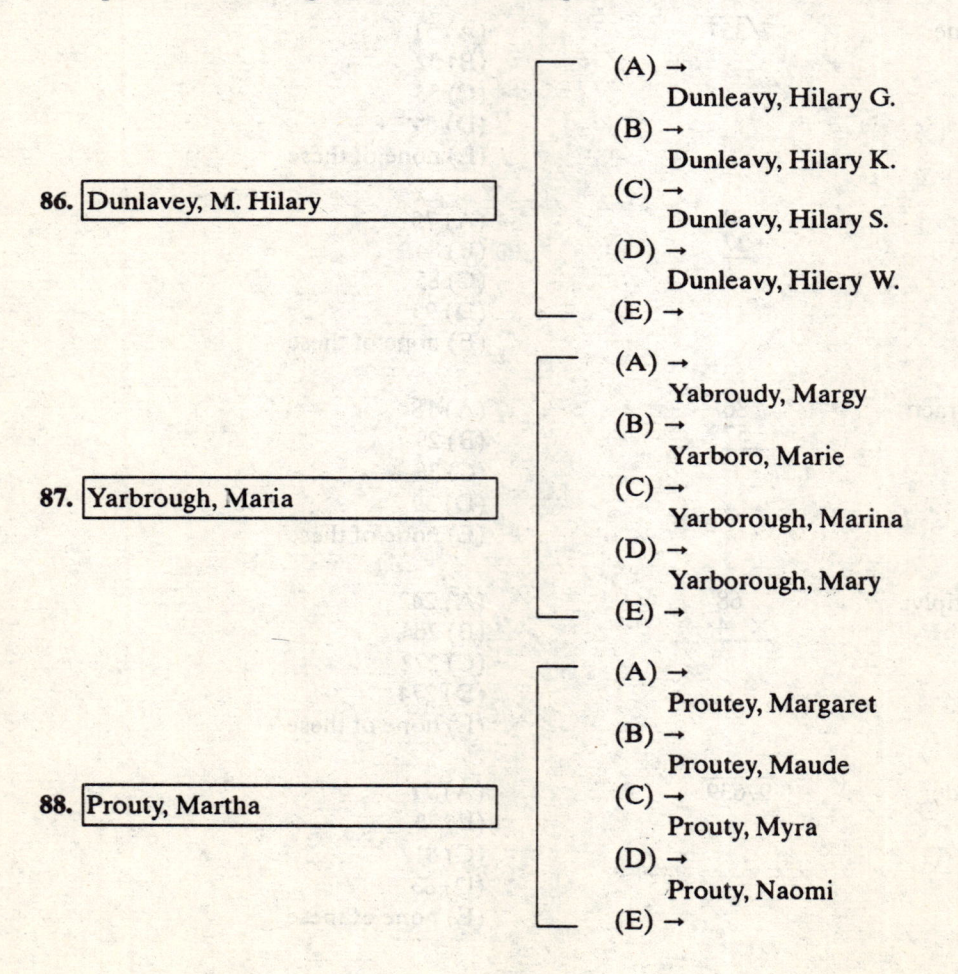

86. Dunlavey, M. Hilary

(A) →
Dunleavy, Hilary G.
(B) →
Dunleavy, Hilary K.
(C) →
Dunleavy, Hilary S.
(D) →
Dunleavy, Hilery W.
(E) →

87. Yarbrough, Maria

(A) →
Yabroudy, Margy
(B) →
Yarboro, Marie
(C) →
Yarborough, Marina
(D) →
Yarborough, Mary
(E) →

88. Prouty, Martha

(A) →
Proutey, Margaret
(B) →
Proutey, Maude
(C) →
Prouty, Myra
(D) →
Prouty, Naomi
(E) →

89. Pawlowicz, Ruth M.

(A) →
Pawalek, Edward
(B) →
Pawelek, Flora G.
(C) →
Pawlowski, Joan M.
(D) →
Pawtowski, Wanda
(E) →

90. Vanstory, George

(A) →
Vanover, Eva
(B) →
VanSwinderen, Floyd
(C) →
VanSyckle, Harry
(D) →
Vanture, Laurence
(E) →

91. Add: 28
           +35

(A) 53
(B) 62
(C) 64
(D) 73
(E) none of these

92. Subtract: 78
              −69

(A) 7
(B) 8
(C) 18
(D) 19
(E) none of these

93. Multiply: 86
             × 6

(A) 492
(B) 506
(C) 516
(D) 526
(E) none of these

94. Divide: 8/648

(A) 71
(B) 76
(C) 81
(D) 89
(E) none of these

95. Add: 97
           +34

(A) 131
(B) 132
(C) 140
(D) 141
(E) none of these

Federal Clerical Examination / 79

For each question below, find which one of the suggested answers appears in that question.

96.	V	5	7	Z	N	9	4	T	
97.	4	6	P	T	2	N	K	9	
98.	6	4	N	2	P	8	Z	K	
99.	7	P	5	2	4	N	K	T	
100.	K	T	8	5	4	N	2	P	

Suggested Answers

- A = 2, 5, N, Z
- B = 4, 5, N, P
- C = 2, 9, P, T
- D = 4, 9, T, Z
- E = none of these

In questions 101 through 105, compare the three names or numbers, and mark the answer:

A if ALL THREE names or numbers are exactly ALIKE
B if only the FIRST and SECOND names or numbers are exactly ALIKE
C if only the FIRST and THIRD names or numbers are exactly ALIKE
D if only the SECOND and THIRD names or numbers are exactly ALIKE
E if ALL THREE names or numbers are DIFFERENT

101.	1592514	1592574	1592574
102.	2010202	2010202	2010220
103.	6177396	6177936	6177396
104.	Drusilla S. Ridgeley	Drusilla S. Ridgeley	Drusilla S. Ridgeley
105.	Andrei I. Toumantzev	Andrei I. Tourmantzev	Andrei I. Toumantzov

In questions 106 through 110, find the correct place for the name in the box.

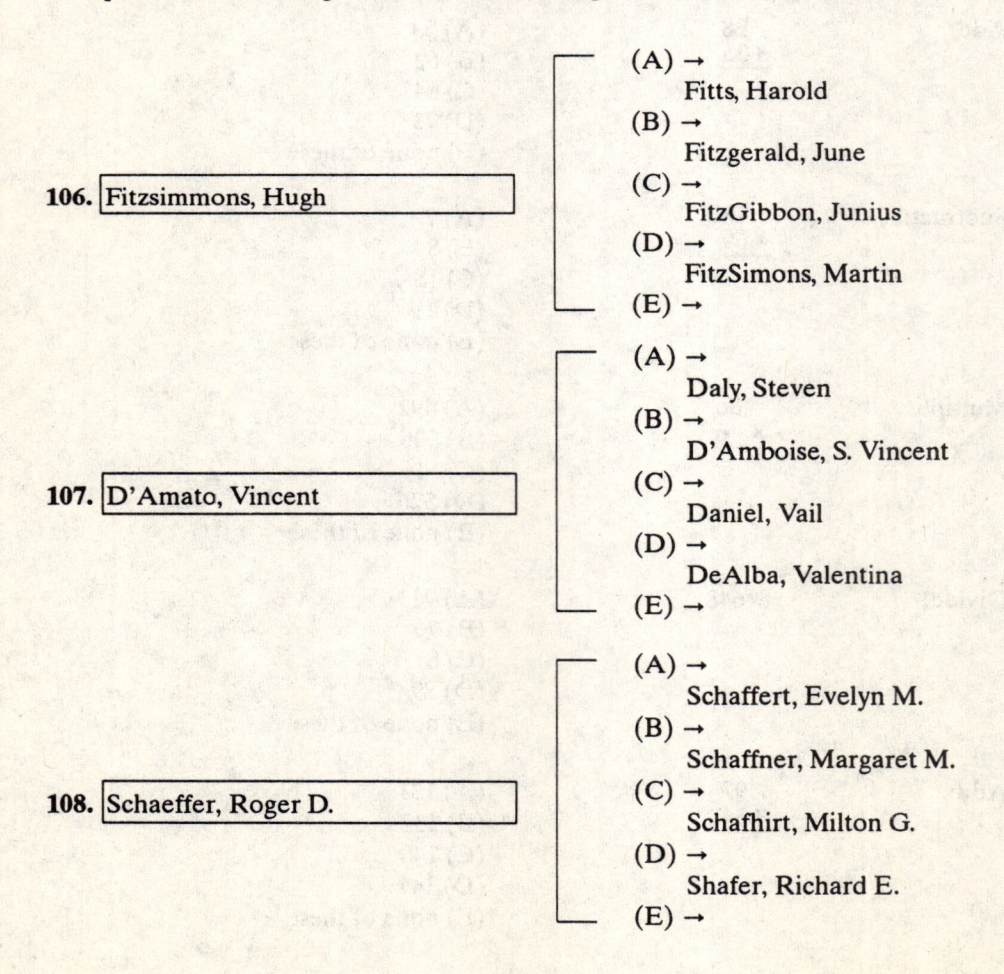

(A) →
Fitts, Harold
(B) →
Fitzgerald, June
(C) →
FitzGibbon, Junius
(D) →
FitzSimons, Martin
(E) →

106. Fitzsimmons, Hugh

(A) →
Daly, Steven
(B) →
D'Amboise, S. Vincent
(C) →
Daniel, Vail
(D) →
DeAlba, Valentina
(E) →

107. D'Amato, Vincent

(A) →
Schaffert, Evelyn M.
(B) →
Schaffner, Margaret M.
(C) →
Schafhirt, Milton G.
(D) →
Shafer, Richard E.
(E) →

108. Schaeffer, Roger D.

109. White-Lewis, Cecil

(A) →
   Whitelaw, Cordelia
(B) →
   White-Leigh, Nancy
(C) →
   Whitely, Rodney
(D) →
   Whitlock, Warren
(E) →

110. VanDerHeggen, Don

(A) →
   VanDemark, Doris
(B) →
   Vandenberg, H. E.
(C) →
   VanDercook, Marie
(D) →
   vanderLinden, Robert
(E) →

111. Add: 75
         +49

(A) 124
(B) 125
(C) 134
(D) 225
(E) none of these

112. Subtract: 69
              −45

(A) 14
(B) 23
(C) 24
(D) 26
(E) none of these

113. Multiply: 36
              × 8

(A) 246
(B) 262
(C) 288
(D) 368
(E) none of these

114. Divide: 8/328

(A) 31
(B) 41
(C) 42
(D) 48
(E) none of these

115. Multiply: 58
              × 9

(A) 472
(B) 513
(C) 521
(D) 522
(E) none of these

For each question below, find which one of the suggested answers appears in that question.

116.	Z	3	N	P	G	5	4	2
117.	6	N	2	8	G	4	P	T
118.	6	N	4	T	V	G	8	2
119.	T	3	P	4	N	8	G	2
120.	6	7	K	G	N	2	L	5

Suggested Answers
- **A** = 2, 3, G, N
- **B** = 2, 6, N, T
- **C** = 3, 4, G, K
- **D** = 4, 6, K, T
- **E** = none of these

END OF CLERICAL TASKS TEST

Correct Answers for Verbal Tasks Test

1. C	15. A	29. D	43. C	57. A	71. D
2. B	16. A	30. A	44. D	58. B	72. A
3. C	17. C	31. B	45. D	59. C	73. C
4. D	18. B	32. A	46. C	60. B	74. D
5. B	19. D	33. B	47. B	61. B	75. A
6. A	20. A	34. D	48. C	62. A	76. D
7. B	21. C	35. D	49. B	63. D	77. C
8. C	22. A	36. B	50. A	64. C	78. A
9. D	23. C	37. C	51. D	65. B	79. C
10. A	24. D	38. A	52. A	66. A	80. B
11. D	25. C	39. C	53. C	67. C	81. B
12. A	26. A	40. B	54. A	68. B	82. C
13. C	27. D	41. C	55. D	69. D	83. B
14. D	28. C	42. B	56. B	70. B	84. A
					85. B

Correct Answers for Clerical Tasks Test

1. B	21. A	41. A	61. C	81. D	101. D
2. E	22. E	42. A	62. B	82. C	102. B
3. D	23. E	43. B	63. E	83. A	103. C
4. A	24. D	44. E	64. E	84. D	104. A
5. E	25. C	45. A	65. C	85. B	105. E
6. E	26. D	46. C	66. A	86. A	106. D
7. A	27. D	47. A	67. D	87. E	107. B
8. D	28. C	48. D	68. C	88. C	108. A
9. B	29. D	49. B	69. D	89. C	109. C
10. E	30. D	50. C	70. E	90. B	110. D
11. D	31. E	51. B	71. A	91. E	111. A
12. B	32. A	52. C	72. C	92. E	112. C
13. B	33. A	53. D	73. B	93. C	113. C
14. B	34. C	54. D	74. C	94. C	114. B
15. B	35. C	55. E	75. A	95. A	115. D
16. A	36. E	56. E	76. D	96. D	116. A
17. D	37. A	57. B	77. D	97. C	117. B
18. E	38. C	58. E	78. A	98. E	118. B
19. B	39. C	59. D	79. E	99. B	119. A
20. A	40. D	60. C	80. C	100. B	120. E

EXPLANATIONS—VERBAL TASKS TEST

1. **(C)** FLEXIBLE means *adjustable* or *pliable*. An office which offers flexible hours may operate from 6 A.M. to 10 P.M.

2. **(B)** An OPTION is a *choice*. When you cast your vote, you are exercising your option.

3. **(C)** To VERIFY is to *check the accuracy of* or to *confirm*. A notary stamp verifies that the signature on the document is the signature of the person named.

4. **(D)** INDOLENT means *idle* or *lazy*. An indolent person is not likely to become a productive employee.

5. **(B)** RESPIRATION is *breathing*. Respiration is the process by which animals inhale and exhale air.

6. **(A)** A BRUSH is a tool of the PAINTER's trade as a WRENCH is a tool of the PLUMBER's trade.

7. **(B)** A PACKAGE transports MERCHANDISE just as a LETTER transmits a MESSAGE.

8. **(C)** SLEEP alleviates WEARINESS just as FOOD alleviates HUNGER.

9. **(D)** The DIAL is an input device of a TELEPHONE just as a KEY is an input device of a TYPEWRITER.

10. **(A)** *Whoever* is the subject of the phrase "whoever has the best record." Choices B and C are wordy and awkward.

11. **(D)** All the other choices contain obvious errors.

12. **(A)** The correct spelling is *collapsible*.

13. **(C)** The correct spelling is *ambiguous*.

14. **(D)** The correct spelling is *predecessor*.

15. **(A)** The correct spelling is *sanctioned*.

16. **(A)** The paragraph presents the problems of fire in fire-resistant buildings. It suggests that the contents of the buildings may burn even though the structural materials themselves do not, and the ensuing fire may even cause the collapse of the buildings. The paragraph does not compare the problem of fire in fire-resistant buildings with that of fire in ordinary buildings.

17. **(C)** The search for truth has speeded the progress of civilization. Choice B is incorrect in its statement that "civilization did not begin until. . . ." Civilization moved ahead slowly even before restrictions on learning were removed.

18. **(B)** VIGILANT means *alert* or *watchful*. A worker must remain vigilant to avoid accidents on the job.

19. **(D)** INCIDENTAL means *happening in connection with something else* or *casual*. Having the windshield washed is incidental to filling the gas tank and checking the oil.

20. **(A)** CONCILIATORY means *tending to reconcile* or *to make peace*. The apology was offered as a conciliatory gesture.

21. **(C)** An ALTERCATION is a *quarrel* or a *controversy*. The two drivers had an angry altercation as to who was at fault in the accident.

Federal Clerical Examination / 85

22. **(A)** IRRESOLUTE means *indecisive* or *wavering*. The couple was irresolute as to the choice of next summer's vacation.

23. **(C)** STILLNESS and SOUND are opposites, as are DARKNESS and SUNLIGHT.

24. **(D)** That which is ACCIDENTAL happens by CHANCE as that which is DESIGNED happens by INTENTION.

25. **(C)** A MUFFLER reduces SOUND as PRACTICE reduces ERRORs.

26. **(A)** The desired result of TRAINING is the development of SKILL as the desired result of RESEARCH is scientific FINDINGS.

27. **(D)** Choices A and C are incorrect in use of the subject form "I" instead of the object of the preposition "me." Choice B incorrectly uses the reflexive "myself." Only I can address a letter to myself.

28. **(C)** All the other choices are quite obviously incorrect.

29. **(D)** The correct spelling is *miniature*.

30. **(A)** The correct spelling is *extemporaneous*.

31. **(B)** The correct spelling is *problematical*.

32. **(A)** The correct spelling of first choice is *descendant*. An alternative spelling which is also correct is *descendent*. A correct spelling is offered among the choices, so A is the answer.

33. **(B)** In a word, we are preserving our natural resources through recycling.

34. **(D)** If you omit all unnecessary words, you use only the words essential to the meaning.

35. **(D)** To COUNTERACT is to *act directly against* or to *neutralize*. My father's vote for the Republican candidate always counteracts my mother's vote for the Democrat.

36. **(B)** DEFERRED means *postponed* or *delayed*. Because I had no money in the bank, I deferred paying my taxes until the due date.

37. **(C)** FEASIBLE means *possible* or *practicable*. It is not feasible for the 92-year-old woman to travel abroad.

38. **(A)** To ENCOUNTER is to *come upon* or to *meet*. If you encounter my brother at the ball game, please give my regards.

39. **(C)** INNATE means *existing naturally* or *native*. Some people argue that the maternal instinct is learned rather than innate.

40. **(B)** The DISCIPLE learns from a MASTER as a STUDENT learns from a TEACHER.

41. **(C)** In this analogy of place, an EXPERIMENT occurs in a LABORATORY as a LECTURE occurs in an AUDITORIUM.

42. **(B)** FUEL powers the ENGINE as FOOD powers the BODY.

43. **(C)** RECREATION occurs in the THEATER as EDUCATION occurs in a SCHOOL.

44. **(D)** Choice A might state either "most" or "all" but not both; choice B should read "persons who"; choice C should read "with regard to. . . ."

45. **(D)** Choice A is incorrect because *both* can refer to only two, but the publisher and authors implies at least three; choice B requires the plural verb "were"; choice C requires the correlative construction "neither...nor."

46. **(C)** The correct spelling is *extricate*.

47. **(B)** The correct spelling is *hereditary*.

48. **(C)** The correct spelling is *auspicious*.

49. **(B)** The correct spelling is *sequence*.

50. **(A)** If instruction in safety rules will help to prevent accidents, some accidents must occur because of ignorance.

51. **(D)** The language that has some representative in English speech has had some of its words absorbed into English.

52. **(A)** To ACQUIESCE is to *give in* or to *assent*. I reluctantly will acquiesce to your request to stay out late with your friends.

53. **(C)** UNANIMITY is *complete agreement* or *harmony*. The plan had such widespread acceptance that the vote resulted in unanimity.

54. **(A)** A PRECEDENT is *an example that sets a standard*. After one employee was permitted to wear jeans in the office, a precedent had been set and soon others also dressed casually.

55. **(D)** VERSATILE means *adaptable* or *many-sided*. This versatile vacuum cleaner can be used indoors or out under both dry and wet conditions.

56. **(B)** AUTHENTIC means *genuine* or *reliable*. The painting attributed to Rembrandt was guaranteed to be authentic.

57. **(A)** The information and substance of a NOVEL is FICTION while the information and substance of BIOGRAPHY is FACT.

58. **(B)** FILM is the medium through which the action of a MOTION PICTURE is projected onto a screen; CARBON PAPER is the medium through which a COPY of words or drawings is transmitted from one piece of paper to another.

59. **(C)** CARELESSNESS earns a REPRIMAND as EFFICIENCY merits a REWARD.

60. **(B)** This analogy refers to the marketplace and the law of supply and demand. That which is SCARCE is likely to be COSTLY while that which is ABUNDANT will be CHEAP.

61. **(B)** In choice A the placement of the apostrophe is inappropriate; choices C and D use the plural, but there is only one company.

62. **(A)** Choices C and D are glaringly poor. Choice B is not incorrect, but choice A is far better.

63. **(D)** The correct spelling is *obliterate*.

64. **(C)** The correct spelling is *diagnosis*.

65. **(B)** The correct spelling is *countenance*.

66. **(A)** The correct spelling is *conceivably*.

67. **(C)** Since manufacturers are assuming risks in attempting to predict what consumers will want, their success depends on the ultimate purchases made by the consumers.

68. **(B)** Humans migrate to various climates and make adjustments to the food supply in each climate; obviously the means by which they supply their needs are varied.

69. **(D)** STRIDENT means *grating* or *harsh-sounding*. The sergeant barked out the orders in strident tones.

70. **(B)** To CONFINE is to *limit* or to *restrict*. If the child's illness is contagious, we must confine him to his home.

71. **(D)** To ACCENTUATE is to *stress, emphasize,* or *intensify*. Life is more pleasant when those we deal with accentuate the positive.

72. **(A)** BANAL means *insipid* or *commonplace*. His commentary was so banal that I had to stifle many yawns.

73. **(C)** One who is INCORRIGIBLE *cannot be changed or corrected*; the person is *irreformable*. Incorrigible offenders should be sentenced to prison for life.

74. **(D)** A DOCTOR promotes HEALTH as a POLICEMAN promotes ORDER.

75. **(A)** A WEAVER creates on a LOOM as an ARTIST creates on an EASEL.

76. **(D)** Many SHIPS make up the FLEET as many PERSONS make up a CROWD.

77. **(C)** MILEAGE is read from a MAP as the DATE is read from a CALENDAR.

78. **(A)** The other choices are quite clearly incorrect.

79. **(C)** Choices A and B use adverbs incorrectly; choice D is awkward and unidiomatic.

80. **(B)** The correct spelling is *competition*.

81. **(B)** The correct spelling is *occasion*.

82. **(C)** The correct spelling is *knowledge*.

83. **(B)** The correct spelling is *deliberate*.

84. **(A)** Time and effort cannot be equated. Efficiency must be measured in terms of results.

85. **(B)** The first sentence of the paragraph makes this statement.

EXPLANATIONS—CLERICAL TASKS TEST

1. **(B)** The last two digits of the third number are reversed.

2. **(E)** The middle digit of the second number is "6" while that of the first and third numbers is "5." The last two digits of the third number are reversed.

3. **(D)** The surname of the second and third names is "Johnson"; the surname of the first name is "Johnston."

4. **(A)** All three names are exactly alike.

5. **(E)** The middle initial of the third name differs from the other two. "Asheton" of the second name differs from "Atherton" of the other two.

6. **(E)** Hachettson; Hackett

7. **(A)** Margenroth; Margeroth

8. **(D)** Bobbitt, Olivia H.; Bobbitt, Olivier E.; Bobbitt, R. Olivia

9. **(B)** Mosely, Albert J.; Mosely, Werner; Mosley, Alvin

10. **(E)** Youmons; Youmuns

11. **(D)** $\begin{array}{r} 43 \\ +32 \\ \hline 75 \end{array}$

12. (B) $\begin{array}{r} 83 \\ -4 \\ \hline 79 \end{array}$

13. (B) $\begin{array}{r} 41 \\ \times7 \\ \hline 287 \end{array}$

14. (B) $6\overline{)306}^{\,51}$

15. (B) $\begin{array}{r} 37 \\ +15 \\ \hline 52 \end{array}$

16. (A) 6 2 5 **K** 4 **P T G**.

17. (D) **L** 4 7 2 **T** 6 **V K**. The answer cannot be (A) because question 17 contains no **5**; it cannot be (B) or (C) because question 17 contains no **G**.

18. (E) The answer cannot be (A) or (B) because question 18 contains no **K**; it cannot be (C) or (D) because question 18 contains no **2**.

19. (B) **G** 4 **K** 7 **L** 3 5 **Z**. The answer cannot be (A) because question 19 contains no **T**.

20. (A) 4 **K** 2 9 **N** 5 **T G**.

21. (A) All three numbers are exactly alike.

22. (E) The last two digits are, respectively, "41," "47," and "14."

23. (E) In the first name, the given name is "Owens" while in the other two it is "Owen." The surname of the second name is "McVey" while in the third name it is "McVay."

24. (D) In the second and third names, the surname is "Rowse"; in the first name it is "Rouse."

25. (C) In the second name the given name is "Merriott"; in the first and third it is "Merritt."

26. (D) Watson; Watters; Wattwood

27. (D) Johnston, Edmund; Johnston, Edward; Johnstone, Edmund A.

28. (C) Remschel; Rensch; Renshaw

29. (C) Schneider, Mertens; Schnyder, Maurice; Schnyder, Newman

30. (D) Freedenberg; Freedenburg; Freedinberg

31. (E) $\begin{array}{r} 68 \\ -47 \\ \hline 21 \end{array}$

32. (A) $\begin{array}{r} 50 \\ \times8 \\ \hline 400 \end{array}$

33. (A) $9\overline{)180}^{\,20}$

34. (C) $\begin{array}{r} 78 \\ +63 \\ \hline 141 \end{array}$

35. (C) $\begin{array}{r} 89 \\ -70 \\ \hline 19 \end{array}$

Federal Clerical Examination / 89

36. **(E)** The answer cannot be (A) because question 36 contains no **V**; it cannot be (B) or (C) because question 36 contains no **5**; it cannot be (D) because question 36 contains no **8** or **V**.

37. **(A)** L 5 N K 4 3 9 V.

38. **(C)** 8 2 V P 9 L Z 5. The answer cannot be (A) or (B) because question 38 contains no **4**.

39. **(C)** V P 9 Z 5 L 8 7. The answer cannot be (A) or (B) because question 39 contains no **4**.

40. **(D)** 5 T 8 N 2 9 V L. The answer cannot be (A) or (B) because question 40 contains no **4**; it cannot be (C) because question 40 contains no **Z**.

41. **(A)** All three numbers are exactly alike.

42. **(A)** All three numbers are exactly alike.

43. **(B)** In the third number, the digits "40" are reversed to read "04."

44. **(E)** The first and third names have the same given name but different surnames. The second name has the same surname as the third, but the given name is different.

45. **(A)** All three names are exactly alike.

46. **(C)** DeMatteo; DeMattia; Derby

47. **(A)** Theriault; Therien

48. **(D)** Gaston, Isabel; Gaston, M. Hubert; Gaston, M. Melvin

49. **(B)** SanLuis; SanMiguel; Santilli

50. **(C)** DeLathouder; DeLaTour; Lathrop

51. **(B)**
$$\begin{array}{r} 62 \\ \times\ 5 \\ \hline 310 \end{array}$$

52. **(C)** $3\overline{)153}^{\,51}$

53. **(D)**
$$\begin{array}{r} 47 \\ +\ 21 \\ \hline 68 \end{array}$$

54. **(D)**
$$\begin{array}{r} 87 \\ -\ 42 \\ \hline 45 \end{array}$$

55. **(E)**
$$\begin{array}{r} 37 \\ \times\ 3 \\ \hline 111 \end{array}$$

56. **(E)** The answer cannot be (A) or (B) because question 56 contains no **8**; it cannot be (C) or (D) because question 56 contains no **9**.

57. **(B)** 8 5 3 V L 2 Z N. The answer cannot be (A) because question 57 contains no **K**.

58. **(E)** The answer cannot be (A) or (B) because question 58 contains no **8**; it cannot be (C) or (D) because question 58 contains no **Z**.

59. **(D)** 9 8 L 2 5 Z K V. The answer cannot be (A) or (C) because question 59 contains no **3**; it cannot be (B) because question 59 contains no **N**.

60. **(C)** Z 6 5 V 9 3 P N. The answer cannot be (A) or (B) because question 60 contains no **8**.

61. **(C)** In the second number, the fifth digit differs from that in the other numbers.

62. **(B)** In the third number, the last two digits are reversed.

63. **(E)** The given name of the third name differs from that of the first two names; the surname of the first name is different from that of the second and third names.

64. **(E)** The middle initial of the first name differs from the middle initials of the other two; the surname of the third name differs from that of the first and second names.

65. **(C)** The surname of the second name is different from the surname of the first and third.

66. **(A)** O'Bannon; O'Beirne

67. **(D)** Entsminger, Jack; Entsminger, Jacob; Entsminger, James

68. **(C)** Iacone, Pedro M.; Iacone, Pete R.; Iacone, Peter F.

69. **(D)** Shephard; Sheppard; Shepperd

70. **(E)** Thackston; Thackton

71. **(A)** $7\overline{)357}^{51}$

72. **(C)** $\begin{array}{r} 58 \\ +27 \\ \hline 85 \end{array}$

73. **(B)** $\begin{array}{r} 86 \\ -57 \\ \hline 29 \end{array}$

74. **(C)** $\begin{array}{r} 68 \\ \times\ 4 \\ \hline 272 \end{array}$

75. **(A)** $9\overline{)639}^{71}$

76. **(D)** 6 Z T N 8 7 4 V. The answer cannot be (A) or (B) because question 76 contains no **2**; it cannot be (C) because question 76 contains no **L**.

77. **(D)** V 7 8 6 N 5 P L. The answer cannot be (A) or (B) because question 77 contains no **2**; it cannot be (C) because question 77 contains no **T**.

78. **(A)** N 7 P V 8 4 2 L.

79. **(E)** The answer cannot be (A) or (B) because question 79 contains no **2**; it cannot be (C) or (D) because question 79 contains no **6**.

80. **(C)** 4 8 G 2 T N 6 L. The answer cannot be (A) because question 80 contains no **7**; it cannot be (B) because question 80 contains no **V**.

81. **(D)** The last digit of the first number differs from the last digit of the second and third numbers.

82. **(C)** The fifth and sixth digits of the middle number are the reverse of the fifth and sixth digits of the first and third numbers.

83. **(A)** All three names are exactly alike.

84. **(D)** In the second and third names, the middle name is "Harloe"; in the first name, it is "Harlor."

85. **(B)** The central initial in the third name differs from the central initial in the first and second names.

86. **(A)** Dunlavey; Dunleavy

87. **(E)** Yarborough; Yarbrough

88. **(C)** Proutey, Maude; Prouty, Martha; Prouty, Myra

89. **(C)** Pawalek; Pawlowicz; Pawlowski

90. **(B)** Vanover; Vanstory; VanSwinderen

91. **(E)** $\begin{array}{r} 28 \\ +\ 35 \\ \hline 63 \end{array}$

92. **(E)** $\begin{array}{r} 78 \\ -\ 69 \\ \hline 9 \end{array}$

93. **(C)** $\begin{array}{r} 86 \\ \times\ 6 \\ \hline 516 \end{array}$

94. **(C)** $8\overline{)648}^{\,81}$

95. **(A)** $\begin{array}{r} 97 \\ +\ 34 \\ \hline 131 \end{array}$

96. **(D)** V 5 7 Z N 9 4 T. The answer cannot be (A) or (C) because question 96 contains no **2**; it cannot be (B) because question 96 contains no **P**.

97. **(C)** 4 6 P T 2 N K 9. The answer cannot be (A) or (B) because question 97 contains no **5**.

98. **(E)** The answer cannot be (A) or (B) because question 98 contains no **5**; it cannot be (C) or (D) because question 98 contains no **9**.

99. **(B)** 7 P 5 2 4 N K T. The answer cannot be (A) because question 99 contains no **Z**.

100. **(B)** K T 8 5 4 N 2 P. The answer cannot be (A) because question 100 contains no **Z**.

101. **(D)** The next to the last digit of the first number differs from that of the other two numbers.

102. **(B)** The last two digits of the third number are reversed.

103. **(C)** The fifth and sixth digits of the second number are reversed.

104. **(A)** All three names are exactly alike.

105. **(E)** All three surnames are different.

106. **(D)** FitzGibbon; Fitzsimmons; FitzSimons

107. **(B)** Daly; D'Amato; D'Amboise

108. **(A)** Schaeffer; Schaffert

109. **(C)** White-Leigh; White-Lewis; Whitely

110. **(D)** VanDercook; VanDerHeggen; vanderLinden

111. **(A)** $\begin{array}{r} 75 \\ + 49 \\ \hline 124 \end{array}$

112. **(C)** $\begin{array}{r} 69 \\ - 45 \\ \hline 24 \end{array}$

113. **(C)** $\begin{array}{r} 36 \\ \times\ 8 \\ \hline 288 \end{array}$

114. **(B)** $8\overline{)328}\ \ 41$

115. **(D)** $\begin{array}{r} 58 \\ \times\ 9 \\ \hline 522 \end{array}$

116. **(A)** Z 3 N P G 5 4 2.

117. **(B)** 6 N 2 8 G 4 P T. The answer cannot be (A) because question 117 contains no **3**.

118. **(B)** 6 N 4 T V G 8 2. The answer cannot be (A) because question 118 contains no **3**.

119. **(A)** T 3 P 4 N 8 G 2.

120. **(E)** The answer cannot be (A) or (C) because question 120 contains no **3**; it cannot be (B) or (D) because question 120 contains no **T**.

Answer Sheet for U.S. Postal Service Clerk, Distribution Clerk (Machine) & Mark-Up Clerk (Automated) Exam

Part A—Address Checking

1. Ⓐ Ⓓ
2. Ⓐ Ⓓ
3. Ⓐ Ⓓ
4. Ⓐ Ⓓ
5. Ⓐ Ⓓ
6. Ⓐ Ⓓ
7. Ⓐ Ⓓ
8. Ⓐ Ⓓ
9. Ⓐ Ⓓ
10. Ⓐ Ⓓ
11. Ⓐ Ⓓ
12. Ⓐ Ⓓ
13. Ⓐ Ⓓ
14. Ⓐ Ⓓ
15. Ⓐ Ⓓ
16. Ⓐ Ⓓ
17. Ⓐ Ⓓ
18. Ⓐ Ⓓ
19. Ⓐ Ⓓ
20. Ⓐ Ⓓ
21. Ⓐ Ⓓ
22. Ⓐ Ⓓ
23. Ⓐ Ⓓ
24. Ⓐ Ⓓ
25. Ⓐ Ⓓ
26. Ⓐ Ⓓ
27. Ⓐ Ⓓ
28. Ⓐ Ⓓ
29. Ⓐ Ⓓ
30. Ⓐ Ⓓ
31. Ⓐ Ⓓ
32. Ⓐ Ⓓ
33. Ⓐ Ⓓ
34. Ⓐ Ⓓ
35. Ⓐ Ⓓ
36. Ⓐ Ⓓ
37. Ⓐ Ⓓ
38. Ⓐ Ⓓ
39. Ⓐ Ⓓ
40. Ⓐ Ⓓ
41. Ⓐ Ⓓ
42. Ⓐ Ⓓ
43. Ⓐ Ⓓ
44. Ⓐ Ⓓ
45. Ⓐ Ⓓ
46. Ⓐ Ⓓ
47. Ⓐ Ⓓ
48. Ⓐ Ⓓ
49. Ⓐ Ⓓ
50. Ⓐ Ⓓ
51. Ⓐ Ⓓ
52. Ⓐ Ⓓ
53. Ⓐ Ⓓ
54. Ⓐ Ⓓ
55. Ⓐ Ⓓ
56. Ⓐ Ⓓ
57. Ⓐ Ⓓ
58. Ⓐ Ⓓ
59. Ⓐ Ⓓ
60. Ⓐ Ⓓ
61. Ⓐ Ⓓ
62. Ⓐ Ⓓ
63. Ⓐ Ⓓ
64. Ⓐ Ⓓ
65. Ⓐ Ⓓ
66. Ⓐ Ⓓ
67. Ⓐ Ⓓ
68. Ⓐ Ⓓ
69. Ⓐ Ⓓ
70. Ⓐ Ⓓ
71. Ⓐ Ⓓ
72. Ⓐ Ⓓ
73. Ⓐ Ⓓ
74. Ⓐ Ⓓ
75. Ⓐ Ⓓ
76. Ⓐ Ⓓ
77. Ⓐ Ⓓ
78. Ⓐ Ⓓ
79. Ⓐ Ⓓ
80. Ⓐ Ⓓ
81. Ⓐ Ⓓ
82. Ⓐ Ⓓ
83. Ⓐ Ⓓ
84. Ⓐ Ⓓ
85. Ⓐ Ⓓ
86. Ⓐ Ⓓ
87. Ⓐ Ⓓ
88. Ⓐ Ⓓ
89. Ⓐ Ⓓ
90. Ⓐ Ⓓ
91. Ⓐ Ⓓ
92. Ⓐ Ⓓ
93. Ⓐ Ⓓ
94. Ⓐ Ⓓ
95. Ⓐ Ⓓ

TEAR HERE

Part B—Memory for Addresses

1. Ⓐ Ⓑ Ⓒ Ⓓ Ⓔ
2. Ⓐ Ⓑ Ⓒ Ⓓ Ⓔ
3. Ⓐ Ⓑ Ⓒ Ⓓ Ⓔ
4. Ⓐ Ⓑ Ⓒ Ⓓ Ⓔ
5. Ⓐ Ⓑ Ⓒ Ⓓ Ⓔ
6. Ⓐ Ⓑ Ⓒ Ⓓ Ⓔ
7. Ⓐ Ⓑ Ⓒ Ⓓ Ⓔ
8. Ⓐ Ⓑ Ⓒ Ⓓ Ⓔ
9. Ⓐ Ⓑ Ⓒ Ⓓ Ⓔ
10. Ⓐ Ⓑ Ⓒ Ⓓ Ⓔ
11. Ⓐ Ⓑ Ⓒ Ⓓ Ⓔ
12. Ⓐ Ⓑ Ⓒ Ⓓ Ⓔ
13. Ⓐ Ⓑ Ⓒ Ⓓ Ⓔ
14. Ⓐ Ⓑ Ⓒ Ⓓ Ⓔ
15. Ⓐ Ⓑ Ⓒ Ⓓ Ⓔ
16. Ⓐ Ⓑ Ⓒ Ⓓ Ⓔ
17. Ⓐ Ⓑ Ⓒ Ⓓ Ⓔ
18. Ⓐ Ⓑ Ⓒ Ⓓ Ⓔ
19. Ⓐ Ⓑ Ⓒ Ⓓ Ⓔ
20. Ⓐ Ⓑ Ⓒ Ⓓ Ⓔ
21. Ⓐ Ⓑ Ⓒ Ⓓ Ⓔ
22. Ⓐ Ⓑ Ⓒ Ⓓ Ⓔ
23. Ⓐ Ⓑ Ⓒ Ⓓ Ⓔ
24. Ⓐ Ⓑ Ⓒ Ⓓ Ⓔ
25. Ⓐ Ⓑ Ⓒ Ⓓ Ⓔ
26. Ⓐ Ⓑ Ⓒ Ⓓ Ⓔ
27. Ⓐ Ⓑ Ⓒ Ⓓ Ⓔ
28. Ⓐ Ⓑ Ⓒ Ⓓ Ⓔ
29. Ⓐ Ⓑ Ⓒ Ⓓ Ⓔ
30. Ⓐ Ⓑ Ⓒ Ⓓ Ⓔ
31. Ⓐ Ⓑ Ⓒ Ⓓ Ⓔ
32. Ⓐ Ⓑ Ⓒ Ⓓ Ⓔ
33. Ⓐ Ⓑ Ⓒ Ⓓ Ⓔ
34. Ⓐ Ⓑ Ⓒ Ⓓ Ⓔ
35. Ⓐ Ⓑ Ⓒ Ⓓ Ⓔ
36. Ⓐ Ⓑ Ⓒ Ⓓ Ⓔ
37. Ⓐ Ⓑ Ⓒ Ⓓ Ⓔ
38. Ⓐ Ⓑ Ⓒ Ⓓ Ⓔ
39. Ⓐ Ⓑ Ⓒ Ⓓ Ⓔ
40. Ⓐ Ⓑ Ⓒ Ⓓ Ⓔ
41. Ⓐ Ⓑ Ⓒ Ⓓ Ⓔ
42. Ⓐ Ⓑ Ⓒ Ⓓ Ⓔ
43. Ⓐ Ⓑ Ⓒ Ⓓ Ⓔ
44. Ⓐ Ⓑ Ⓒ Ⓓ Ⓔ
45. Ⓐ Ⓑ Ⓒ Ⓓ Ⓔ
46. Ⓐ Ⓑ Ⓒ Ⓓ Ⓔ
47. Ⓐ Ⓑ Ⓒ Ⓓ Ⓔ
48. Ⓐ Ⓑ Ⓒ Ⓓ Ⓔ
49. Ⓐ Ⓑ Ⓒ Ⓓ Ⓔ
50. Ⓐ Ⓑ Ⓒ Ⓓ Ⓔ
51. Ⓐ Ⓑ Ⓒ Ⓓ Ⓔ
52. Ⓐ Ⓑ Ⓒ Ⓓ Ⓔ
53. Ⓐ Ⓑ Ⓒ Ⓓ Ⓔ
54. Ⓐ Ⓑ Ⓒ Ⓓ Ⓔ
55. Ⓐ Ⓑ Ⓒ Ⓓ Ⓔ
56. Ⓐ Ⓑ Ⓒ Ⓓ Ⓔ
57. Ⓐ Ⓑ Ⓒ Ⓓ Ⓔ
58. Ⓐ Ⓑ Ⓒ Ⓓ Ⓔ
59. Ⓐ Ⓑ Ⓒ Ⓓ Ⓔ
60. Ⓐ Ⓑ Ⓒ Ⓓ Ⓔ
61. Ⓐ Ⓑ Ⓒ Ⓓ Ⓔ
62. Ⓐ Ⓑ Ⓒ Ⓓ Ⓔ
63. Ⓐ Ⓑ Ⓒ Ⓓ Ⓔ
64. Ⓐ Ⓑ Ⓒ Ⓓ Ⓔ
65. Ⓐ Ⓑ Ⓒ Ⓓ Ⓔ
66. Ⓐ Ⓑ Ⓒ Ⓓ Ⓔ
67. Ⓐ Ⓑ Ⓒ Ⓓ Ⓔ
68. Ⓐ Ⓑ Ⓒ Ⓓ Ⓔ
69. Ⓐ Ⓑ Ⓒ Ⓓ Ⓔ
70. Ⓐ Ⓑ Ⓒ Ⓓ Ⓔ
71. Ⓐ Ⓑ Ⓒ Ⓓ Ⓔ
72. Ⓐ Ⓑ Ⓒ Ⓓ Ⓔ
73. Ⓐ Ⓑ Ⓒ Ⓓ Ⓔ
74. Ⓐ Ⓑ Ⓒ Ⓓ Ⓔ
75. Ⓐ Ⓑ Ⓒ Ⓓ Ⓔ
76. Ⓐ Ⓑ Ⓒ Ⓓ Ⓔ
77. Ⓐ Ⓑ Ⓒ Ⓓ Ⓔ
78. Ⓐ Ⓑ Ⓒ Ⓓ Ⓔ
79. Ⓐ Ⓑ Ⓒ Ⓓ Ⓔ
80. Ⓐ Ⓑ Ⓒ Ⓓ Ⓔ
81. Ⓐ Ⓑ Ⓒ Ⓓ Ⓔ
82. Ⓐ Ⓑ Ⓒ Ⓓ Ⓔ
83. Ⓐ Ⓑ Ⓒ Ⓓ Ⓔ
84. Ⓐ Ⓑ Ⓒ Ⓓ Ⓔ
85. Ⓐ Ⓑ Ⓒ Ⓓ Ⓔ
86. Ⓐ Ⓑ Ⓒ Ⓓ Ⓔ
87. Ⓐ Ⓑ Ⓒ Ⓓ Ⓔ
88. Ⓐ Ⓑ Ⓒ Ⓓ Ⓔ

Part C—Number Series

1. Ⓐ Ⓑ Ⓒ Ⓓ Ⓔ
2. Ⓐ Ⓑ Ⓒ Ⓓ Ⓔ
3. Ⓐ Ⓑ Ⓒ Ⓓ Ⓔ
4. Ⓐ Ⓑ Ⓒ Ⓓ Ⓔ
5. Ⓐ Ⓑ Ⓒ Ⓓ Ⓔ
6. Ⓐ Ⓑ Ⓒ Ⓓ Ⓔ
7. Ⓐ Ⓑ Ⓒ Ⓓ Ⓔ
8. Ⓐ Ⓑ Ⓒ Ⓓ Ⓔ
9. Ⓐ Ⓑ Ⓒ Ⓓ Ⓔ
10. Ⓐ Ⓑ Ⓒ Ⓓ Ⓔ
11. Ⓐ Ⓑ Ⓒ Ⓓ Ⓔ
12. Ⓐ Ⓑ Ⓒ Ⓓ Ⓔ
13. Ⓐ Ⓑ Ⓒ Ⓓ Ⓔ
14. Ⓐ Ⓑ Ⓒ Ⓓ Ⓔ
15. Ⓐ Ⓑ Ⓒ Ⓓ Ⓔ
16. Ⓐ Ⓑ Ⓒ Ⓓ Ⓔ
17. Ⓐ Ⓑ Ⓒ Ⓓ Ⓔ
18. Ⓐ Ⓑ Ⓒ Ⓓ Ⓔ
19. Ⓐ Ⓑ Ⓒ Ⓓ Ⓔ
20. Ⓐ Ⓑ Ⓒ Ⓓ Ⓔ
21. Ⓐ Ⓑ Ⓒ Ⓓ Ⓔ
22. Ⓐ Ⓑ Ⓒ Ⓓ Ⓔ
23. Ⓐ Ⓑ Ⓒ Ⓓ Ⓔ
24. Ⓐ Ⓑ Ⓒ Ⓓ Ⓔ

PART D—FOLLOWING ORAL INSTRUCTIONS

1. Ⓐ Ⓑ Ⓒ Ⓓ Ⓔ
2. Ⓐ Ⓑ Ⓒ Ⓓ Ⓔ
3. Ⓐ Ⓑ Ⓒ Ⓓ Ⓔ
4. Ⓐ Ⓑ Ⓒ Ⓓ Ⓔ
5. Ⓐ Ⓑ Ⓒ Ⓓ Ⓔ
6. Ⓐ Ⓑ Ⓒ Ⓓ Ⓔ
7. Ⓐ Ⓑ Ⓒ Ⓓ Ⓔ
8. Ⓐ Ⓑ Ⓒ Ⓓ Ⓔ
9. Ⓐ Ⓑ Ⓒ Ⓓ Ⓔ
10. Ⓐ Ⓑ Ⓒ Ⓓ Ⓔ
11. Ⓐ Ⓑ Ⓒ Ⓓ Ⓔ
12. Ⓐ Ⓑ Ⓒ Ⓓ Ⓔ
13. Ⓐ Ⓑ Ⓒ Ⓓ Ⓔ
14. Ⓐ Ⓑ Ⓒ Ⓓ Ⓔ
15. Ⓐ Ⓑ Ⓒ Ⓓ Ⓔ
16. Ⓐ Ⓑ Ⓒ Ⓓ Ⓔ
17. Ⓐ Ⓑ Ⓒ Ⓓ Ⓔ
18. Ⓐ Ⓑ Ⓒ Ⓓ Ⓔ
19. Ⓐ Ⓑ Ⓒ Ⓓ Ⓔ
20. Ⓐ Ⓑ Ⓒ Ⓓ Ⓔ
21. Ⓐ Ⓑ Ⓒ Ⓓ Ⓔ
22. Ⓐ Ⓑ Ⓒ Ⓓ Ⓔ

23. Ⓐ Ⓑ Ⓒ Ⓓ Ⓔ
24. Ⓐ Ⓑ Ⓒ Ⓓ Ⓔ
25. Ⓐ Ⓑ Ⓒ Ⓓ Ⓔ
26. Ⓐ Ⓑ Ⓒ Ⓓ Ⓔ
27. Ⓐ Ⓑ Ⓒ Ⓓ Ⓔ
28. Ⓐ Ⓑ Ⓒ Ⓓ Ⓔ
29. Ⓐ Ⓑ Ⓒ Ⓓ Ⓔ
30. Ⓐ Ⓑ Ⓒ Ⓓ Ⓔ
31. Ⓐ Ⓑ Ⓒ Ⓓ Ⓔ
32. Ⓐ Ⓑ Ⓒ Ⓓ Ⓔ
33. Ⓐ Ⓑ Ⓒ Ⓓ Ⓔ
34. Ⓐ Ⓑ Ⓒ Ⓓ Ⓔ
35. Ⓐ Ⓑ Ⓒ Ⓓ Ⓔ
36. Ⓐ Ⓑ Ⓒ Ⓓ Ⓔ
37. Ⓐ Ⓑ Ⓒ Ⓓ Ⓔ
38. Ⓐ Ⓑ Ⓒ Ⓓ Ⓔ
39. Ⓐ Ⓑ Ⓒ Ⓓ Ⓔ
40. Ⓐ Ⓑ Ⓒ Ⓓ Ⓔ
41. Ⓐ Ⓑ Ⓒ Ⓓ Ⓔ
42. Ⓐ Ⓑ Ⓒ Ⓓ Ⓔ
43. Ⓐ Ⓑ Ⓒ Ⓓ Ⓔ
44. Ⓐ Ⓑ Ⓒ Ⓓ Ⓔ

45. Ⓐ Ⓑ Ⓒ Ⓓ Ⓔ
46. Ⓐ Ⓑ Ⓒ Ⓓ Ⓔ
47. Ⓐ Ⓑ Ⓒ Ⓓ Ⓔ
48. Ⓐ Ⓑ Ⓒ Ⓓ Ⓔ
49. Ⓐ Ⓑ Ⓒ Ⓓ Ⓔ
50. Ⓐ Ⓑ Ⓒ Ⓓ Ⓔ
51. Ⓐ Ⓑ Ⓒ Ⓓ Ⓔ
52. Ⓐ Ⓑ Ⓒ Ⓓ Ⓔ
53. Ⓐ Ⓑ Ⓒ Ⓓ Ⓔ
54. Ⓐ Ⓑ Ⓒ Ⓓ Ⓔ
55. Ⓐ Ⓑ Ⓒ Ⓓ Ⓔ
56. Ⓐ Ⓑ Ⓒ Ⓓ Ⓔ
57. Ⓐ Ⓑ Ⓒ Ⓓ Ⓔ
58. Ⓐ Ⓑ Ⓒ Ⓓ Ⓔ
59. Ⓐ Ⓑ Ⓒ Ⓓ Ⓔ
60. Ⓐ Ⓑ Ⓒ Ⓓ Ⓔ
61. Ⓐ Ⓑ Ⓒ Ⓓ Ⓔ
62. Ⓐ Ⓑ Ⓒ Ⓓ Ⓔ
63. Ⓐ Ⓑ Ⓒ Ⓓ Ⓔ
64. Ⓐ Ⓑ Ⓒ Ⓓ Ⓔ
65. Ⓐ Ⓑ Ⓒ Ⓓ Ⓔ
66. Ⓐ Ⓑ Ⓒ Ⓓ Ⓔ

67. Ⓐ Ⓑ Ⓒ Ⓓ Ⓔ
68. Ⓐ Ⓑ Ⓒ Ⓓ Ⓔ
69. Ⓐ Ⓑ Ⓒ Ⓓ Ⓔ
70. Ⓐ Ⓑ Ⓒ Ⓓ Ⓔ
71. Ⓐ Ⓑ Ⓒ Ⓓ Ⓔ
72. Ⓐ Ⓑ Ⓒ Ⓓ Ⓔ
73. Ⓐ Ⓑ Ⓒ Ⓓ Ⓔ
74. Ⓐ Ⓑ Ⓒ Ⓓ Ⓔ
75. Ⓐ Ⓑ Ⓒ Ⓓ Ⓔ
76. Ⓐ Ⓑ Ⓒ Ⓓ Ⓔ
77. Ⓐ Ⓑ Ⓒ Ⓓ Ⓔ
78. Ⓐ Ⓑ Ⓒ Ⓓ Ⓔ
79. Ⓐ Ⓑ Ⓒ Ⓓ Ⓔ
80. Ⓐ Ⓑ Ⓒ Ⓓ Ⓔ
81. Ⓐ Ⓑ Ⓒ Ⓓ Ⓔ
82. Ⓐ Ⓑ Ⓒ Ⓓ Ⓔ
83. Ⓐ Ⓑ Ⓒ Ⓓ Ⓔ
84. Ⓐ Ⓑ Ⓒ Ⓓ Ⓔ
85. Ⓐ Ⓑ Ⓒ Ⓓ Ⓔ
86. Ⓐ Ⓑ Ⓒ Ⓓ Ⓔ
87. Ⓐ Ⓑ Ⓒ Ⓓ Ⓔ
88. Ⓐ Ⓑ Ⓒ Ⓓ Ⓔ

TEAR HERE

Score Sheet

Address Checking

Your score on the Address Checking part is based upon the number of questions you answered correctly minus the number of questions you answered incorrectly. To determine your score, subtract the number of wrong answers from the number of correct answers.

Number Right   −   Number Wrong   =   Raw Score

_____ − _____ = _____

Memory for Addresses

Your score on the Memory for Addresses part is based upon the number of questions you answered correctly minus one-fourth of the questions you answered incorrectly (number wrong divided by 4). Calculate this now:

Number Wrong ÷ 4 = _____ .

Number Right   −   Number Wrong ÷ 4   =   Raw Score

_____ − _____ = _____

Number Series

Your score on the Number Series part is based only on the number of questions you answered correctly. Wrong answers do not count against you.

Number Right   =   Raw Score

_____ = _____

Following Oral Instructions

Your score on the Following Oral Instructions part is based only upon the number of questions you marked correctly on the answer sheet. The worksheet is not scored, and wrong answers on the answer sheet do not count against you.

Number Right   =   Raw Score

_____ = _____

TOTAL SCORE

To find your total raw score, add together the raw scores for each section of the exam.

Address Checking Score　　　　　　_____

\+

Memory for Addresses Score　　　　_____

\+

Number Series Score　　　　　　　_____

\+

Following Oral Instructions Score　　_____

=

Total Raw Score　　　　　　　　　_____

Self Evaluation Chart

Calculate your raw score for each test as shown above. Then check to see where your score falls on the scale from Poor to Excellent. Lightly shade in the boxes in which your scores fall.

Part	Excellent	Good	Average	Fair	Poor
Address Checking	80–95	65–79	50–64	35–49	1–34
Memory for Addresses	75–88	60–74	45–59	30–44	1–29
Number Series	21–24	18–20	14–17	11–13	1–10
Following Oral Instructions	27–31	23–26	19–22	14–18	1–13

U.S. POSTAL SERVICE CLERK, DISTRIBUTION CLERK (MACHINE) & MARK-UP CLERK (AUTOMATED) EXAM

Part A—Address Checking

SAMPLE QUESTIONS

You will be allowed three minutes to read the directions and answer the five sample questions that follow. On the actual test, however, you will have only six minutes to answer 95 questions, so see how quickly you can compare addresses and still get the correct answer.

Directions: Each question consists of two addresses. If the two addresses are alike in EVERY way, mark A on your answer sheet. If the two addresses are different in ANY way, mark D on your answer sheet.

1. Ft Collins CO 80523   Ft Collins CO 85023
2. 3626 Pennsylvania Ave NE   3626 Pennsylvania Ave NE
3. 2418 E 514th St   2418 E 515th St
4. 4437 Continental Tpke   4437 Continental Tpke
5. 682 Dunbarton Rd   682 Dunbarton Dr

Sample Answer Sheet

1. Ⓐ Ⓓ   4. Ⓐ Ⓓ
2. Ⓐ Ⓓ   5. Ⓐ Ⓓ
3. Ⓐ Ⓓ

Correct Answers

1. Ⓐ ●   4. ● Ⓓ
2. ● Ⓓ   5. Ⓐ ●
3. Ⓐ ●

Address Checking

Time: 6 Minutes. 95 Questions.

Directions: For each question, compare the address in the left column with the address in the right column. If the two addresses are ALIKE IN **EVERY** WAY, blacken space A on your answer sheet. If the two addresses are DIFFERENT IN **ANY** WAY, blacken space D on your answer sheet. Correct answers for this test are on page 121.

1. 1897 Smicksburg Rd — 1897 Smithsburg Rd
2. 3609 E Paseo Aldeano — 3909 E Paseo Aldeano
3. 11787 Ornamental Ln — 1787 Ornamental Ln
4. 1096 Camino Grande E — 1096 Camino Grande E
5. 2544 E Radcliff Ave — 2544 E Redcliff Ave
6. 5796 E Narragansett Dr — 5796 E Narragasett Dr
7. 12475 Ebbtide Way W — 12475 Ebbtide Way W
8. 14396 N Via Armando — 14396 S Via Armando
9. 2155 S Del Giorgio Rd — 2155 S Del Giorgio Rd
10. 16550 Bainbridge Cir — 16505 Bainbridge Cir
11. 1826 Milneburg Rd — 1826 Milneburg St
12. Eureka KS 67045 — Eureka KY 67045
13. 4010 Glenaddie Ave — 4010 Glenaddie Ave
14. 13501 Stratford Rd — 13501 Standford Rd
15. 3296 W 64th St — 3296 E 64th St
16. 2201 Tennessee Cir — 2201 Tennessee Cir
17. 1502 Avenue M NE — 1502 Avenue N NE
18. 1096 SE Longrone Dr — 1096 SE Longrone Dr
19. 1267 Darthmouth Ct — 1267 Darthmont Ct
20. 825 Ophanage Rd — 825 Ophanage Rd
21. 1754 Golden Springs Rd — 1754 Golden Springs Road
22. 1015 Tallwoods Ln — 1015 Tallwoods Ln
23. 1097 Lambada Dr — 1097 Lambadd Dr
24. Vredenburgh AL 36481 — Verdenburgh AL 36481
25. 1800 Monticello Ave — 1800 Monticello Ave
26. 1723 Yellowbird Ln — 1723 Yellowbird Ct
27. 700 Valca Materials Rd — 700 Valca Materials Rd
28. 1569 Ladywood Ln N — 1569 Ladywood Ln W
29. 3256 Interurban Dr — 3256 Interurban Dr
30. 1507 Haughton Cir — 1507 Haughton Ct
31. 8971 Robertson Ave — 8971 Robinson Ave
32. 3801 NE 49th Street — 3801 NW 49th Street
33. 4102 Chalkville Rd — 4102 Chalkview Rd
34. 1709 Ingersoll Cir — 1709 Ingersoll Cir
35. 6800 N Nantucket Ln — 6800 N Nantucket Ln
36. 12401 Tarrymore Dr — 12401 Terrymore Dr
37. 1097 Huntsville Ave — 1097 Huntsville Ave
38. 3566 Lornaridge Pl — 3566 Lornaridge Pl
39. 2039 Klondike Ave SW — 2039 Klondie Ave SW
40. 3267 Mayland Ln — 3267 Maryland Ln
41. 12956 Strawberry Ln — 12596 Strawberry Ln
42. De Armanville AL 36257 — De Armanville AL 36257
43. 6015 Anniston Dr — 6015 Anneston Dr

44.	1525 E 90th St	1525 E 90th St
45.	1299 Chappaque Rd	1266 Chappaque Rd
46.	2156 Juliette Dr	2156 Juliaetta Dr
47.	999 N Hollingsworth St	999 S Hollingsworth St
48.	16901 Odum Crest Ln	19601 Odum Crest Ln
49.	9787 Zellmark Dr	9787 Zealmark Dr
50.	11103 NE Feasell Ave	11103 NE Feasell Ave
51.	51121 N Mattison Rd	51121 S Mattison Rd
52.	8326 Blackjack Ln	8326 Blackjack Blvd
53.	18765 Lagarde Ave	18765 Lagrande Ave
54.	11297 Gallatin Ln	11297 Gallatin Ln
55.	Wormleysburg PA 17043	Wormleysburg PA 17043
56.	22371 N Sprague Ave	22371 S Sprague Ave
57.	15014 Warrior River Rd	15014 Warrior River Rd
58.	45721 Hueytown Plaza	45721 Hueytowne Plaza
59.	8973 Tedescki Dr	8793 Tedescki Dr
60.	12995 Raimond Muscoda Pl	12995 Raimont Muscoda Pl
61.	Phippsburg CO 80469	Phippsburg CA 80469
62.	52003 W 49th Ave	52003 W 46th Ave
63.	17201 Zenobia Cir	17210 Zenobia Cir
64.	4800 Garrison Cir	4800 Garrison Dr
65.	Los Angeles CA 90070	Los Angeles CA 90076
66.	14798 W 62nd Ave	14198 W 62nd Ave
67.	7191 E Eldridge Way	7191 E Eldridge Way
68.	1279 S Quintard Dr	1279 S Guintard Dr
69.	21899 Dellwood Ave	21899 Dillwood Ave
70.	7191 Zenophone Cir	7191 Zenohone Cir
71.	4301 Los Encinos Way	4301 Los Encinas Way
72.	19700 Ostronic Dr NW	19700 Ostronic Dr NE
73.	23291 Van Velsire Dr	23219 Van Velsire Dr
74.	547 Paradise Valley Rd	547 Paradise Valley Ct
75.	23167 Saltillo Ave	23167 Santillo Ave
76.	43001 Mourning Dove Way	43001 Mourning Dove Way
77.	21183 Declaration Ave	21183 Declaration Ave
78.	10799 Via Sierra Ramal Ave	10799 Via Sierra Ramel Ave
79.	16567 Hermosillia Ct	16597 Hermosillia Ct
80.	Villamont VA 24178	Villamont VA 24178
81.	18794 Villaboso Ave	18794 Villeboso Ave
82.	24136 Ranthom Ave	24136 Ranthon Ave
83.	13489 Golondrina Pl	13489 Golondrina St
84.	6598 Adamsville Ave	6598 Adamsville Ave
85.	12641 Indals Pl NE	12641 Indals Pl NW
86.	19701 SE 2nd Avenue	19701 NE 2nd Avenue
87.	22754 Cachalote Ln	22754 Cachalott Ln
88.	12341 Kingfisher Rd	12341 Kingfisher Rd
89.	24168 Lorenzana Dr	24168 Lorenzano Dr
90.	32480 Blackfriar Rd	32480 Blackfriar Rd
91.	16355 Wheeler Dr	16355 Wheelen Dr
92.	5100 Magna Carta Rd	5100 Magna Certa Rd
93.	2341 N Federalist Pl	2341 N Federalist Pl
94.	22200 Timpangos Rd	22200 Timpangos Rd
95.	19704 Calderon Rd	19704 Calderon Rd

END OF ADDRESS CHECKING

Part B—Memory for Addresses

Sample Questions

The sample questions for this part are based upon the addresses in the five boxes below. Your task is to mark on your answer sheet the letter of the box in which each address belongs. You will have five minutes now to study the locations of the addresses. Then cover the boxes and try to mark the location of the sample questions. You may look back at the boxes if you cannot yet mark the address locations from memory.

The exam itself provides three practice sessions before the question set that really counts. Practice I and Practice III supply you with the boxes and permit you to refer to them if necessary. Practice II and the Memory for Addresses test itself do not permit you to look at the boxes. The test itself is based on memory.

A	B	C	D	E
8100-8399 Test Pigeon 7600-8099 City Webb 6800-6999 Mark	6800-6999 Test Vampire 7000-7599 City Yak 8400-8699 Mark	7600-8099 Test Octopus 8100-8399 City Fleet 7000-7599 Mark	8400-8699 Test Ghost 6800-6999 City Hammer 7600-8099 Mark	7000-7599 Test Lever 8400-8699 City Nougat 8100-8399 Mark

1. 7000-7599 Test
2. Octopus
3. Nougat
4. 8100-8399 Mark
5. 7000-7599 City
6. 8100-8399 City
7. Pigeon
8. 6800-6999 Mark
9. Vampire
10. Yak
11. 8400-8699 Test
12. 7600-8099 City
13. 7000-7599 Mark
14. Hammer

Sample Answer Sheet

1. Ⓐ Ⓑ Ⓒ Ⓓ Ⓔ
2. Ⓐ Ⓑ Ⓒ Ⓓ Ⓔ
3. Ⓐ Ⓑ Ⓒ Ⓓ Ⓔ
4. Ⓐ Ⓑ Ⓒ Ⓓ Ⓔ
5. Ⓐ Ⓑ Ⓒ Ⓓ Ⓔ
6. Ⓐ Ⓑ Ⓒ Ⓓ Ⓔ
7. Ⓐ Ⓑ Ⓒ Ⓓ Ⓔ
8. Ⓐ Ⓑ Ⓒ Ⓓ Ⓔ
9. Ⓐ Ⓑ Ⓒ Ⓓ Ⓔ
10. Ⓐ Ⓑ Ⓒ Ⓓ Ⓔ
11. Ⓐ Ⓑ Ⓒ Ⓓ Ⓔ
12. Ⓐ Ⓑ Ⓒ Ⓓ Ⓔ
13. Ⓐ Ⓑ Ⓒ Ⓓ Ⓔ
14. Ⓐ Ⓑ Ⓒ Ⓓ Ⓔ

Correct Answers

1. Ⓐ Ⓑ Ⓒ Ⓓ ●
2. Ⓐ Ⓑ ● Ⓓ Ⓔ
3. Ⓐ Ⓑ Ⓒ Ⓓ ●
4. Ⓐ Ⓑ Ⓒ Ⓓ ●
5. Ⓐ ● Ⓒ Ⓓ Ⓔ
6. Ⓐ Ⓑ ● Ⓓ Ⓔ
7. ● Ⓑ Ⓒ Ⓓ Ⓔ
8. ● Ⓑ Ⓒ Ⓓ Ⓔ
9. Ⓐ ● Ⓒ Ⓓ Ⓔ
10. Ⓐ ● Ⓒ Ⓓ Ⓔ
11. Ⓐ Ⓑ Ⓒ ● Ⓔ
12. Ⓐ ● Ⓒ Ⓓ Ⓔ
13. Ⓐ Ⓑ ● Ⓓ Ⓔ
14. Ⓐ Ⓑ Ⓒ ● Ⓔ

Practice for Memory for Addresses

Directions: The five boxes below are labelled A, B, C, D, and E. In each box are three sets of number spans with names and two names that are not associated with numbers. In the next THREE MINUTES, you must try to memorize the box location of each name and number span. The position of a name or number span within its box is not important. You need only remember the letter of the box in which the item is to be found. You will use these names and numbers to answer three sets of practice questions that are NOT scored and one actual test that is scored. Correct answers are on page 122.

A	B	C	D	E
8100-8399 Test Pigeon 7600-8099 City Webb 6800-6999 Mark	6800-6999 Test Vampire 7000-7599 City Yak 8400-8699 Mark	7600-8099 Test Octopus 8100-8399 City Fleet 7000-7599 Mark	8400-8699 Test Ghost 6800-6999 City Hammer 7600-8099 Mark	7000-7599 Test Lever 8400-8699 City Nougat 8100-8399 Mark

PRACTICE I

Directions: Use the next THREE MINUTES to mark on the Practice I answer sheet the letter of the box in which each item that follows is to be found. Try to mark each item without looking back at the boxes. If, however, you get stuck, you may refer to the boxes during this practice exercise. If you find that you must look at the boxes, try to memorize as you do so. This test is for practice only. It will not be scored.

1. 6800-6999 Test
2. 7000-7599 City
3. 8100-8399 Mark
4. Octopus
5. Webb
6. 7000-7599 Test
7. Nougat
8. 7600-8099 Mark
9. 7000-7599 City
10. Fleet
11. Hammer
12. 7000-7599 Mark
13. 7600-8099 City
14. 8400-8699 Test
15. 8400-8699 Mark
16. 7600-8099 City
17. Vampire
18. Lever
19. Ghost
20. 6800-6999 Mark
21. 8100-8399 City
22. 8400-8699 City
23. 8400-8699 Mark
24. Pigeon
25. Fleet
26. 8400-8699 Test
27. 7000-7599 Mark
28. 6800-6999 Test
29. 7600-8099 City
30. Yak
31. Nougat
32. 8100-8399 Test
33. 7000-7599 Test
34. Lever
35. 7000-7599 City
36. 7600-8099 Mark
37. Octopus
38. Webb
39. Hammer
40. 8100-8399 Mark
41. 7600-8099 Test
42. 6800-6999 City
43. 7600-8099 Test
44. Fleet
45. 6800-6999 Mark
46. 8100-8399 City
47. 8400-8699 City
48. 8400-8699 Mark
49. Yak
50. Vampire
51. 7000-7599 Test
52. 8100-8399 Mark
53. 8100-8399 Test
54. Ghost
55. Fleet
56. 6800-6999 Mark
57. 7000-7599 Mark
58. 7000-7599 City
59. Lever
60. Octopus
61. 7600-8099 Test
62. 8400-8699 Test
63. 7600-8099 City
64. Hammer
65. Pigeon
66. 7600-8099 Mark
67. 6800-6999 City
68. 6800-6999 Test
69. 8100-8399 City
70. Webb
71. Nougat
72. 7600-8099 Test
73. 8400-8699 City
74. 8400-8699 Mark
75. 8100-8399 Test
76. 7000-7599 City
77. 7000-7599 Mark
78. Hammer
79. Lever
80. Pigeon
81. 7600-8099 Test
82. 7000-7599 Test
83. 8100-8399 Mark
84. Vampire
85. Fleet
86. 7600-8099 City
87. 6800-6999 Mark
88. 8400-8699 City

Practice I Answer Sheet

1. Ⓐ Ⓑ Ⓒ Ⓓ Ⓔ
2. Ⓐ Ⓑ Ⓒ Ⓓ Ⓔ
3. Ⓐ Ⓑ Ⓒ Ⓓ Ⓔ
4. Ⓐ Ⓑ Ⓒ Ⓓ Ⓔ
5. Ⓐ Ⓑ Ⓒ Ⓓ Ⓔ
6. Ⓐ Ⓑ Ⓒ Ⓓ Ⓔ
7. Ⓐ Ⓑ Ⓒ Ⓓ Ⓔ
8. Ⓐ Ⓑ Ⓒ Ⓓ Ⓔ
9. Ⓐ Ⓑ Ⓒ Ⓓ Ⓔ
10. Ⓐ Ⓑ Ⓒ Ⓓ Ⓔ
11. Ⓐ Ⓑ Ⓒ Ⓓ Ⓔ
12. Ⓐ Ⓑ Ⓒ Ⓓ Ⓔ
13. Ⓐ Ⓑ Ⓒ Ⓓ Ⓔ
14. Ⓐ Ⓑ Ⓒ Ⓓ Ⓔ
15. Ⓐ Ⓑ Ⓒ Ⓓ Ⓔ
16. Ⓐ Ⓑ Ⓒ Ⓓ Ⓔ
17. Ⓐ Ⓑ Ⓒ Ⓓ Ⓔ
18. Ⓐ Ⓑ Ⓒ Ⓓ Ⓔ
19. Ⓐ Ⓑ Ⓒ Ⓓ Ⓔ
20. Ⓐ Ⓑ Ⓒ Ⓓ Ⓔ
21. Ⓐ Ⓑ Ⓒ Ⓓ Ⓔ
22. Ⓐ Ⓑ Ⓒ Ⓓ Ⓔ
23. Ⓐ Ⓑ Ⓒ Ⓓ Ⓔ
24. Ⓐ Ⓑ Ⓒ Ⓓ Ⓔ
25. Ⓐ Ⓑ Ⓒ Ⓓ Ⓔ
26. Ⓐ Ⓑ Ⓒ Ⓓ Ⓔ
27. Ⓐ Ⓑ Ⓒ Ⓓ Ⓔ
28. Ⓐ Ⓑ Ⓒ Ⓓ Ⓔ
29. Ⓐ Ⓑ Ⓒ Ⓓ Ⓔ
30. Ⓐ Ⓑ Ⓒ Ⓓ Ⓔ
31. Ⓐ Ⓑ Ⓒ Ⓓ Ⓔ
32. Ⓐ Ⓑ Ⓒ Ⓓ Ⓔ
33. Ⓐ Ⓑ Ⓒ Ⓓ Ⓔ
34. Ⓐ Ⓑ Ⓒ Ⓓ Ⓔ
35. Ⓐ Ⓑ Ⓒ Ⓓ Ⓔ
36. Ⓐ Ⓑ Ⓒ Ⓓ Ⓔ
37. Ⓐ Ⓑ Ⓒ Ⓓ Ⓔ
38. Ⓐ Ⓑ Ⓒ Ⓓ Ⓔ
39. Ⓐ Ⓑ Ⓒ Ⓓ Ⓔ
40. Ⓐ Ⓑ Ⓒ Ⓓ Ⓔ
41. Ⓐ Ⓑ Ⓒ Ⓓ Ⓔ
42. Ⓐ Ⓑ Ⓒ Ⓓ Ⓔ
43. Ⓐ Ⓑ Ⓒ Ⓓ Ⓔ
44. Ⓐ Ⓑ Ⓒ Ⓓ Ⓔ
45. Ⓐ Ⓑ Ⓒ Ⓓ Ⓔ
46. Ⓐ Ⓑ Ⓒ Ⓓ Ⓔ
47. Ⓐ Ⓑ Ⓒ Ⓓ Ⓔ
48. Ⓐ Ⓑ Ⓒ Ⓓ Ⓔ
49. Ⓐ Ⓑ Ⓒ Ⓓ Ⓔ
50. Ⓐ Ⓑ Ⓒ Ⓓ Ⓔ
51. Ⓐ Ⓑ Ⓒ Ⓓ Ⓔ
52. Ⓐ Ⓑ Ⓒ Ⓓ Ⓔ
53. Ⓐ Ⓑ Ⓒ Ⓓ Ⓔ
54. Ⓐ Ⓑ Ⓒ Ⓓ Ⓔ
55. Ⓐ Ⓑ Ⓒ Ⓓ Ⓔ
56. Ⓐ Ⓑ Ⓒ Ⓓ Ⓔ
57. Ⓐ Ⓑ Ⓒ Ⓓ Ⓔ
58. Ⓐ Ⓑ Ⓒ Ⓓ Ⓔ
59. Ⓐ Ⓑ Ⓒ Ⓓ Ⓔ
60. Ⓐ Ⓑ Ⓒ Ⓓ Ⓔ
61. Ⓐ Ⓑ Ⓒ Ⓓ Ⓔ
62. Ⓐ Ⓑ Ⓒ Ⓓ Ⓔ
63. Ⓐ Ⓑ Ⓒ Ⓓ Ⓔ
64. Ⓐ Ⓑ Ⓒ Ⓓ Ⓔ
65. Ⓐ Ⓑ Ⓒ Ⓓ Ⓔ
66. Ⓐ Ⓑ Ⓒ Ⓓ Ⓔ
67. Ⓐ Ⓑ Ⓒ Ⓓ Ⓔ
68. Ⓐ Ⓑ Ⓒ Ⓓ Ⓔ
69. Ⓐ Ⓑ Ⓒ Ⓓ Ⓔ
70. Ⓐ Ⓑ Ⓒ Ⓓ Ⓔ
71. Ⓐ Ⓑ Ⓒ Ⓓ Ⓔ
72. Ⓐ Ⓑ Ⓒ Ⓓ Ⓔ
73. Ⓐ Ⓑ Ⓒ Ⓓ Ⓔ
74. Ⓐ Ⓑ Ⓒ Ⓓ Ⓔ
75. Ⓐ Ⓑ Ⓒ Ⓓ Ⓔ
76. Ⓐ Ⓑ Ⓒ Ⓓ Ⓔ
77. Ⓐ Ⓑ Ⓒ Ⓓ Ⓔ
78. Ⓐ Ⓑ Ⓒ Ⓓ Ⓔ
79. Ⓐ Ⓑ Ⓒ Ⓓ Ⓔ
80. Ⓐ Ⓑ Ⓒ Ⓓ Ⓔ
81. Ⓐ Ⓑ Ⓒ Ⓓ Ⓔ
82. Ⓐ Ⓑ Ⓒ Ⓓ Ⓔ
83. Ⓐ Ⓑ Ⓒ Ⓓ Ⓔ
84. Ⓐ Ⓑ Ⓒ Ⓓ Ⓔ
85. Ⓐ Ⓑ Ⓒ Ⓓ Ⓔ
86. Ⓐ Ⓑ Ⓒ Ⓓ Ⓔ
87. Ⓐ Ⓑ Ⓒ Ⓓ Ⓔ
88. Ⓐ Ⓑ Ⓒ Ⓓ Ⓔ

Practice II

Directions: The next 88 questions constitute another practice exercise. Mark your answers on the Practice II answer sheet. Again, the time limit is THREE MINUTES. This time, however, you must NOT look at the boxes while answering the questions. You must rely on your memory in marking the box location of each item. This practice test will not be scored.

1. 7000-7599 Mark
2. 6800-6999 City
3. 6800-6999 Test
4. Pigeon
5. Nougat
6. 8400-8699 Test
7. 7000-7599 City
8. 6800-6999 Mark
9. Hammer
10. Ghost
11. 7600-8099 City
12. 8100-8399 Mark
13. 7600-8099 Mark
14. 7600-8099 Test
15. Octopus
16. Webb
17. 8100-8399 City
18. 8400-8699 City
19. 6800-6999 Mark
20. Fleet
21. Lever
22. Yak
23. 8100-8399 Test
24. 7000-7599 Test
25. Vampire
26. Octopus
27. 6800-6999 Test
28. 6800-6999 City
29. 6800-6999 Mark
30. Lever
31. Nougat
32. 7000-7599 City
33. 8100-8399 Mark
34. 8100-8399 City
35. 8100-8399 Test
36. 8400-8699 Mark
37. Yak
38. Webb
39. 7600-8099 Test
40. 7000-7599 Mark
41. Fleet
42. 8400-8699 City
43. 7600-8099 City
44. 8400-8699 Test
45. Pigeon
46. Ghost
47. Hammer
48. 7600-8099 Mark
49. 7000-7599 Test
50. 8100-8399 Mark
51. 6800-6999 City
52. 7600-8099 Test
53. Lever
54. Hammer
55. 8100-8399 Test
56. 7000-7599 City
57. 7000-7599 Mark
58. Pigeon
59. Vampire
60. 8100-8399 City
61. 7600-8099 City
62. 7000-7599 Test
63. 6800-6999 Mark
64. Nougat
65. Yak
66. Webb
67. 8400-8699 Mark
68. 7600-8099 Mark

69. 8400-8699 City	74. 8400-8699 Test	79. Webb	84. Octopus
70. 6800-6999 Test	75. 7600-8099 Test	80. 6800-6999 City	85. 7000-7599 Test
71. Ghost	76. 6800-6999 Mark	81. 6800-6999 Test	86. 8100-8399 City
72. Octopus	77. 7600-8099 City	82. 7600-8099 Mark	87. 6800-6999 Mark
73. Fleet	78. Nougat	83. Vampire	88. 8100-8399 Test

Practice II Answer Sheet

1. Ⓐ Ⓑ Ⓒ Ⓓ Ⓔ   23. Ⓐ Ⓑ Ⓒ Ⓓ Ⓔ   45. Ⓐ Ⓑ Ⓒ Ⓓ Ⓔ   67. Ⓐ Ⓑ Ⓒ Ⓓ Ⓔ
2. Ⓐ Ⓑ Ⓒ Ⓓ Ⓔ   24. Ⓐ Ⓑ Ⓒ Ⓓ Ⓔ   46. Ⓐ Ⓑ Ⓒ Ⓓ Ⓔ   68. Ⓐ Ⓑ Ⓒ Ⓓ Ⓔ
3. Ⓐ Ⓑ Ⓒ Ⓓ Ⓔ   25. Ⓐ Ⓑ Ⓒ Ⓓ Ⓔ   47. Ⓐ Ⓑ Ⓒ Ⓓ Ⓔ   69. Ⓐ Ⓑ Ⓒ Ⓓ Ⓔ
4. Ⓐ Ⓑ Ⓒ Ⓓ Ⓔ   26. Ⓐ Ⓑ Ⓒ Ⓓ Ⓔ   48. Ⓐ Ⓑ Ⓒ Ⓓ Ⓔ   70. Ⓐ Ⓑ Ⓒ Ⓓ Ⓔ
5. Ⓐ Ⓑ Ⓒ Ⓓ Ⓔ   27. Ⓐ Ⓑ Ⓒ Ⓓ Ⓔ   49. Ⓐ Ⓑ Ⓒ Ⓓ Ⓔ   71. Ⓐ Ⓑ Ⓒ Ⓓ Ⓔ
6. Ⓐ Ⓑ Ⓒ Ⓓ Ⓔ   28. Ⓐ Ⓑ Ⓒ Ⓓ Ⓔ   50. Ⓐ Ⓑ Ⓒ Ⓓ Ⓔ   72. Ⓐ Ⓑ Ⓒ Ⓓ Ⓔ
7. Ⓐ Ⓑ Ⓒ Ⓓ Ⓔ   29. Ⓐ Ⓑ Ⓒ Ⓓ Ⓔ   51. Ⓐ Ⓑ Ⓒ Ⓓ Ⓔ   73. Ⓐ Ⓑ Ⓒ Ⓓ Ⓔ
8. Ⓐ Ⓑ Ⓒ Ⓓ Ⓔ   30. Ⓐ Ⓑ Ⓒ Ⓓ Ⓔ   52. Ⓐ Ⓑ Ⓒ Ⓓ Ⓔ   74. Ⓐ Ⓑ Ⓒ Ⓓ Ⓔ
9. Ⓐ Ⓑ Ⓒ Ⓓ Ⓔ   31. Ⓐ Ⓑ Ⓒ Ⓓ Ⓔ   53. Ⓐ Ⓑ Ⓒ Ⓓ Ⓔ   75. Ⓐ Ⓑ Ⓒ Ⓓ Ⓔ
10. Ⓐ Ⓑ Ⓒ Ⓓ Ⓔ   32. Ⓐ Ⓑ Ⓒ Ⓓ Ⓔ   54. Ⓐ Ⓑ Ⓒ Ⓓ Ⓔ   76. Ⓐ Ⓑ Ⓒ Ⓓ Ⓔ
11. Ⓐ Ⓑ Ⓒ Ⓓ Ⓔ   33. Ⓐ Ⓑ Ⓒ Ⓓ Ⓔ   55. Ⓐ Ⓑ Ⓒ Ⓓ Ⓔ   77. Ⓐ Ⓑ Ⓒ Ⓓ Ⓔ
12. Ⓐ Ⓑ Ⓒ Ⓓ Ⓔ   34. Ⓐ Ⓑ Ⓒ Ⓓ Ⓔ   56. Ⓐ Ⓑ Ⓒ Ⓓ Ⓔ   78. Ⓐ Ⓑ Ⓒ Ⓓ Ⓔ
13. Ⓐ Ⓑ Ⓒ Ⓓ Ⓔ   35. Ⓐ Ⓑ Ⓒ Ⓓ Ⓔ   57. Ⓐ Ⓑ Ⓒ Ⓓ Ⓔ   79. Ⓐ Ⓑ Ⓒ Ⓓ Ⓔ
14. Ⓐ Ⓑ Ⓒ Ⓓ Ⓔ   36. Ⓐ Ⓑ Ⓒ Ⓓ Ⓔ   58. Ⓐ Ⓑ Ⓒ Ⓓ Ⓔ   80. Ⓐ Ⓑ Ⓒ Ⓓ Ⓔ
15. Ⓐ Ⓑ Ⓒ Ⓓ Ⓔ   37. Ⓐ Ⓑ Ⓒ Ⓓ Ⓔ   59. Ⓐ Ⓑ Ⓒ Ⓓ Ⓔ   81. Ⓐ Ⓑ Ⓒ Ⓓ Ⓔ
16. Ⓐ Ⓑ Ⓒ Ⓓ Ⓔ   38. Ⓐ Ⓑ Ⓒ Ⓓ Ⓔ   60. Ⓐ Ⓑ Ⓒ Ⓓ Ⓔ   82. Ⓐ Ⓑ Ⓒ Ⓓ Ⓔ
17. Ⓐ Ⓑ Ⓒ Ⓓ Ⓔ   39. Ⓐ Ⓑ Ⓒ Ⓓ Ⓔ   61. Ⓐ Ⓑ Ⓒ Ⓓ Ⓔ   83. Ⓐ Ⓑ Ⓒ Ⓓ Ⓔ
18. Ⓐ Ⓑ Ⓒ Ⓓ Ⓔ   40. Ⓐ Ⓑ Ⓒ Ⓓ Ⓔ   62. Ⓐ Ⓑ Ⓒ Ⓓ Ⓔ   84. Ⓐ Ⓑ Ⓒ Ⓓ Ⓔ
19. Ⓐ Ⓑ Ⓒ Ⓓ Ⓔ   41. Ⓐ Ⓑ Ⓒ Ⓓ Ⓔ   63. Ⓐ Ⓑ Ⓒ Ⓓ Ⓔ   85. Ⓐ Ⓑ Ⓒ Ⓓ Ⓔ
20. Ⓐ Ⓑ Ⓒ Ⓓ Ⓔ   42. Ⓐ Ⓑ Ⓒ Ⓓ Ⓔ   64. Ⓐ Ⓑ Ⓒ Ⓓ Ⓔ   86. Ⓐ Ⓑ Ⓒ Ⓓ Ⓔ
21. Ⓐ Ⓑ Ⓒ Ⓓ Ⓔ   43. Ⓐ Ⓑ Ⓒ Ⓓ Ⓔ   65. Ⓐ Ⓑ Ⓒ Ⓓ Ⓔ   87. Ⓐ Ⓑ Ⓒ Ⓓ Ⓔ
22. Ⓐ Ⓑ Ⓒ Ⓓ Ⓔ   44. Ⓐ Ⓑ Ⓒ Ⓓ Ⓔ   66. Ⓐ Ⓑ Ⓒ Ⓓ Ⓔ   88. Ⓐ Ⓑ Ⓒ Ⓓ Ⓔ

Practice III

Directions: The names and addresses are repeated for you in the boxes below. Each name and each number span is in the same box in which you found it in the original set. You will now be allowed FIVE MINUTES to study the locations again. Do your best to memorize the letter of the box in which each item is located. This is your last chance to see the boxes.

A	B	C	D	E
8100-8399 Test Pigeon 7600-8099 City Webb 6800-6999 Mark	6800-6999 Test Vampire 7000-7599 City Yak 8400-8699 Mark	7600-8099 Test Octopus 8100-8399 City Fleet 7000-7599 Mark	8400-8699 Test Ghost 6800-6999 City Hammer 7600-8099 Mark	7000-7599 Test Lever 8400-8699 City Nougat 8100-8399 Mark

106 / Clerical Exams Handbook

Directions: This is your last practice test. Mark the location of each of the 88 items on your answer sheet. You will have FIVE MINUTES to answer these questions. Do NOT look back at the boxes. This practice test will not be scored.

1. Fleet	23. 8400-8699 Test	45. Vampire	67. 6800-6999 Mark
2. Lever	24. 7000-7599 Mark	46. 6800-6999 Test	68. 7600-8099 City
3. 8400-8699 Test	25. Octopus	47. 6800-6999 Mark	69. Octopus
4. 7000-7599 City	26. Fleet	48. 7600-8099 Mark	70. Fleet
5. 6800-6999 Mark	27. 8100-8399 City	49. Hammer	71. 8400-8699 City
6. Vampire	28. 8100-8399 Test	50. Yak	72. 7000-7599 Mark
7. Pigeon	29. 7000-7599 City	51. 8400-8699 City	73. 7600-8099 Test
8. 8100-8399 Test	30. 7000-7599 Test	52. 8400-8699 Test	74. 7600-8099 Mark
9. 8100-8399 Mark	31. 8100-8399 Test	53. 7600-8099 Test	75. 6800-6999 City
10. 7000-7599 Test	32. 7000-7599 City	54. Lever	76. 6800-6999 Test
11. 8100-8399 City	33. 7000-7599 Mark	55. Octopus	77. Webb
12. Octopus	34. Nougat	56. 7000-7599 Test	78. Pigeon
13. Ghost	35. Ghost	57. 7000-7599 Mark	79. Lever
14. Yak	36. 6800-6999 City	58. 7000-7599 City	80. 8400-8699 Test
15. 6800-6999 City	37. 7000-7599 Test	59. 8100-8399 Test	81. 8400-8699 Mark
16. 6800-6999 Test	38. 8100-8399 Mark	60. Vampire	82. Nougat
17. 7600-8099 Mark	39. Pigeon	61. 8100-8399 City	83. 8400-8699 City
18. 7600-8099 City	40. Webb	62. Hammer	84. 7000-7599 City
19. Hammer	41. 7600-8099 City	63. 8100-8399 Mark	85. 7000-7599 Test
20. Nougat	42. 8100-8399 City	64. 7000-7599 Test	86. Hammer
21. 8400-8699 Mark	43. 8400-8699 Mark	65. Ghost	87. 6800-6999 Mark
22. 8400-8699 City	44. Fleet	66. Yak	88. Yak

PRACTICE III ANSWER SHEET

1. Ⓐ Ⓑ Ⓒ Ⓓ Ⓔ   23. Ⓐ Ⓑ Ⓒ Ⓓ Ⓔ   45. Ⓐ Ⓑ Ⓒ Ⓓ Ⓔ   67. Ⓐ Ⓑ Ⓒ Ⓓ Ⓔ
2. Ⓐ Ⓑ Ⓒ Ⓓ Ⓔ   24. Ⓐ Ⓑ Ⓒ Ⓓ Ⓔ   46. Ⓐ Ⓑ Ⓒ Ⓓ Ⓔ   68. Ⓐ Ⓑ Ⓒ Ⓓ Ⓔ
3. Ⓐ Ⓑ Ⓒ Ⓓ Ⓔ   25. Ⓐ Ⓑ Ⓒ Ⓓ Ⓔ   47. Ⓐ Ⓑ Ⓒ Ⓓ Ⓔ   69. Ⓐ Ⓑ Ⓒ Ⓓ Ⓔ
4. Ⓐ Ⓑ Ⓒ Ⓓ Ⓔ   26. Ⓐ Ⓑ Ⓒ Ⓓ Ⓔ   48. Ⓐ Ⓑ Ⓒ Ⓓ Ⓔ   70. Ⓐ Ⓑ Ⓒ Ⓓ Ⓔ
5. Ⓐ Ⓑ Ⓒ Ⓓ Ⓔ   27. Ⓐ Ⓑ Ⓒ Ⓓ Ⓔ   49. Ⓐ Ⓑ Ⓒ Ⓓ Ⓔ   71. Ⓐ Ⓑ Ⓒ Ⓓ Ⓔ
6. Ⓐ Ⓑ Ⓒ Ⓓ Ⓔ   28. Ⓐ Ⓑ Ⓒ Ⓓ Ⓔ   50. Ⓐ Ⓑ Ⓒ Ⓓ Ⓔ   72. Ⓐ Ⓑ Ⓒ Ⓓ Ⓔ
7. Ⓐ Ⓑ Ⓒ Ⓓ Ⓔ   29. Ⓐ Ⓑ Ⓒ Ⓓ Ⓔ   51. Ⓐ Ⓑ Ⓒ Ⓓ Ⓔ   73. Ⓐ Ⓑ Ⓒ Ⓓ Ⓔ
8. Ⓐ Ⓑ Ⓒ Ⓓ Ⓔ   30. Ⓐ Ⓑ Ⓒ Ⓓ Ⓔ   52. Ⓐ Ⓑ Ⓒ Ⓓ Ⓔ   74. Ⓐ Ⓑ Ⓒ Ⓓ Ⓔ
9. Ⓐ Ⓑ Ⓒ Ⓓ Ⓔ   31. Ⓐ Ⓑ Ⓒ Ⓓ Ⓔ   53. Ⓐ Ⓑ Ⓒ Ⓓ Ⓔ   75. Ⓐ Ⓑ Ⓒ Ⓓ Ⓔ
10. Ⓐ Ⓑ Ⓒ Ⓓ Ⓔ   32. Ⓐ Ⓑ Ⓒ Ⓓ Ⓔ   54. Ⓐ Ⓑ Ⓒ Ⓓ Ⓔ   76. Ⓐ Ⓑ Ⓒ Ⓓ Ⓔ
11. Ⓐ Ⓑ Ⓒ Ⓓ Ⓔ   33. Ⓐ Ⓑ Ⓒ Ⓓ Ⓔ   55. Ⓐ Ⓑ Ⓒ Ⓓ Ⓔ   77. Ⓐ Ⓑ Ⓒ Ⓓ Ⓔ
12. Ⓐ Ⓑ Ⓒ Ⓓ Ⓔ   34. Ⓐ Ⓑ Ⓒ Ⓓ Ⓔ   56. Ⓐ Ⓑ Ⓒ Ⓓ Ⓔ   78. Ⓐ Ⓑ Ⓒ Ⓓ Ⓔ
13. Ⓐ Ⓑ Ⓒ Ⓓ Ⓔ   35. Ⓐ Ⓑ Ⓒ Ⓓ Ⓔ   57. Ⓐ Ⓑ Ⓒ Ⓓ Ⓔ   79. Ⓐ Ⓑ Ⓒ Ⓓ Ⓔ
14. Ⓐ Ⓑ Ⓒ Ⓓ Ⓔ   36. Ⓐ Ⓑ Ⓒ Ⓓ Ⓔ   58. Ⓐ Ⓑ Ⓒ Ⓓ Ⓔ   80. Ⓐ Ⓑ Ⓒ Ⓓ Ⓔ
15. Ⓐ Ⓑ Ⓒ Ⓓ Ⓔ   37. Ⓐ Ⓑ Ⓒ Ⓓ Ⓔ   59. Ⓐ Ⓑ Ⓒ Ⓓ Ⓔ   81. Ⓐ Ⓑ Ⓒ Ⓓ Ⓔ
16. Ⓐ Ⓑ Ⓒ Ⓓ Ⓔ   38. Ⓐ Ⓑ Ⓒ Ⓓ Ⓔ   60. Ⓐ Ⓑ Ⓒ Ⓓ Ⓔ   82. Ⓐ Ⓑ Ⓒ Ⓓ Ⓔ
17. Ⓐ Ⓑ Ⓒ Ⓓ Ⓔ   39. Ⓐ Ⓑ Ⓒ Ⓓ Ⓔ   61. Ⓐ Ⓑ Ⓒ Ⓓ Ⓔ   83. Ⓐ Ⓑ Ⓒ Ⓓ Ⓔ
18. Ⓐ Ⓑ Ⓒ Ⓓ Ⓔ   40. Ⓐ Ⓑ Ⓒ Ⓓ Ⓔ   62. Ⓐ Ⓑ Ⓒ Ⓓ Ⓔ   84. Ⓐ Ⓑ Ⓒ Ⓓ Ⓔ
19. Ⓐ Ⓑ Ⓒ Ⓓ Ⓔ   41. Ⓐ Ⓑ Ⓒ Ⓓ Ⓔ   63. Ⓐ Ⓑ Ⓒ Ⓓ Ⓔ   85. Ⓐ Ⓑ Ⓒ Ⓓ Ⓔ
20. Ⓐ Ⓑ Ⓒ Ⓓ Ⓔ   42. Ⓐ Ⓑ Ⓒ Ⓓ Ⓔ   64. Ⓐ Ⓑ Ⓒ Ⓓ Ⓔ   86. Ⓐ Ⓑ Ⓒ Ⓓ Ⓔ
21. Ⓐ Ⓑ Ⓒ Ⓓ Ⓔ   43. Ⓐ Ⓑ Ⓒ Ⓓ Ⓔ   65. Ⓐ Ⓑ Ⓒ Ⓓ Ⓔ   87. Ⓐ Ⓑ Ⓒ Ⓓ Ⓔ
22. Ⓐ Ⓑ Ⓒ Ⓓ Ⓔ   44. Ⓐ Ⓑ Ⓒ Ⓓ Ⓔ   66. Ⓐ Ⓑ Ⓒ Ⓓ Ⓔ   88. Ⓐ Ⓑ Ⓒ Ⓓ Ⓔ

Memory for Addresses

Time: 5 Minutes. 88 Questions.

Directions: Mark your answers on the answer sheet in the section headed "MEMORY FOR ADDRESSES." This test will be scored. You are NOT permitted to look at the boxes. Work from memory, as quickly and as accurately as you can. Correct answers are on page 123.

1. 8400-8699 Test
2. 7000-7599 City
3. 8400-8699 Mark
4. Nougat
5. Pigeon
6. 6800-6999 Test
7. 8100-8399 Test
8. 8400-8699 City
9. 7000-7599 Mark
10. Ghost
11. Hammer
12. Vampire
13. 7600-8099 City
14. 7600-8099 Mark
15. 6800-6999 Mark
16. Octopus
17. Yak
18. 7600-8099 Test
19. 7000-7599 Test
20. 8400-8699 City
21. 8100-8399 Mark
22. Vampire
23. Lever
24. 7600-8099 Test
25. 7600-8099 City
26. 8100-8399 Mark
27. Webb
28. Ghost
29. 6800-6999 Mark
30. 7000-7599 Test
31. 8100-8399 City
32. 8400-8699 City
33. Pigeon
34. Yak
35. 7600-8099 Mark
36. 8400-8699 Mark
37. 8100-8399 Test
38. 6800-6999 City
39. Octopus
40. Hammer
41. Nougat
42. 7000-7599 City
43. 6800-6999 Test
44. 7600-8099 Mark
45. Nougat
46. 8400-8699 City
47. 6800-6999 Mark
48. 7600-8099 Test
49. 7000-7599 City
50. Ghost
51. Fleet
52. Yak
53. 7000-7599 Test
54. 8100-8399 City
55. 7600-8099 City
56. Pigeon
57. Octopus
58. 6800-6999 City
59. 8400-8699 Mark
60. 8100-8399 Mark
61. 8100-8399 Test
62. Webb
63. Hammer
64. 8400-8699 Test
65. 7000-7599 Mark
66. 8100-8399 City
67. Lever
68. Vampire
69. 8100-8399 Test
70. 8400-8699 City
71. 7000-7599 Test
72. 6800-6999 Mark
73. 8100-8399 City
74. 6800-6999 City
75. Yak
76. Nougat
77. Fleet
78. 6800-6999 Test
79. 7000-7599 Mark
80. 7000-7599 City
81. 8100-8399 Test
82. 8100-8399 Mark
83. Pigeon
84. Lever
85. Hammer
86. 8400-8699 Test
87. 8400-8699 Mark
88. 7600-8099 City

END OF MEMORY FOR ADDRESSES

Part C—Number Series

SAMPLE QUESTIONS

The following sample questions show you the type of question that will be used in Part C. You will have three minutes to answer the sample questions and to study the explanations.

Directions: Each number series question consists of a series of numbers that follows some definite order. The numbers progress from left to right according to some rule. One pair of numbers to the right of the series comprises the next two numbers in the series. Study each series to try to find a pattern to the series and to figure out the rule that governs the progression. Choose the answer pair that continues the series according to the pattern established and mark its letter on your answer sheet.

1. 75 75 72 72 69 69 66 . . . . . (A) 66 66   (B) 66 68   (C) 63 63   (D) 66 63   (E) 63 60

The pattern established in this series is: repeat the number, −3; repeat the number, −3 . . . . To continue the series, repeat 66, then subtract 3. The answer is (**D**).

2. 12 16 21 27 31 36 42 . . . . . (A) 48 56   (B) 44 48   (C) 48 52   (D) 46 52   (E) 46 51

By marking the amount and direction of change from one number of the series to the next, you can see that the pattern is: +4, +5, +6; +4, +5, +6; +4, +5, +6. Continuing the series: 42 + 4 = 46 + 5 = 51. (**E**) is the correct answer.

3. 22 24 12 26 28 12 30 . . . . . (A) 12 32   (B) 32 34   (C) 32 12   (D) 12 12   (E) 32 36

In this series the basic pattern is +2. The series may be read: 22 24 26 28 30 32. After each two numbers of the series we find the number 12, which serves no function except for repetition. To continue the series, add 2 to 30 to get 32. After 30 and 32, you must put in the number 12, so (**C**) is the correct answer.

4. 5 70 10 68 15 66 20 . . . . . . (A) 25 64   (B) 64 25   (C) 24 63   (D) 25 30   (E) 64 62

In this problem there are two distinct series alternating with one another. The first series is going up by a factor of +5. It reads: 10 15 20. The alternating series is going down by a factor of −2. It reads: 70 68 66. At the point where you must continue the series, the next number must be a member of the descending series, so it must be 64. Following that number must come the next number of the ascending series, which is 25. (**B**) is the answer.

5. 13 22 32 43 55 68 82 . . . . . (A) 97 113   (B) 100 115   (C) 96 110   (D) 95 105   (E) 99 112

The numbers are large, but the progression is simple. If you mark the differences between numbers, you can readily recognize: +9, +10, +11, +12, +13, +14. Continuing the series: 82 + 15 = 97 + 16 = 113. (**A**) is the correct answer.

Sample Answer Sheet

1. Ⓐ Ⓑ Ⓒ Ⓓ Ⓔ   4. Ⓐ Ⓑ Ⓒ Ⓓ Ⓔ
2. Ⓐ Ⓑ Ⓒ Ⓓ Ⓔ   5. Ⓐ Ⓑ Ⓒ Ⓓ Ⓔ
3. Ⓐ Ⓑ Ⓒ Ⓓ Ⓔ

Correct Answers

1. Ⓐ Ⓑ Ⓒ ● Ⓔ   4. Ⓐ ● Ⓒ Ⓓ Ⓔ
2. Ⓐ Ⓑ Ⓒ Ⓓ ●   5. ● Ⓑ Ⓒ Ⓓ Ⓔ
3. Ⓐ Ⓑ ● Ⓓ Ⓔ

U.S. Postal Service Clerk, Distribution Clerk & Mark-Up Clerk Exam / 109

Number Series

Time: 20 Minutes. 24 Questions.

Directions: Each number series question consists of a series of numbers that follows some definite order. The numbers progress from left to right according to some rule. One lettered pair of numbers comprises the next two numbers in the series. Study each series to try to find a pattern to the series and to figure the rule that governs the progression. Choose the answer pair that continues the series according to the pattern established and mark its letter on your answer sheet. Correct answers are on page 123.

1. 3 8 4 9 5 10 6 .... (A) 7 11 (B) 7 8 (C) 11 8 (D) 12 7 (E) 11 7
2. 18 14 19 17 20 20 21 .... (A) 22 24 (B) 14 19 (C) 24 21 (D) 21 23 (E) 23 22
3. 6 9 10 7 11 12 8 .... (A) 9 10 (B) 9 13 (C) 16 14 (D) 13 14 (E) 14 15
4. 7 5 3 9 7 5 11 .... (A) 13 12 (B) 7 5 (C) 9 7 (D) 13 7 (E) 9 9
5. 7 9 18 10 12 18 13 ...... (A) 18 14 (B) 15 18 (C) 14 15 (D) 15 14 (E) 14 18
6. 2 6 4 8 6 10 8 .... (A) 12 10 (B) 6 10 (C) 10 12 (D) 12 16 (E) 6 4
7. 7 9 12 14 17 19 22 ...... (A) 25 27 (B) 23 24 (C) 23 25 (D) 24 27 (E) 26 27
8. 3 23 5 25 7 27 9 .... (A) 10 11 (B) 27 29 (C) 29 11 (D) 11 28 (E) 28 10
9. 1 2 2 3 4 12 5 6 .... (A) 7 8 (B) 11 7 (C) 11 56 (D) 56 7 (E) 30 7
10. 1 2 3 6 4 5 6 6 7 ...... (A) 6 5 (B) 8 9 (C) 6 8 (D) 7 6 (E) 8 6
11. 1 3 40 5 7 37 9 .... (A) 11 39 (B) 9 11 (C) 34 11 (D) 11 34 (E) 11 35
12. 25 27 29 31 33 35 37 .... (A) 39 41 (B) 38 39 (C) 37 39 (D) 37 38 (E) 39 40
13. 91 85 17 81 75 15 71 .... (A) 74 14 (B) 61 51 (C) 65 13 (D) 65 10 (E) 66 33
14. 41 37 46 42 51 47 56 .... (A) 51 70 (B) 52 61 (C) 49 60 (D) 60 43 (E) 55 65
15. 6 6 6 18 18 18 54 .... (A) 54 108 (B) 54 162 (C) 108 108 (D) 108 162 (E) 54 54
16. 13 23 14 22 15 21 16 .... (A) 17 20 (B) 20 17 (C) 17 18 (D) 20 19 (E) 16 20
17. 52 10 48 20 44 30 40 .... (A) 36 50 (B) 50 36 (C) 36 40 (D) 40 36 (E) 40 40
18. 94 84 75 67 60 54 49 .... (A) 45 42 (B) 49 45 (C) 44 40 (D) 46 42 (E) 45 40
19. 76 38 38 48 24 24 34 .... (A) 34 44 (B) 34 34 (C) 17 17 (D) 34 17 (E) 17 27
20. 83 38 84 48 85 58 86 .... (A) 86 68 (B) 87 78 (C) 59 95 (D) 68 88 (E) 68 87
21. 19 21 21 24 24 24 28 .... (A) 28 31 (B) 28 33 (C) 32 36 (D) 28 28 (E) 28 32
22. 52 45 38 32 26 21 16 .... (A) 16 12 (B) 12 8 (C) 11 6 (D) 11 7 (E) 12 9
23. 100 81 64 49 36 25 16 ... (A) 12 10 (B) 8 4 (C) 8 2 (D) 9 4 (E) 9 2
24. 4 40 44 5 50 55 6 ...... (A) 60 66 (B) 6 60 (C) 6 66 (D) 7 70 (E) 70 77

END OF NUMBER SERIES

Part D—Following Oral Instructions

Directions and Sample Questions

LISTENING TO INSTRUCTIONS: When you are ready to try these sample questions, give the following instructions to a friend and have the friend read them aloud to you at the rate of 80 words per minute. Do not read them to yourself. Your friend will need a watch with a second hand. Listen carefully and do exactly what your friend tells you to do with the worksheet and answer sheet. Your friend will tell you some things to do with each item on the worksheet. After each set of instructions, your friend will give you time to mark your answer by darkening a circle on the sample answer sheet. Since B and D sound very much alike, your friend will say "B as in baker" when he or she means B and "D as in dog" when he or she means D.

Before proceeding further, tear out the worksheet on page 113. Then hand this book to your friend.

TO THE PERSON WHO IS TO READ THE INSTRUCTIONS: The instructions are to be read at the rate of 80 words per minute. Do not read aloud the material that is in parentheses. Do not repeat any instructions.

Read Aloud to the Candidate

Look at line 1 on your worksheet. (Pause slightly.) Draw a line under the third letter in the line. (Pause 2 seconds.) Now, on your answer sheet, find the number that is 2 less than 17 and darken the space for the letter under which you drew a line. (Pause 10 seconds.)

Look at line 2 on your worksheet. (Pause slightly.) Locate the smallest number and draw a circle around it. (Pause 5 seconds.) Now, on your answer sheet, darken the space for the letter C for the number you have circled. (Pause 5 seconds.)

Look at line 3 on your worksheet. (Pause slightly.) There are 5 boxes. Each box has a number. In each box containing a number that can be found on a foot-long ruler, write the letter E. (Pause 10 seconds.) Now, on your answer sheet, darken the space for the number-letter combination that is in each box you wrote in. (Pause 10 seconds.)

Look at line 4 on your worksheet. (Pause slightly.) If in a week Wednesday comes before Thursday, write D as in dog in the box with the largest number. (Pause 5 seconds.) If it does not, write E in the box of the second-to-largest number. (Pause 5 seconds.) Now, on your answer sheet, darken the space for the number-letter combination that is in the box you just wrote in. (Pause 5 seconds.)

U.S. Postal Service Clerk, Distribution Clerk & Mark-Up Clerk Exam / 113

Sample Worksheet

Directions: Listening carefully to each set of instructions, mark each item on this worksheet as directed. Then complete each question by marking the sample answer sheet below as directed. For each answer you will darken the answer for a number-letter combination. Should you fall behind and miss an instruction, don't become excited. Let that one go and listen for the next one. If, when you start to darken a space for a number, you find that you have already darkened another space for that number, either erase the first mark and darken the space for the new combination or let the first mark stay and do not darken a space for the new combination. Write with a pencil that has a clean eraser. When you finish, you should have no more than one space darkened for each number.

1. E C A D R

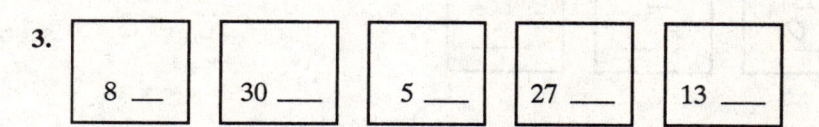

2. 6 3 12 14 5 8

3. | 8 ___ | 30 ___ | 5 ___ | 27 ___ | 13 ___ |

4. | 6 ___ | 13 ___ | 12 ___ | 9 ___ |

TEAR HERE

Sample Answer Sheet

1. Ⓐ Ⓑ Ⓒ Ⓓ Ⓔ   6. Ⓐ Ⓑ Ⓒ Ⓓ Ⓔ   11. Ⓐ Ⓑ Ⓒ Ⓓ Ⓔ
2. Ⓐ Ⓑ Ⓒ Ⓓ Ⓔ   7. Ⓐ Ⓑ Ⓒ Ⓓ Ⓔ   12. Ⓐ Ⓑ Ⓒ Ⓓ Ⓔ
3. Ⓐ Ⓑ Ⓒ Ⓓ Ⓔ   8. Ⓐ Ⓑ Ⓒ Ⓓ Ⓔ   13. Ⓐ Ⓑ Ⓒ Ⓓ Ⓔ
4. Ⓐ Ⓑ Ⓒ Ⓓ Ⓔ   9. Ⓐ Ⓑ Ⓒ Ⓓ Ⓔ   14. Ⓐ Ⓑ Ⓒ Ⓓ Ⓔ
5. Ⓐ Ⓑ Ⓒ Ⓓ Ⓔ   10. Ⓐ Ⓑ Ⓒ Ⓓ Ⓔ   15. Ⓐ Ⓑ Ⓒ Ⓓ Ⓔ

114 / *Clerical Exams Handbook*

Correct Answers to Sample Questions

1. Ⓐ Ⓑ Ⓒ Ⓓ Ⓔ	6. Ⓐ Ⓑ Ⓒ Ⓓ Ⓔ	11. Ⓐ Ⓑ Ⓒ Ⓓ Ⓔ
2. Ⓐ Ⓑ Ⓒ Ⓓ Ⓔ	7. Ⓐ Ⓑ Ⓒ Ⓓ Ⓔ	12. Ⓐ Ⓑ Ⓒ Ⓓ Ⓔ
3. Ⓐ Ⓑ ● Ⓓ Ⓔ	8. Ⓐ Ⓑ Ⓒ Ⓓ ●	13. Ⓐ Ⓑ Ⓒ ● Ⓔ
4. Ⓐ Ⓑ Ⓒ Ⓓ Ⓔ	9. Ⓐ Ⓑ Ⓒ Ⓓ Ⓔ	14. Ⓐ Ⓑ Ⓒ Ⓓ Ⓔ
5. Ⓐ Ⓑ Ⓒ Ⓓ ●	10. Ⓐ Ⓑ Ⓒ Ⓓ Ⓔ	15. ● Ⓑ Ⓒ Ⓓ Ⓔ

1. E   C   *A*   D   R

2. 6   ⟨3⟩   12   14   5   8

3. | 8 *E* | 30 ___ | 5 *E* | 27 ___ | 13 ___ |

4. | 6 ___ | 13 *D* | 12 ___ | 9 ___ |

U.S. Postal Service Clerk, Distribution Clerk & Mark-Up Clerk Exam / 115

Following Oral Instructions

Time: 25 Minutes.

LISTENING TO INSTRUCTIONS

Directions: When you are ready to try this test of the Model Exam, give the following instructions to a friend and have the friend read them aloud to you at the rate of 80 words per minute. Do NOT read them to yourself. Your friend will need a watch with a second hand. Listen carefully and do exactly what your friend tells you to do with the worksheet and with the answer sheet. Your friend will tell you some things to do with each item on the worksheet. After each set of instructions, your friend will give you time to mark your answer by darkening a circle on the answer sheet. Since B and D sound very much alike, your friend will say "B as in baker" when he or she means B and "D as in dog" when he or she means D.

Before proceeding further, tear out the worksheet on page 119 of this test. Then hand this book to your friend.

TO THE PERSON WHO IS TO READ THE INSTRUCTIONS: The instructions are to be read at the rate of 80 words per minute. Do not read aloud the material that is in parentheses. Once you have begun the test itself, do not repeat any instructions. The next three paragraphs consist of approximately 120 words. Read these three paragraphs aloud to the candidate in about one and one-half minutes. You may reread these paragraphs as often as necessary to establish an 80-words-per-minute reading speed.

READ ALOUD TO THE CANDIDATE

On the job you will have to listen to directions and then do what you have been told to do. In this test, I will read instructions to you. Try to understand them as I read them; I cannot repeat them. Once we begin, you may not ask any questions until the end of the test.

On the job you won't have to deal with pictures, numbers, and letters like those in the test, but you will have to listen to instructions and follow them. We are using this test to see how well you can follow instructions.

You are to mark your test booklet according to the instructions that I'll read to you. After each set of instructions, I'll give you time to record your answers on the separate answer sheet.

The actual test begins now.

Look at line 1 on your worksheet. (Pause slightly.) Underline the fifth number on line 1. (Pause 2 seconds.) Now, on your answer sheet, find the number you have underlined and mark D as in dog. (Pause 5 seconds.)

Now look at line 2 on your worksheet. (Pause slightly.) In each box that contains a vowel, write that vowel next to the number in the box. (Pause 5 seconds.) Now, on your answer sheet, blacken the spaces for the number-letter combinations in the box or boxes in which you just wrote. (Pause 10 seconds.)

Look at line 3 on your worksheet. (Pause slightly.) Find the smallest number on line 3 and multiply it by 2. Write the number at the end of line 3. (Pause 5 seconds.) Now, on your answer sheet, darken space C for that number. (Pause 5 seconds.)

Look at line 3 again. (Pause slightly.) Divide the third number by 10 and write that number at the end of the line. (Pause 2 seconds.) Now, on your answer sheet, darken space A for the number you just wrote. (Pause 5 seconds.)

Now look at line 4 on your worksheet. (Pause slightly.) Mail for Detroit and Hartford is to be put in box 3. (Pause slightly.) Mail for Cleveland and St. Louis is to be put in box 26. (Pause slightly.) Write C in the box in which you put mail for St. Louis. (Pause 2 seconds.) Now, on your answer sheet, darken the space for the number-letter combination that is in the box you just wrote in. (Pause 5 seconds.)

Look at line 5 on your worksheet. (Pause slightly.) Write B as in baker on the line next to the highest number. (Pause 2 seconds.) Now, on your answer sheet, blacken the space for the number-letter combination in the circle in which you just wrote. (Pause 5 seconds.)

Look at line 5 again. (Pause slightly.) Write the letter C on the line next to the lowest number. (Pause 2 seconds.) Now, on your answer sheet, blacken the space for the number-letter combination in the circle in which you just wrote. (Pause 5 seconds.)

Look at the boxes and words on line 6 of your worksheet. (Pause 2 seconds.) In Box 1, write the first letter of the third word. (Pause 5 seconds.) In Box 2, write the last letter of the first word. (Pause 5 seconds.) In Box 3, write the last letter of the second word. (Pause 5 seconds.) Now, on your answer sheet, blacken spaces for the number-letter combinations in all three boxes. (Pause 15 seconds.)

Look at line 7 on your worksheet. (Pause slightly.) Write the number 33 next to the letter in the mid-size circle. (Pause 2 seconds.) Now, on your answer sheet, darken the space for the number-letter combination in the circle in which you just wrote. (Pause 5 seconds.)

Look at line 8 on your worksheet. (Pause slightly.) If July comes before June, write D as in dog on the line after the second number; if not, write A on the line after the first number. (Pause 10 seconds.) Now, on your answer sheet, darken the space for the number-letter combination you just wrote. (Pause 5 seconds.)

Look at line 9 on your worksheet. (Pause slightly.) The number on each sack represents the number of pieces of mail in that sack. Next to the letter, write the last two figures of the sack containing the most pieces of mail. (Pause 2 seconds.) On your answer sheet, darken the space for the number-letter combination in the sack you just wrote in. (Pause 5 seconds.)

Look at line 9 again. (Pause slightly.) Now, write next to the letter the first two figures in the sack containing the fewest pieces of mail. (Pause 2 seconds.) On your answer sheet, darken the space for the number-letter combination in the sack you just wrote in. (Pause 5 seconds.)

Look at line 10 on your worksheet. (Pause slightly.) Answer this question: What is the sum of 8 plus 13? (Pause 2 seconds.) If the answer is 25, write 25 in the second box; if not, write the correct answer in the fourth box. (Pause 2 seconds.) Now, on your answer sheet, blacken the number-letter combination in the box you just wrote in. (Pause 5 seconds.)

Look at line 10 again. (Pause slightly.) In the fifth box, write the number of ounces in a pound. (Pause 2 seconds.) Now, on your answer sheet, blacken the number-letter combination in the box you just wrote in. (Pause 5 seconds.)

Look at line 11 on your worksheet. (Pause slightly.) If the number in the circle is greater than the number in the star, write B as in baker in the triangle; if not, write E in the box.

(Pause 5 seconds.) Now, on your answer sheet, darken the number-letter combination in the figure you just wrote in. (Pause 5 seconds.)

Look at line 12 on your worksheet. (Pause slightly.) Draw one line under each P in line 12. (Pause 5 seconds.) Draw two lines under each Q in line 12. (Pause 5 seconds.) Count the number of P's and the number of Q's. (Pause 5 seconds.) If there are more P's than Q's, blacken 71A on your answer sheet; if there are not more P's than Q's, blacken 71C on your answer sheet. (Pause 5 seconds.)

Look at line 13 on your worksheet. (Pause slightly.) Circle each odd number that falls between 65 and 85. (Pause 10 seconds.) Now, on your answer sheet, darken space D as in dog for each number that you circled. (Pause 10 seconds.)

Look at line 13 again. (Pause slightly.) Find the number that is divisible by 6 and underline it. (Pause 2 seconds.) Now, on your answer sheet, darken space A for that number. (Pause 5 seconds.)

Look at line 14 on your worksheet. (Pause slightly.) Each circled time represents a pickup time from a street letter box. Find the pickup time which is furthest from noon and write the last two figures of that time on the line in the circle. (Pause 2 seconds.) Now, on your answer sheet, darken the number-letter combination that is in the circle you just wrote in. (Pause 5 seconds.)

Look at line 14 again. (Pause slightly.) Find the pickup time that is closest to noon and write the last two figures of that time on the line in the circle. (Pause 2 seconds.) Now, on your answer sheet, darken the number-letter combination that is in the circle you just wrote in. (Pause 5 seconds.)

Look at line 15 on your worksheet. (Pause slightly.) Write the highest number in the small box. (Pause 2 seconds.) Write the lowest number in the large box. (Pause 2 seconds.) Now, on your answer sheet, darken the number-letter combinations in the boxes you just wrote in. (Pause 10 seconds.)

Look at line 16 on your worksheet. (Pause slightly.) If, in the alphabet, the fourth letter on line 16 comes before the first letter on line 16, draw a line under the fourth letter (pause 2 seconds); if not, draw a line under the first letter on line 16. (Pause 2 seconds.) Now, on your answer sheet, find number 39 and blacken the space for the letter you underlined. (Pause 5 seconds.)

Look at line 17 on your worksheet. (Pause slightly.) Find the number that does not belong on line 17 and circle that number. (Pause 2 seconds.) Now, on your answer sheet, darken D as in dog for the number you just circled. (Pause 5 seconds.)

Look at line 17 again. (Pause slightly.) Find the number that answers this question: 60 minus 20 equals . . . and draw two lines under that number. (Pause 2 seconds.) Now, on your answer sheet, darken space C for the number under which you just drew two lines. (Pause 5 seconds.)

Look at line 18 on your worksheet. (Pause slightly.) If 3 is less than 7 and 4 is more than 6, write the number 12 in the first box (pause 5 seconds); if not, write the number 48 in the third box. (Pause 5 seconds.) Now, on your answer sheet, darken the space for the number-letter combination in the box you just wrote in. (Pause 5 seconds.)

Look at line 19 on your worksheet. (Pause slightly.) Draw a circle around the number that represents the product of 5 × 6. (Pause 5 seconds.) Now, on your answer sheet, find the number that you just circled and darken space A for that number. (Pause 5 seconds.)

U.S. Postal Service Clerk, Distribution Clerk & Mark-Up Clerk Exam / 119

Following Oral Instructions

WORKSHEET

Directions: Listening carefully to each set of instructions, mark each item on this worksheet as directed. Then complete each question by marking the answer sheet as directed. For each answer you will darken the answer for a number-letter combination. Should you fall behind and miss an instruction, don't become excited. Let that one go and listen for the next one. If, when you start to darken a space for a number, you find that you have already darkened another space for that number, either erase the first mark and darken the space for the new combination or let the first mark stay and do not darken a space for the new combination. Write with a pencil that has a clean eraser. When you finish, you should have no more than one space darkened for each number. Correct answers are on page 125.

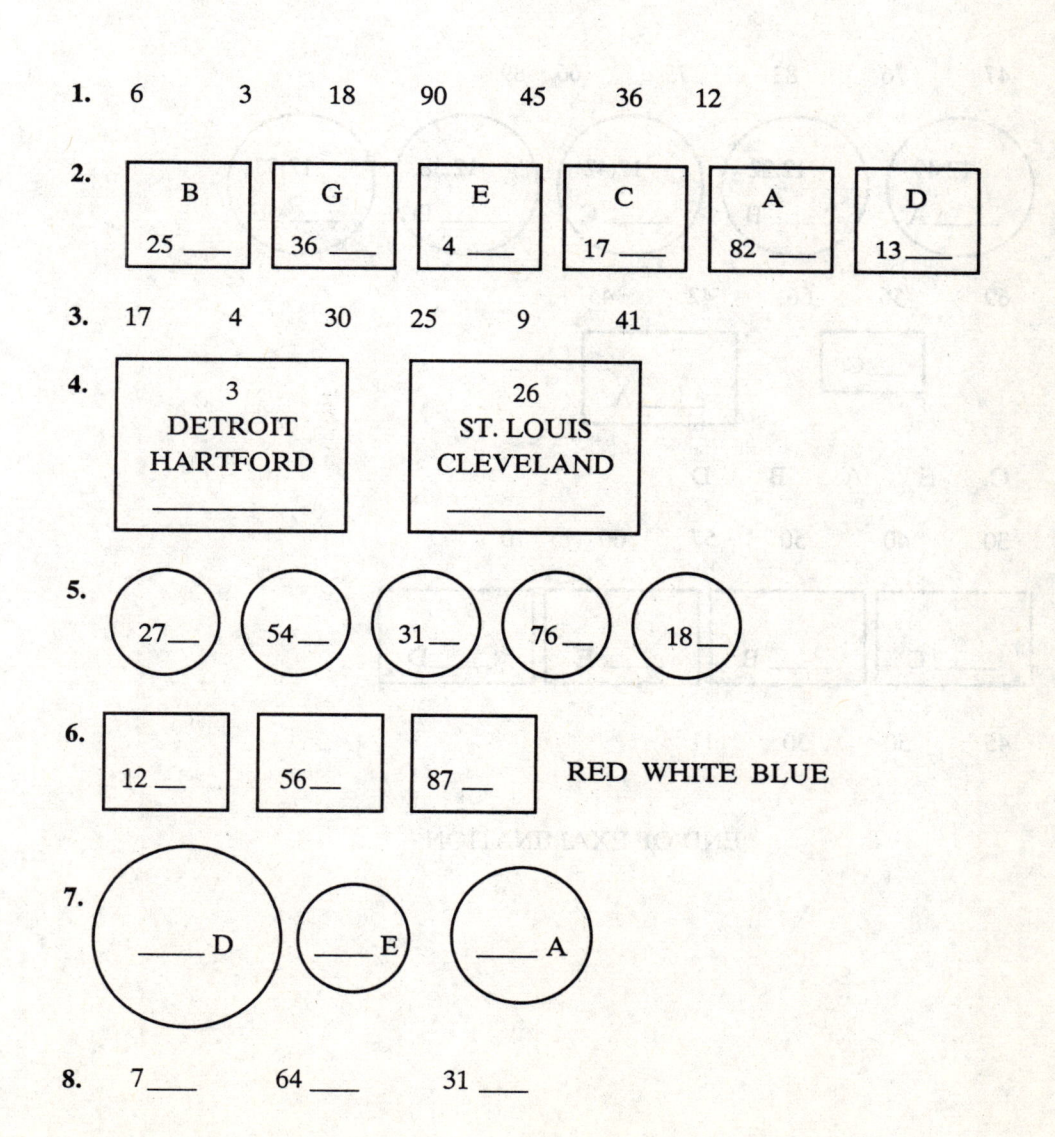

TEAR HERE

1.   6   3   18   90   45   36   12

2. [B 25 ___]   [G 36 ___]   [E 4 ___]   [C 17 ___]   [A 82 ___]   [D 13 ___]

3.   17   4   30   25   9   41

4. [3 DETROIT HARTFORD _____]   [26 ST. LOUIS CLEVELAND _____]

5. (27 __)   (54 __)   (31 __)   (76 __)   (18 __)

6. [12 __]   [56 __]   [87 __]   RED   WHITE   BLUE

7. (__ D)   (__ E)   (__ A)

8.   7 ___   64 ___   31 ___

9. (bag) 432 __D (bag) 863 __C (bag) 729 __A (bag) 366 __B

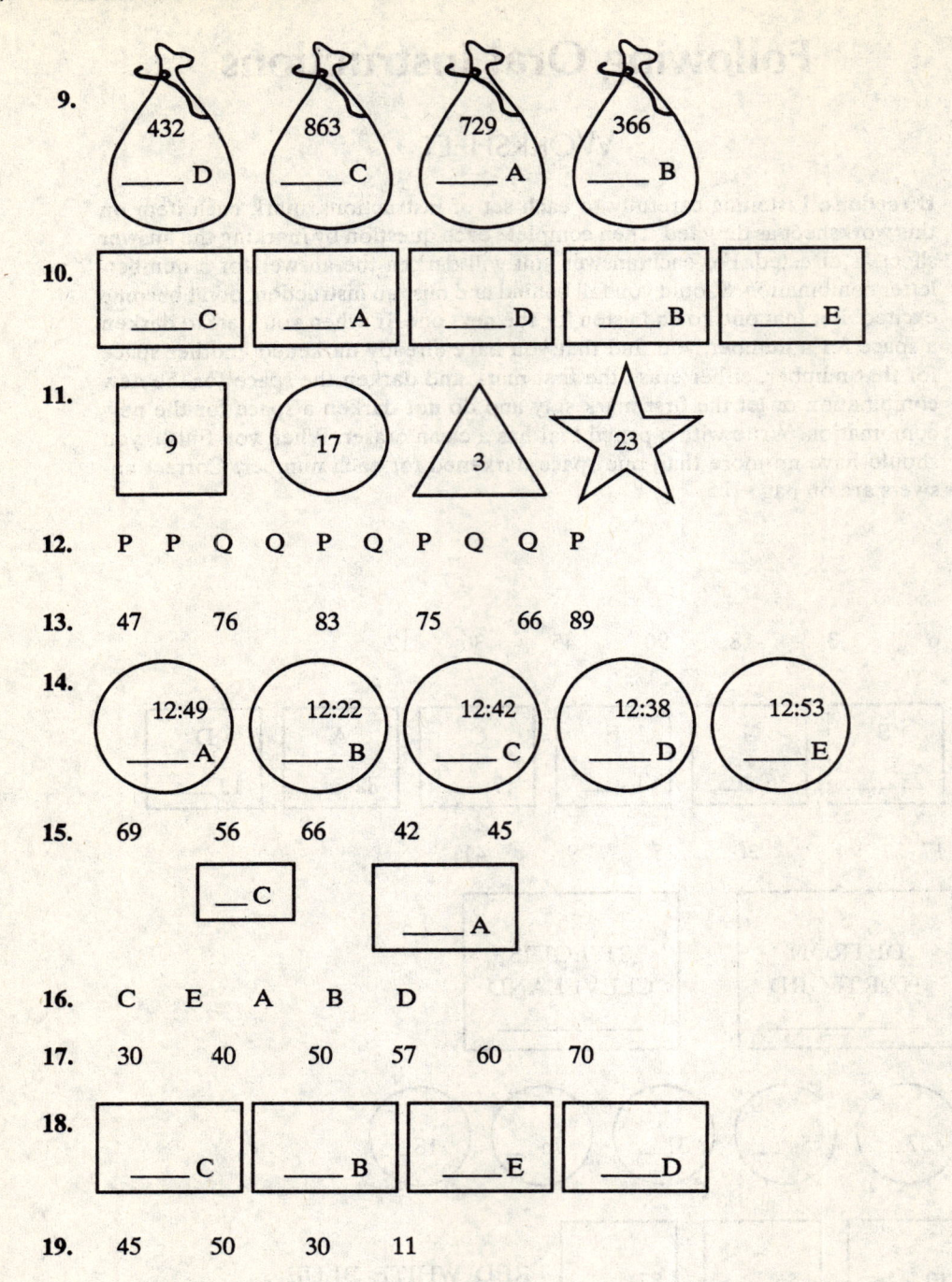

10. [__C] [__A] [__D] [__B] [__E]

11. [square: 9] (circle: 17) (triangle: 3) (star: 23)

12. P P Q Q P Q P Q Q P

13. 47   76   83   75   66   89

14. (12:49 __A) (12:22 __B) (12:42 __C) (12:38 __D) (12:53 __E)

15. 69   56   66   42   45

[__C]   [__A]

16. C E A B D

17. 30   40   50   57   60   70

18. [__C] [__B] [__E] [__D]

19. 45   50   30   11

END OF EXAMINATION

Correct Answers for U.S. Postal Service Clerk, Distribution Clerk (Machine) & Mark-Up Clerk (Automated) Exam

PART A—ADDRESS CHECKING

1. **D**	13. **A**	25. **A**	37. **A**	49. **D**	61. **D**	73. **D**	85. **D**
2. **D**	14. **D**	26. **D**	38. **A**	50. **A**	62. **D**	74. **D**	86. **D**
3. **D**	15. **D**	27. **A**	39. **D**	51. **D**	63. **D**	75. **D**	87. **D**
4. **A**	16. **A**	28. **D**	40. **D**	52. **D**	64. **D**	76. **A**	88. **D**
5. **D**	17. **D**	29. **A**	41. **D**	53. **D**	65. **D**	77. **A**	89. **D**
6. **D**	18. **A**	30. **D**	42. **A**	54. **A**	66. **D**	78. **D**	90. **A**
7. **A**	19. **D**	31. **D**	43. **D**	55. **A**	67. **A**	79. **D**	91. **D**
8. **D**	20. **A**	32. **D**	44. **A**	56. **D**	68. **D**	80. **A**	92. **D**
9. **A**	21. **D**	33. **D**	45. **D**	57. **A**	69. **D**	81. **D**	93. **A**
10. **D**	22. **A**	34. **A**	46. **D**	58. **D**	70. **D**	82. **D**	94. **A**
11. **D**	23. **D**	35. **A**	47. **D**	59. **D**	71. **D**	83. **D**	95. **A**
12. **D**	24. **D**	36. **D**	48. **D**	60. **D**	72. **D**	84. **A**	

ANALYZING YOUR ERRORS

This Address Checking Test contains 30 address pairs that are exactly alike and 65 address pairs that are different. The chart below shows what kind of difference occurs in each of the addresses that contains a difference. Check your answers against this chart to see which kind of difference you missed most often. Note also the questions in which you thought you saw a difference but in which there really was none. Becoming aware of your errors will help you to eliminate those errors on the actual exam.

Type of Difference	Question Numbers	Number of Questions You Missed
Difference in NUMBERS	2, 3, 10, 41, 45, 48, 59, 62, 63, 65, 66, 73, 79	
Difference in ABBREVIATIONS	8, 11, 12, 15, 17, 21, 26, 28, 30, 32, 47, 51, 52, 56, 61, 64, 72, 74, 83, 85, 86	
Difference in NAMES	1, 5, 6, 14, 19, 23, 24, 31, 33, 36, 39, 40, 43, 46, 49, 53, 58, 60, 68, 69, 70, 71, 75, 78, 81, 82, 87, 88, 89, 91, 92	
No Difference	4, 7, 9, 13, 16, 18, 20, 22, 25, 27, 29, 34, 35, 37, 38, 42, 44, 50, 54, 55, 57, 67, 76, 77, 80, 84, 90, 93, 94, 95	

Part B—Memory for Addresses

Practice I

1. B	12. C	23. B	34. E	45. A	56. A	67. D	78. D
2. B	13. A	24. A	35. B	46. C	57. C	68. B	79. E
3. E	14. D	25. C	36. D	47. E	58. B	69. C	80. A
4. C	15. B	26. D	37. C	48. B	59. E	70. A	81. C
5. A	16. A	27. C	38. A	49. B	60. C	71. E	82. E
6. E	17. B	28. B	39. D	50. B	61. C	72. C	83. E
7. E	18. E	29. A	40. E	51. E	62. D	73. E	84. B
8. D	19. D	30. B	41. C	52. E	63. A	74. B	85. C
9. B	20. A	31. E	42. D	53. A	64. D	75. A	86. A
10. C	21. C	32. A	43. C	54. D	65. A	76. B	87. A
11. D	22. E	33. E	44. C	55. C	66. D	77. C	88. E

Practice II

1. C	12. E	23. A	34. C	45. A	56. B	67. B	78. E
2. D	13. D	24. E	35. A	46. D	57. C	68. D	79. A
3. B	14. C	25. B	36. B	47. D	58. A	69. E	80. D
4. A	15. C	26. C	37. B	48. D	59. B	70. B	81. B
5. E	16. A	27. B	38. A	49. E	60. C	71. D	82. D
6. D	17. C	28. D	39. C	50. E	61. A	72. C	83. B
7. B	18. E	29. A	40. C	51. D	62. E	73. C	84. C
8. A	19. A	30. E	41. C	52. C	63. A	74. D	85. E
9. D	20. C	31. E	42. E	53. E	64. E	75. C	86. C
10. D	21. E	32. B	43. A	54. D	65. B	76. A	87. A
11. A	22. B	33. E	44. D	55. A	66. A	77. A	88. A

Practice III

1. C	12. C	23. D	34. E	45. B	56. E	67. A	78. A
2. E	13. D	24. C	35. D	46. B	57. C	68. A	79. E
3. D	14. B	25. C	36. D	47. A	58. B	69. C	80. D
4. B	15. D	26. C	37. E	48. D	59. A	70. C	81. B
5. A	16. B	27. C	38. E	49. D	60. B	71. E	82. E
6. B	17. D	28. A	39. A	50. B	61. C	72. C	83. E
7. A	18. A	29. B	40. A	51. E	62. D	73. C	84. B
8. A	19. D	30. E	41. A	52. D	63. E	74. D	85. E
9. E	20. E	31. A	42. C	53. C	64. E	75. D	86. D
10. E	21. B	32. B	43. B	54. E	65. D	76. B	87. A
11. C	22. E	33. C	44. C	55. C	66. B	77. A	88. B

MEMORY FOR ADDRESSES

1. D	12. B	23. E	34. B	45. E	56. A	67. E	78. B
2. B	13. A	24. C	35. D	46. E	57. C	68. B	79. C
3. B	14. D	25. A	36. B	47. A	58. D	69. A	80. B
4. E	15. A	26. E	37. A	48. C	59. B	70. E	81. A
5. A	16. C	27. A	38. D	49. B	60. E	71. E	82. E
6. B	17. B	28. D	39. C	50. D	61. A	72. A	83. A
7. A	18. C	29. A	40. D	51. C	62. A	73. C	84. E
8. E	19. E	30. E	41. E	52. B	63. D	74. D	85. D
9. C	20. E	31. C	42. B	53. E	64. D	75. B	86. D
10. D	21. E	32. E	43. B	54. C	65. C	76. E	87. B
11. D	22. B	33. A	44. D	55. A	66. C	77. C	88. A

PART C—NUMBER SERIES

1. E	4. C	7. D	10. B	13. C	16. B	19. C	22. B
2. E	5. B	8. C	11. D	14. B	17. D	20. E	23. D
3. D	6. A	9. E	12. A	15. E	18. A	21. D	24. A

EXPLANATIONS

1. **(E)** There are two alternating series, each ascending by +1. One series begins with 3, the other with 8.

2. **(E)** The two alternating series progress at different rates. The first, beginning with 18, moves up one number at a time. The alternating series, beginning with 14, increases by +3.

3. **(D)** There are two alternating series, but this time two numbers of one series interpose between steps of the other series. Thus, one series reads 6 7 8 while the other reads 9 10 11 12 13 14.

4. **(C)** Here we have a series of mini-series. The pattern in each mini-series is −2, −2. Then the pattern repeats with the first number of the next mini-series two numbers higher than the first number of the preceding mini-series.

5. **(B)** The series really is +2, +1, with the number 18 appearing between the two numbers at the +1 phase.

6. **(A)** Two series alternate, both ascending by +2.

7. **(D)** Here the progression is +2, +3; +2, +3; and so on.

8. **(C)** Both alternating series move up by +2.

9. **(E)** The series is essentially 1 2 3 4 5 6 7, but after each two numbers in the series we find the product of the multiplication of those two numbers: 1 × 2 = 2; 3 × 4 = 12; 5 × 6 = 30; 7 . . . .

10. **(B)** The series is simply 1 2 3 4 5 6 7 8 9. After each three numbers of the series, we find the number <u>6</u>.

11. **(D)** There are two series. The ascending series increases by +2. The descending series intervenes after every two members of the ascending series. The descending series moves in steps of −3.

12. **(A)** Weren't you ready for an easy one? There is no catch. The series moves by +2.

13. **(C)** You may feel the rhythm of this series and spot the pattern without playing around with the numbers. If you cannot solve the problem by inspection, then you might see three parallel series. The first series descends by −10 (91 81 71); the second series also descends by minus 10 (85 75 65); the third series descends by −2 (17 15 13). Or, you might see a series of mini-series. Each mini-series begins with a number 10 lower than the first number of the previous mini-series. Within each mini-series the pattern is −6, ÷5.

14. **(B)** The pattern is −4, +9; −4, +9 . . . Or, there are two alternating series. The first series ascends at the rate of +5; the alternating series also ascends at the rate of +5.

15. **(E)** Each number appears three times, then is multiplied by 3.

16. **(B)** There are two alternating series. One starts at <u>13</u> and moves up by +1, and the other starts at <u>23</u> and moves down by −1.

17. **(D)** There are two alternating series. The first series begins with <u>52</u> and descends at the rate of −4. The alternating series begins with <u>10</u> and ascends at the rate of +10.

18. **(A)** The pattern is: −10, −9, −8, −7, −6, −5, −4, −3.

19. **(C)** The pattern is: ÷2, repeat the number, +10; ÷2, repeat the number, +10; ÷2, repeat the number, +10.

20. **(E)** You see a simple series, 83 84 85 86 . . . . After each number in this series you see its mirror image, that is, the mirror image of 83 is 38; the mirror image of 84 is 48; and so forth. Or you might see a series that increases by +1 alternating with a series that increases by +10.

21. **(D)** The pattern is: +2, repeat the number 2 times; +3, repeat the number 3 times; +4, repeat the number 4 times.

22. **(B)** The pattern is −7, −7, −6, −6, −5, −5, −4, −4.

23. **(D)** The series consists of the squares of the whole numbers in descending order.

24. **(A)** You can probably get this one by inspection. If not, notice the series of mini-series. In each mini-series the pattern is 10 times the first number, 11 times the first number.

PART D—FOLLOWING ORAL INSTRUCTIONS

Correctly Filled Answer Grid

1. Ⓐ Ⓑ Ⓒ Ⓓ Ⓔ	23. Ⓐ Ⓑ Ⓒ Ⓓ Ⓔ	45. Ⓐ Ⓑ Ⓒ ● Ⓔ	67. Ⓐ Ⓑ Ⓒ Ⓓ Ⓔ
2. Ⓐ Ⓑ Ⓒ Ⓓ Ⓔ	24. Ⓐ Ⓑ Ⓒ Ⓓ Ⓔ	46. Ⓐ Ⓑ Ⓒ Ⓓ Ⓔ	68. Ⓐ Ⓑ Ⓒ Ⓓ Ⓔ
3. ● Ⓑ Ⓒ Ⓓ Ⓔ	25. Ⓐ Ⓑ Ⓒ Ⓓ Ⓔ	47. Ⓐ Ⓑ Ⓒ Ⓓ Ⓔ	69. Ⓐ Ⓑ ● Ⓓ Ⓔ
4. Ⓐ Ⓑ Ⓒ Ⓓ ●	26. Ⓐ Ⓑ ● Ⓓ Ⓔ	48. Ⓐ Ⓑ Ⓒ Ⓓ ●	70. Ⓐ Ⓑ Ⓒ Ⓓ Ⓔ
5. Ⓐ Ⓑ Ⓒ Ⓓ Ⓔ	27. Ⓐ Ⓑ Ⓒ Ⓓ Ⓔ	49. Ⓐ Ⓑ Ⓒ Ⓓ Ⓔ	71. Ⓐ Ⓑ ● Ⓓ Ⓔ
6. Ⓐ Ⓑ Ⓒ Ⓓ Ⓔ	28. Ⓐ Ⓑ Ⓒ Ⓓ Ⓔ	50. Ⓐ Ⓑ Ⓒ Ⓓ Ⓔ	72. Ⓐ Ⓑ Ⓒ Ⓓ Ⓔ
7. ● Ⓑ Ⓒ Ⓓ Ⓔ	29. Ⓐ Ⓑ Ⓒ Ⓓ Ⓔ	51. Ⓐ Ⓑ Ⓒ Ⓓ Ⓔ	73. Ⓐ Ⓑ Ⓒ Ⓓ Ⓔ
8. Ⓐ Ⓑ ● Ⓓ Ⓔ	30. ● Ⓑ Ⓒ Ⓓ Ⓔ	52. Ⓐ Ⓑ Ⓒ Ⓓ Ⓔ	74. Ⓐ Ⓑ Ⓒ Ⓓ Ⓔ
9. Ⓐ Ⓑ Ⓒ Ⓓ ●	31. Ⓐ Ⓑ Ⓒ Ⓓ Ⓔ	53. Ⓐ Ⓑ Ⓒ Ⓓ ●	75. Ⓐ Ⓑ Ⓒ ● Ⓔ
10. Ⓐ Ⓑ Ⓒ Ⓓ Ⓔ	32. Ⓐ Ⓑ Ⓒ Ⓓ Ⓔ	54. Ⓐ Ⓑ Ⓒ Ⓓ Ⓔ	76. Ⓐ ● Ⓒ Ⓓ Ⓔ
11. Ⓐ Ⓑ Ⓒ Ⓓ Ⓔ	33. Ⓐ ● Ⓒ Ⓓ Ⓔ	55. Ⓐ Ⓑ Ⓒ Ⓓ Ⓔ	77. Ⓐ Ⓑ Ⓒ Ⓓ Ⓔ
12. Ⓐ ● Ⓒ Ⓓ Ⓔ	34. Ⓐ Ⓑ Ⓒ Ⓓ Ⓔ	56. Ⓐ Ⓑ Ⓒ ● Ⓔ	78. Ⓐ Ⓑ Ⓒ Ⓓ Ⓔ
13. Ⓐ Ⓑ Ⓒ Ⓓ Ⓔ	35. Ⓐ Ⓑ Ⓒ Ⓓ Ⓔ	57. Ⓐ Ⓑ Ⓒ ● Ⓔ	79. Ⓐ Ⓑ Ⓒ Ⓓ Ⓔ
14. Ⓐ Ⓑ Ⓒ Ⓓ Ⓔ	36. Ⓐ ● Ⓒ Ⓓ Ⓔ	58. Ⓐ Ⓑ Ⓒ Ⓓ Ⓔ	80. Ⓐ Ⓑ Ⓒ Ⓓ Ⓔ
15. Ⓐ Ⓑ Ⓒ Ⓓ Ⓔ	37. Ⓐ Ⓑ Ⓒ Ⓓ Ⓔ	59. Ⓐ Ⓑ Ⓒ Ⓓ Ⓔ	81. Ⓐ Ⓑ Ⓒ Ⓓ Ⓔ
16. Ⓐ Ⓑ Ⓒ Ⓓ ●	38. Ⓐ Ⓑ Ⓒ Ⓓ Ⓔ	60. Ⓐ Ⓑ Ⓒ Ⓓ Ⓔ	82. ● Ⓑ Ⓒ Ⓓ Ⓔ
17. Ⓐ Ⓑ Ⓒ Ⓓ Ⓔ	39. Ⓐ ● Ⓒ Ⓓ Ⓔ	61. Ⓐ Ⓑ Ⓒ Ⓓ Ⓔ	83. Ⓐ Ⓑ Ⓒ ● Ⓔ
18. Ⓐ Ⓑ ● Ⓓ Ⓔ	40. Ⓐ Ⓑ ● Ⓓ Ⓔ	62. Ⓐ Ⓑ Ⓒ Ⓓ Ⓔ	84. Ⓐ Ⓑ Ⓒ Ⓓ Ⓔ
19. Ⓐ Ⓑ Ⓒ Ⓓ Ⓔ	41. Ⓐ Ⓑ Ⓒ Ⓓ Ⓔ	63. Ⓐ Ⓑ ● Ⓓ Ⓔ	85. Ⓐ Ⓑ Ⓒ Ⓓ Ⓔ
20. Ⓐ Ⓑ Ⓒ Ⓓ Ⓔ	42. ● Ⓑ Ⓒ Ⓓ Ⓔ	64. Ⓐ Ⓑ Ⓒ Ⓓ Ⓔ	86. Ⓐ Ⓑ Ⓒ Ⓓ Ⓔ
21. Ⓐ ● Ⓒ Ⓓ Ⓔ	43. Ⓐ Ⓑ Ⓒ Ⓓ Ⓔ	65. Ⓐ Ⓑ Ⓒ Ⓓ Ⓔ	87. Ⓐ Ⓑ Ⓒ Ⓓ ●
22. Ⓐ ● Ⓒ Ⓓ Ⓔ	44. Ⓐ Ⓑ Ⓒ Ⓓ Ⓔ	66. ● Ⓑ Ⓒ Ⓓ Ⓔ	88. Ⓐ Ⓑ Ⓒ Ⓓ Ⓔ

Correctly Filled Worksheet

1. 6   3   18   90   <u>45</u>   36   12

2.
B	G	E	C	A	D
25 ___	36 ___	4 <u>E</u>	17 ___	82 <u>A</u>	13 ___

3. 17   4   30   25   9   41   **8**

4.
3 DETROIT HARTFORD _____	26 ST. LOUIS CLEVELAND <u>C</u>

5. (27 ___) (54 ___) (31 ___) (76 <u>B</u>) (18 <u>C</u>)

6. | 12 <u>B</u> | 56 <u>D</u> | 87 <u>E</u> | RED   WHITE   BLUE

7. (___ D) (___ E) (<u>33</u> A)

8. 7 <u>A</u>   64 ___   31 ___

9. (bag 432 ___ D) (bag 863 <u>63</u> C) (bag 729 ___ A) (bag 366 <u>36</u> B)

10. | ___ C | ___ A | ___ D | <u>21</u> B | <u>16</u> E |

11. [square: E/9]   [circle: 17]   [triangle: 3]   [star: 23]

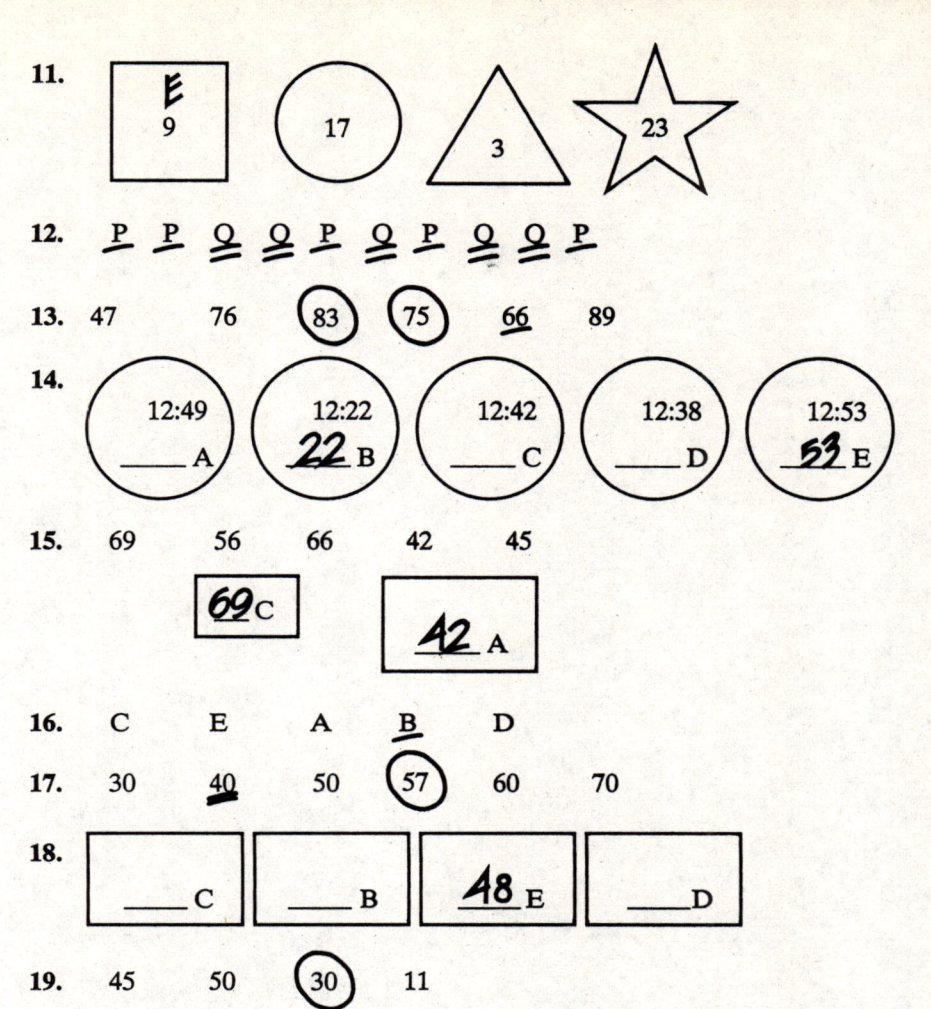

12. P̲ P̲ Q̳ Q̳ P̲ Q̳ P̲ Q̳ Q̳ P̲

13. 47   76   ⓛ83   ⓛ75   66̲   89

14. (12:49 ___A) (12:22 **22** B) (12:42 ___C) (12:38 ___D) (12:53 **53** E)

15. 69   56   66   42   45

     [square: **69** C]   [rectangle: **42** A]

16. C   E   A   B̲   D
17. 30   **40̲**   50   ⓛ57   60   70

18. [___C]   [___B]   [**48** E]   [___D]

19. 45   50   ⓛ30   11

Answer Sheet for U.S. Postal Service Clerk-Typist and Clerk-Stenographer Exams

Exam 710 (Parts A & B)

Clerk-Typist
Clerk-Stenographer

Exam 711 (Part C)

Clerk-Stenographer only

Part A

1. Ⓐ Ⓑ Ⓒ Ⓓ Ⓔ
2. Ⓐ Ⓑ Ⓒ Ⓓ Ⓔ
3. Ⓐ Ⓑ Ⓒ Ⓓ Ⓔ
4. Ⓐ Ⓑ Ⓒ Ⓓ Ⓔ
5. Ⓐ Ⓑ Ⓒ Ⓓ Ⓔ
6. Ⓐ Ⓑ Ⓒ Ⓓ Ⓔ
7. Ⓐ Ⓑ Ⓒ Ⓓ Ⓔ
8. Ⓐ Ⓑ Ⓒ Ⓓ Ⓔ
9. Ⓐ Ⓑ Ⓒ Ⓓ Ⓔ
10. Ⓐ Ⓑ Ⓒ Ⓓ Ⓔ
11. Ⓐ Ⓑ Ⓒ Ⓓ Ⓔ
12. Ⓐ Ⓑ Ⓒ Ⓓ Ⓔ
13. Ⓐ Ⓑ Ⓒ Ⓓ Ⓔ
14. Ⓐ Ⓑ Ⓒ Ⓓ Ⓔ
15. Ⓐ Ⓑ Ⓒ Ⓓ Ⓔ
16. Ⓐ Ⓑ Ⓒ Ⓓ Ⓔ
17. Ⓐ Ⓑ Ⓒ Ⓓ Ⓔ
18. Ⓐ Ⓑ Ⓒ Ⓓ Ⓔ
19. Ⓐ Ⓑ Ⓒ Ⓓ Ⓔ
20. Ⓐ Ⓑ Ⓒ Ⓓ Ⓔ
21. Ⓐ Ⓑ Ⓒ Ⓓ Ⓔ
22. Ⓐ Ⓑ Ⓒ Ⓓ Ⓔ
23. Ⓐ Ⓑ Ⓒ Ⓓ Ⓔ
24. Ⓐ Ⓑ Ⓒ Ⓓ Ⓔ
25. Ⓐ Ⓑ Ⓒ Ⓓ Ⓔ
26. Ⓐ Ⓑ Ⓒ Ⓓ Ⓔ
27. Ⓐ Ⓑ Ⓒ Ⓓ Ⓔ
28. Ⓐ Ⓑ Ⓒ Ⓓ Ⓔ
29. Ⓐ Ⓑ Ⓒ Ⓓ Ⓔ
30. Ⓐ Ⓑ Ⓒ Ⓓ Ⓔ
31. Ⓐ Ⓑ Ⓒ Ⓓ Ⓔ
32. Ⓐ Ⓑ Ⓒ Ⓓ Ⓔ
33. Ⓐ Ⓑ Ⓒ Ⓓ Ⓔ
34. Ⓐ Ⓑ Ⓒ Ⓓ Ⓔ
35. Ⓐ Ⓑ Ⓒ Ⓓ Ⓔ
36. Ⓐ Ⓑ Ⓒ Ⓓ Ⓔ
37. Ⓐ Ⓑ Ⓒ Ⓓ Ⓔ
38. Ⓐ Ⓑ Ⓒ Ⓓ Ⓔ
39. Ⓐ Ⓑ Ⓒ Ⓓ Ⓔ
40. Ⓐ Ⓑ Ⓒ Ⓓ Ⓔ
41. Ⓐ Ⓑ Ⓒ Ⓓ Ⓔ
42. Ⓐ Ⓑ Ⓒ Ⓓ Ⓔ
43. Ⓐ Ⓑ Ⓒ Ⓓ Ⓔ
44. Ⓐ Ⓑ Ⓒ Ⓓ Ⓔ
45. Ⓐ Ⓑ Ⓒ Ⓓ Ⓔ
46. Ⓐ Ⓑ Ⓒ Ⓓ Ⓔ
47. Ⓐ Ⓑ Ⓒ Ⓓ Ⓔ
48. Ⓐ Ⓑ Ⓒ Ⓓ Ⓔ
49. Ⓐ Ⓑ Ⓒ Ⓓ Ⓔ
50. Ⓐ Ⓑ Ⓒ Ⓓ Ⓔ
51. Ⓐ Ⓑ Ⓒ Ⓓ Ⓔ
52. Ⓐ Ⓑ Ⓒ Ⓓ Ⓔ
53. Ⓐ Ⓑ Ⓒ Ⓓ Ⓔ
54. Ⓐ Ⓑ Ⓒ Ⓓ Ⓔ
55. Ⓐ Ⓑ Ⓒ Ⓓ Ⓔ
56. Ⓐ Ⓑ Ⓒ Ⓓ Ⓔ
57. Ⓐ Ⓑ Ⓒ Ⓓ Ⓔ
58. Ⓐ Ⓑ Ⓒ Ⓓ Ⓔ
59. Ⓐ Ⓑ Ⓒ Ⓓ Ⓔ
60. Ⓐ Ⓑ Ⓒ Ⓓ Ⓔ
61. Ⓐ Ⓑ Ⓒ Ⓓ Ⓔ
62. Ⓐ Ⓑ Ⓒ Ⓓ Ⓔ
63. Ⓐ Ⓑ Ⓒ Ⓓ Ⓔ
64. Ⓐ Ⓑ Ⓒ Ⓓ Ⓔ
65. Ⓐ Ⓑ Ⓒ Ⓓ Ⓔ
66. Ⓐ Ⓑ Ⓒ Ⓓ Ⓔ
67. Ⓐ Ⓑ Ⓒ Ⓓ Ⓔ
68. Ⓐ Ⓑ Ⓒ Ⓓ Ⓔ
69. Ⓐ Ⓑ Ⓒ Ⓓ Ⓔ
70. Ⓐ Ⓑ Ⓒ Ⓓ Ⓔ
71. Ⓐ Ⓑ Ⓒ Ⓓ Ⓔ
72. Ⓐ Ⓑ Ⓒ Ⓓ Ⓔ
73. Ⓐ Ⓑ Ⓒ Ⓓ Ⓔ
74. Ⓐ Ⓑ Ⓒ Ⓓ Ⓔ
75. Ⓐ Ⓑ Ⓒ Ⓓ Ⓔ
76. Ⓐ Ⓑ Ⓒ Ⓓ Ⓔ
77. Ⓐ Ⓑ Ⓒ Ⓓ Ⓔ
78. Ⓐ Ⓑ Ⓒ Ⓓ Ⓔ
79. Ⓐ Ⓑ Ⓒ Ⓓ Ⓔ
80. Ⓐ Ⓑ Ⓒ Ⓓ Ⓔ
81. Ⓐ Ⓑ Ⓒ Ⓓ Ⓔ
82. Ⓐ Ⓑ Ⓒ Ⓓ Ⓔ
83. Ⓐ Ⓑ Ⓒ Ⓓ Ⓔ
84. Ⓐ Ⓑ Ⓒ Ⓓ Ⓔ
85. Ⓐ Ⓑ Ⓒ Ⓓ Ⓔ

TEAR HERE

PART B

1. Ⓐ Ⓑ Ⓒ Ⓓ Ⓔ
2. Ⓐ Ⓑ Ⓒ Ⓓ Ⓔ
3. Ⓐ Ⓑ Ⓒ Ⓓ Ⓔ
4. Ⓐ Ⓑ Ⓒ Ⓓ Ⓔ
5. Ⓐ Ⓑ Ⓒ Ⓓ Ⓔ
6. Ⓐ Ⓑ Ⓒ Ⓓ Ⓔ
7. Ⓐ Ⓑ Ⓒ Ⓓ Ⓔ
8. Ⓐ Ⓑ Ⓒ Ⓓ Ⓔ
9. Ⓐ Ⓑ Ⓒ Ⓓ Ⓔ
10. Ⓐ Ⓑ Ⓒ Ⓓ Ⓔ
11. Ⓐ Ⓑ Ⓒ Ⓓ Ⓔ
12. Ⓐ Ⓑ Ⓒ Ⓓ Ⓔ
13. Ⓐ Ⓑ Ⓒ Ⓓ Ⓔ
14. Ⓐ Ⓑ Ⓒ Ⓓ Ⓔ
15. Ⓐ Ⓑ Ⓒ Ⓓ Ⓔ
16. Ⓐ Ⓑ Ⓒ Ⓓ Ⓔ
17. Ⓐ Ⓑ Ⓒ Ⓓ Ⓔ
18. Ⓐ Ⓑ Ⓒ Ⓓ Ⓔ
19. Ⓐ Ⓑ Ⓒ Ⓓ Ⓔ
20. Ⓐ Ⓑ Ⓒ Ⓓ Ⓔ
21. Ⓐ Ⓑ Ⓒ Ⓓ Ⓔ
22. Ⓐ Ⓑ Ⓒ Ⓓ Ⓔ
23. Ⓐ Ⓑ Ⓒ Ⓓ Ⓔ
24. Ⓐ Ⓑ Ⓒ Ⓓ Ⓔ
25. Ⓐ Ⓑ Ⓒ Ⓓ Ⓔ
26. Ⓐ Ⓑ Ⓒ Ⓓ Ⓔ
27. Ⓐ Ⓑ Ⓒ Ⓓ Ⓔ
28. Ⓐ Ⓑ Ⓒ Ⓓ Ⓔ
29. Ⓐ Ⓑ Ⓒ Ⓓ Ⓔ
30. Ⓐ Ⓑ Ⓒ Ⓓ Ⓔ
31. Ⓐ Ⓑ Ⓒ Ⓓ Ⓔ
32. Ⓐ Ⓑ Ⓒ Ⓓ Ⓔ
33. Ⓐ Ⓑ Ⓒ Ⓓ Ⓔ
34. Ⓐ Ⓑ Ⓒ Ⓓ Ⓔ
35. Ⓐ Ⓑ Ⓒ Ⓓ Ⓔ
36. Ⓐ Ⓑ Ⓒ Ⓓ Ⓔ
37. Ⓐ Ⓑ Ⓒ Ⓓ Ⓔ
38. Ⓐ Ⓑ Ⓒ Ⓓ Ⓔ
39. Ⓐ Ⓑ Ⓒ Ⓓ Ⓔ
40. Ⓐ Ⓑ Ⓒ Ⓓ Ⓔ
41. Ⓐ Ⓑ Ⓒ Ⓓ Ⓔ
42. Ⓐ Ⓑ Ⓒ Ⓓ Ⓔ
43. Ⓐ Ⓑ Ⓒ Ⓓ Ⓔ
44. Ⓐ Ⓑ Ⓒ Ⓓ Ⓔ
45. Ⓐ Ⓑ Ⓒ Ⓓ Ⓔ
46. Ⓐ Ⓑ Ⓒ Ⓓ Ⓔ
47. Ⓐ Ⓑ Ⓒ Ⓓ Ⓔ
48. Ⓐ Ⓑ Ⓒ Ⓓ Ⓔ
49. Ⓐ Ⓑ Ⓒ Ⓓ Ⓔ
50. Ⓐ Ⓑ Ⓒ Ⓓ Ⓔ
51. Ⓐ Ⓑ Ⓒ Ⓓ Ⓔ
52. Ⓐ Ⓑ Ⓒ Ⓓ Ⓔ
53. Ⓐ Ⓑ Ⓒ Ⓓ Ⓔ
54. Ⓐ Ⓑ Ⓒ Ⓓ Ⓔ
55. Ⓐ Ⓑ Ⓒ Ⓓ Ⓔ
56. Ⓐ Ⓑ Ⓒ Ⓓ Ⓔ
57. Ⓐ Ⓑ Ⓒ Ⓓ Ⓔ
58. Ⓐ Ⓑ Ⓒ Ⓓ Ⓔ
59. Ⓐ Ⓑ Ⓒ Ⓓ Ⓔ
60. Ⓐ Ⓑ Ⓒ Ⓓ Ⓔ
61. Ⓐ Ⓑ Ⓒ Ⓓ Ⓔ
62. Ⓐ Ⓑ Ⓒ Ⓓ Ⓔ
63. Ⓐ Ⓑ Ⓒ Ⓓ Ⓔ
64. Ⓐ Ⓑ Ⓒ Ⓓ Ⓔ
65. Ⓐ Ⓑ Ⓒ Ⓓ Ⓔ
66. Ⓐ Ⓑ Ⓒ Ⓓ Ⓔ
67. Ⓐ Ⓑ Ⓒ Ⓓ Ⓔ
68. Ⓐ Ⓑ Ⓒ Ⓓ Ⓔ
69. Ⓐ Ⓑ Ⓒ Ⓓ Ⓔ
70. Ⓐ Ⓑ Ⓒ Ⓓ Ⓔ
71. Ⓐ Ⓑ Ⓒ Ⓓ Ⓔ
72. Ⓐ Ⓑ Ⓒ Ⓓ Ⓔ
73. Ⓐ Ⓑ Ⓒ Ⓓ Ⓔ
74. Ⓐ Ⓑ Ⓒ Ⓓ Ⓔ
75. Ⓐ Ⓑ Ⓒ Ⓓ Ⓔ
76. Ⓐ Ⓑ Ⓒ Ⓓ Ⓔ
77. Ⓐ Ⓑ Ⓒ Ⓓ Ⓔ
78. Ⓐ Ⓑ Ⓒ Ⓓ Ⓔ
79. Ⓐ Ⓑ Ⓒ Ⓓ Ⓔ
80. Ⓐ Ⓑ Ⓒ Ⓓ Ⓔ
81. Ⓐ Ⓑ Ⓒ Ⓓ Ⓔ
82. Ⓐ Ⓑ Ⓒ Ⓓ Ⓔ
83. Ⓐ Ⓑ Ⓒ Ⓓ Ⓔ
84. Ⓐ Ⓑ Ⓒ Ⓓ Ⓔ
85. Ⓐ Ⓑ Ⓒ Ⓓ Ⓔ
86. Ⓐ Ⓑ Ⓒ Ⓓ Ⓔ
87. Ⓐ Ⓑ Ⓒ Ⓓ Ⓔ
88. Ⓐ Ⓑ Ⓒ Ⓓ Ⓔ
89. Ⓐ Ⓑ Ⓒ Ⓓ Ⓔ
90. Ⓐ Ⓑ Ⓒ Ⓓ Ⓔ
91. Ⓐ Ⓑ Ⓒ Ⓓ Ⓔ
92. Ⓐ Ⓑ Ⓒ Ⓓ Ⓔ
93. Ⓐ Ⓑ Ⓒ Ⓓ Ⓔ
94. Ⓐ Ⓑ Ⓒ Ⓓ Ⓔ
95. Ⓐ Ⓑ Ⓒ Ⓓ Ⓔ
96. Ⓐ Ⓑ Ⓒ Ⓓ Ⓔ
97. Ⓐ Ⓑ Ⓒ Ⓓ Ⓔ
98. Ⓐ Ⓑ Ⓒ Ⓓ Ⓔ
99. Ⓐ Ⓑ Ⓒ Ⓓ Ⓔ
100. Ⓐ Ⓑ Ⓒ Ⓓ Ⓔ
101. Ⓐ Ⓑ Ⓒ Ⓓ Ⓔ
102. Ⓐ Ⓑ Ⓒ Ⓓ Ⓔ
103. Ⓐ Ⓑ Ⓒ Ⓓ Ⓔ
104. Ⓐ Ⓑ Ⓒ Ⓓ Ⓔ
105. Ⓐ Ⓑ Ⓒ Ⓓ Ⓔ
106. Ⓐ Ⓑ Ⓒ Ⓓ Ⓔ
107. Ⓐ Ⓑ Ⓒ Ⓓ Ⓔ
108. Ⓐ Ⓑ Ⓒ Ⓓ Ⓔ
109. Ⓐ Ⓑ Ⓒ Ⓓ Ⓔ
110. Ⓐ Ⓑ Ⓒ Ⓓ Ⓔ
111. Ⓐ Ⓑ Ⓒ Ⓓ Ⓔ
112. Ⓐ Ⓑ Ⓒ Ⓓ Ⓔ
113. Ⓐ Ⓑ Ⓒ Ⓓ Ⓔ
114. Ⓐ Ⓑ Ⓒ Ⓓ Ⓔ
115. Ⓐ Ⓑ Ⓒ Ⓓ Ⓔ
116. Ⓐ Ⓑ Ⓒ Ⓓ Ⓔ
117. Ⓐ Ⓑ Ⓒ Ⓓ Ⓔ
118. Ⓐ Ⓑ Ⓒ Ⓓ Ⓔ
119. Ⓐ Ⓑ Ⓒ Ⓓ Ⓔ
120. Ⓐ Ⓑ Ⓒ Ⓓ Ⓔ
121. Ⓐ Ⓑ Ⓒ Ⓓ Ⓔ
122. Ⓐ Ⓑ Ⓒ Ⓓ Ⓔ
123. Ⓐ Ⓑ Ⓒ Ⓓ Ⓔ
124. Ⓐ Ⓑ Ⓒ Ⓓ Ⓔ
125. Ⓐ Ⓑ Ⓒ Ⓓ Ⓔ

PART C

1. Ⓐ Ⓑ Ⓒ Ⓓ Ⓔ
2. Ⓐ Ⓑ Ⓒ Ⓓ Ⓔ
3. Ⓐ Ⓑ Ⓒ Ⓓ Ⓔ
4. Ⓐ Ⓑ Ⓒ Ⓓ Ⓔ
5. Ⓐ Ⓑ Ⓒ Ⓓ Ⓔ
6. Ⓐ Ⓑ Ⓒ Ⓓ Ⓔ
7. Ⓐ Ⓑ Ⓒ Ⓓ Ⓔ
8. Ⓐ Ⓑ Ⓒ Ⓓ Ⓔ
9. Ⓐ Ⓑ Ⓒ Ⓓ Ⓔ
10. Ⓐ Ⓑ Ⓒ Ⓓ Ⓔ
11. Ⓐ Ⓑ Ⓒ Ⓓ Ⓔ
12. Ⓐ Ⓑ Ⓒ Ⓓ Ⓔ
13. Ⓐ Ⓑ Ⓒ Ⓓ Ⓔ
14. Ⓐ Ⓑ Ⓒ Ⓓ Ⓔ
15. Ⓐ Ⓑ Ⓒ Ⓓ Ⓔ
16. Ⓐ Ⓑ Ⓒ Ⓓ Ⓔ
17. Ⓐ Ⓑ Ⓒ Ⓓ Ⓔ
18. Ⓐ Ⓑ Ⓒ Ⓓ Ⓔ
19. Ⓐ Ⓑ Ⓒ Ⓓ Ⓔ
20. Ⓐ Ⓑ Ⓒ Ⓓ Ⓔ
21. Ⓐ Ⓑ Ⓒ Ⓓ Ⓔ
22. Ⓐ Ⓑ Ⓒ Ⓓ Ⓔ
23. Ⓐ Ⓑ Ⓒ Ⓓ Ⓔ
24. Ⓐ Ⓑ Ⓒ Ⓓ Ⓔ
25. Ⓐ Ⓑ Ⓒ Ⓓ Ⓔ
26. Ⓐ Ⓑ Ⓒ Ⓓ Ⓔ
27. Ⓐ Ⓑ Ⓒ Ⓓ Ⓔ
28. Ⓐ Ⓑ Ⓒ Ⓓ Ⓔ
29. Ⓐ Ⓑ Ⓒ Ⓓ Ⓔ
30. Ⓐ Ⓑ Ⓒ Ⓓ Ⓔ
31. Ⓐ Ⓑ Ⓒ Ⓓ Ⓔ
32. Ⓐ Ⓑ Ⓒ Ⓓ Ⓔ
33. Ⓐ Ⓑ Ⓒ Ⓓ Ⓔ
34. Ⓐ Ⓑ Ⓒ Ⓓ Ⓔ
35. Ⓐ Ⓑ Ⓒ Ⓓ Ⓔ
36. Ⓐ Ⓑ Ⓒ Ⓓ Ⓔ
37. Ⓐ Ⓑ Ⓒ Ⓓ Ⓔ
38. Ⓐ Ⓑ Ⓒ Ⓓ Ⓔ
39. Ⓐ Ⓑ Ⓒ Ⓓ Ⓔ
40. Ⓐ Ⓑ Ⓒ Ⓓ Ⓔ
41. Ⓐ Ⓑ Ⓒ Ⓓ Ⓔ
42. Ⓐ Ⓑ Ⓒ Ⓓ Ⓔ
43. Ⓐ Ⓑ Ⓒ Ⓓ Ⓔ
44. Ⓐ Ⓑ Ⓒ Ⓓ Ⓔ
45. Ⓐ Ⓑ Ⓒ Ⓓ Ⓔ
46. Ⓐ Ⓑ Ⓒ Ⓓ Ⓔ
47. Ⓐ Ⓑ Ⓒ Ⓓ Ⓔ
48. Ⓐ Ⓑ Ⓒ Ⓓ Ⓔ
49. Ⓐ Ⓑ Ⓒ Ⓓ Ⓔ
50. Ⓐ Ⓑ Ⓒ Ⓓ Ⓔ
51. Ⓐ Ⓑ Ⓒ Ⓓ Ⓔ
52. Ⓐ Ⓑ Ⓒ Ⓓ Ⓔ
53. Ⓐ Ⓑ Ⓒ Ⓓ Ⓔ
54. Ⓐ Ⓑ Ⓒ Ⓓ Ⓔ
55. Ⓐ Ⓑ Ⓒ Ⓓ Ⓔ

U.S. POSTAL SERVICE CLERK-TYPIST AND CLERK-STENOGRAPHER EXAM

Part A—Clerical Ability

SAMPLE QUESTIONS

There are four kinds of questions in Part A. Each kind of question has its own set of directions, and each portion of the part is timed separately. The four kinds of questions are:

Sequencing	3 minutes,	20 questions
Comparisons	5 minutes,	30 questions
Spelling	3 minutes,	20 questions
Computations	8 minutes,	15 questions

Directions for sequencing questions: For each question there is a name, number, or code in a box at the left and four other names or codes in alphabetical or numerical order at the right. Find the correct space for the boxed name or number so that it will be in alphabetical and/or numerical order with the others and mark the letter of that space on your answer sheet.

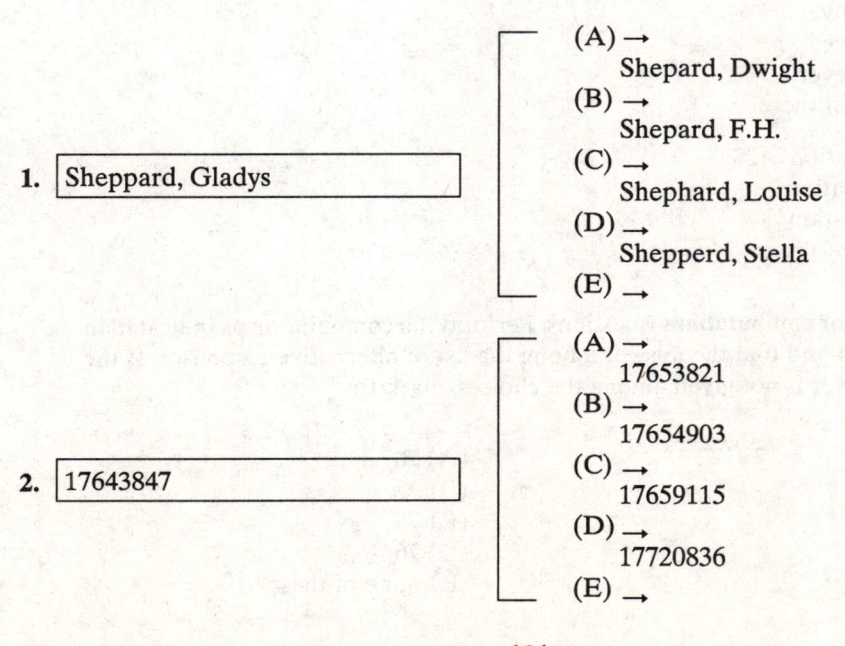

1. Sheppard, Gladys

   (A) →
   Shepard, Dwight
   (B) →
   Shepard, F.H.
   (C) →
   Shephard, Louise
   (D) →
   Shepperd, Stella
   (E) →

2. 17643847

   (A) →
   17653821
   (B) →
   17654903
   (C) →
   17659115
   (D) →
   17720836
   (E) →

3. GGG-2483

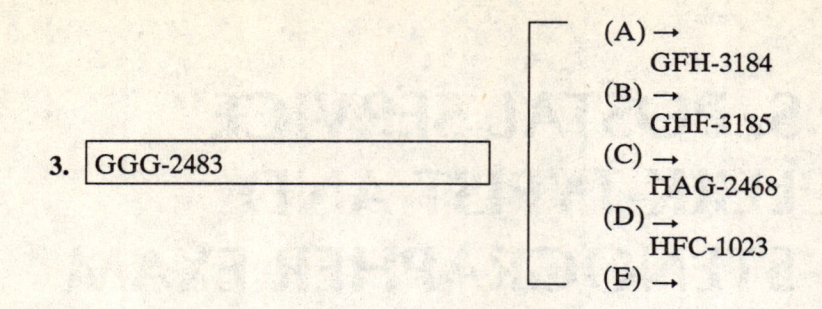

(A) → GFH-3184
(B) → GHF-3185
(C) → HAG-2468
(D) → HFC-1023
(E) →

Directions for comparisons questions: In each line across the page there are three names, addresses, or codes that are very much alike. Compare the three and decide which ones are EXACTLY alike. On your answer sheet, mark:

A if **ALL THREE** names, addresses, or codes are exactly **ALIKE**
B if only the **FIRST** and **SECOND** names, addresses, or codes are exactly **ALIKE**
C if only the **FIRST** and **THIRD** names, addresses, or codes are exactly **ALIKE**
D if only the **SECOND** and **THIRD** names, addresses, or codes are exactly **ALIKE**
E if **ALL THREE** names, addresses, or codes are **DIFFERENT**

4. H. Merritt Audubon	H. Merriott Audubon	H. Merritt Audubon
5. 2395890	2395890	2395890
6. 3418 W. 42nd St.	3418 W. 42nd Ave.	3148 W. 42nd Ave.

Directions for spelling questions: Find the correct spelling of the word and darken the appropriate space on the answer sheet. If none of the spellings is correct, darken space D.

7. (A) exceed
   (B) excede
   (C) exseed
   (D) none of these

8. (A) maneuver
   (B) manuver
   (C) manuever
   (D) none of these

9. (A) corellation
   (B) corrolation
   (C) corralation
   (D) none of these

Directions for computations questions: Perform the computation as indicated in the question and find the answer among the list of alternative responses. If the correct answer is not given among the choices, mark E.

10. $2\sqrt{142}$

(A) 70
(B) 72
(C) 74
(D) 76
(E) none of these

11. 25   (A) 5
    −10   (B) 10
                  (C) 15
                  (D) 20
                  (E) none of these

12. 18   (A) 108
    × 6   (B) 116
                  (C) 118
                  (D) 124
                  (E) none of these

Sample Answer Sheet

1. Ⓐ Ⓑ Ⓒ Ⓓ Ⓔ   5. Ⓐ Ⓑ Ⓒ Ⓓ Ⓔ   9. Ⓐ Ⓑ Ⓒ Ⓓ Ⓔ
2. Ⓐ Ⓑ Ⓒ Ⓓ Ⓔ   6. Ⓐ Ⓑ Ⓒ Ⓓ Ⓔ   10. Ⓐ Ⓑ Ⓒ Ⓓ Ⓔ
3. Ⓐ Ⓑ Ⓒ Ⓓ Ⓔ   7. Ⓐ Ⓑ Ⓒ Ⓓ Ⓔ   11. Ⓐ Ⓑ Ⓒ Ⓓ Ⓔ
4. Ⓐ Ⓑ Ⓒ Ⓓ Ⓔ   8. Ⓐ Ⓑ Ⓒ Ⓓ Ⓔ   12. Ⓐ Ⓑ Ⓒ Ⓓ Ⓔ

Correct Answers to Sample Questions

1. Ⓐ Ⓑ Ⓒ ● Ⓔ   5. ● Ⓑ Ⓒ Ⓓ Ⓔ   9. Ⓐ Ⓑ Ⓒ ● Ⓔ
2. ● Ⓑ Ⓒ Ⓓ Ⓔ   6. Ⓐ Ⓑ Ⓒ Ⓓ ●   10. Ⓐ Ⓑ Ⓒ Ⓓ ●
3. Ⓐ ● Ⓒ Ⓓ Ⓔ   7. ● Ⓑ Ⓒ Ⓓ Ⓔ   11. Ⓐ Ⓑ ● Ⓓ Ⓔ
4. Ⓐ Ⓑ ● Ⓓ Ⓔ   8. ● Ⓑ Ⓒ Ⓓ Ⓔ   12. ● Ⓑ Ⓒ Ⓓ Ⓔ

Sequencing

Time: 3 Minutes. 20 Questions.

Directions: For each question there is a name, number, or code in a box at the left and four other names, numbers, or codes in alphabetical or numerical order at the right. Find the correct space for the boxed name or number so that it will be in alphabetical and/or numerical order with the others and mark the letter of that space on your answer sheet.

1. Hackett, Gerald

   (A) →
   Habert, James
   (B) →
   Hachett, J.J.
   (C) →
   Hachetts, K. Larson
   (D) →
   Hachettson, Leroy
   (E) →

2. 59233362

   (A) →
   58146020
   (B) →
   59233162
   (C) →
   59233262
   (D) →
   59233662
   (E) →

3. MYP-6734

   (A) →
   NYP-6733
   (B) →
   NYS-7412
   (C) →
   NZT-4899
   (D) →
   PYZ-3636
   (E) →

4. Bobbitt, Olivier E.

   (A) →
   Bobbitt, D. Olivier
   (B) →
   Bobbitt, Olive B.
   (C) →
   Bobbitt, Olivia H.
   (D) →
   Bobbitt, R. Olivia
   (E) →

5. 00102032

(A) → 00120312
(B) → 00120323
(C) → 00120324
(D) → 00200303
(E) →

6. LPD-6100

(A) → LPD-5865
(B) → LPD-6001
(C) → LPD-6101
(D) → LPD-6106
(E) →

7. Vanstory, George

(A) → Vanover, Eva
(B) → VanSwinderen, Floyd
(C) → VanSyckle, Harry
(D) → Vanture, Laurence
(E) →

8. Fitzsimmons, Hugh

(A) → Fitts, Harold
(B) → Fitzgerald, June
(C) → FitzGibbon, Junius
(D) → FitzSimons, Martin
(E) →

9. 01066010

(A) → 01006040
(B) → 01006051
(C) → 01016053
(D) → 01016060
(E) →

10. AAZ-2687

(A) → AAA-2132
(B) → AAS-4623
(C) → ASA-3216
(D) → ASZ-5490
(E) →

11. Pawlowicz, Ruth M.

(A) → Pawalek, Edward
(B) → Pawelek, Flora G.
(C) → Pawlowski, Joan M.
(D) → Pawtowski, Wanda
(E) →

12. NCD-7834

(A) → NBJ-4682
(B) → NBT-5066
(C) → NCD-7710
(D) → NCD-7868
(E) →

13. 36270013

(A) → 36260006
(B) → 36270000
(C) → 36270030
(D) → 36670012
(E) →

14. Freedenburg, C. Erma

(A) → Freedenburg, Emerson
(B) → Freedenburg, Erma
(C) → Freedenburg, Erma E.
(D) → Freedinburg, Erma F.
(E) →

15. Prouty, Martha

(A) →
Proutey, Margaret
(B) →
Proutey, Maude
(C) →
Prouty, Myra
(D) →
Prouty, Naomi
(E) →

16. 58006021

(A) →
58006130
(B) →
58097222
(C) →
59000599
(D) →
59909000
(E) →

17. EKK-1443

(A) →
EGK-1164
(B) →
EKG-1329
(C) →
EKK-1331
(D) →
EKK-1403
(E) →

18. D'Amato, Vincent

(A) →
Daly, Steven
(B) →
D'Amboise, S. Vincent
(C) →
Daniel, Vail
(D) →
DeAlba, Valentina
(E) →

19. Schaeffer, Roger D.

(A) →
Schaffert, Evelyn M.
(B) →
Schaffner, Margaret M.
(C) →
Schafhirt, Milton G.
(D) →
Shafer, Richard E.
(E) →

20. SPP-4856

(A) →
PPS-4838
(B) →
PSP-4921
(C) →
SPS-4906
(D) →
SSP-4911
(E) →

END OF SEQUENCING QUESTIONS

U.S. Postal Service Clerk-Typist and Clerk-Stenographer Exam / 139

Comparisons

Time: 5 Minutes. 30 Questions.

Directions: In each line across the page there are three names, addresses, or codes that are very much alike. Compare the three and decide which ones are EXACTLY alike. On your answer sheet, mark:

A   if **ALL THREE** names, addresses, or codes are exactly **ALIKE**
B   if only the **FIRST** and **SECOND** names, addresses, or codes are exactly **ALIKE**
C   if only the **FIRST** and **THIRD** names, addresses, or codes are exactly **ALIKE**
D   if only the **SECOND** and **THIRD** names, addresses, or codes are exactly **ALIKE**
E   if **ALL THREE** names, addresses, or codes are **DIFFERENT**

21.	Drusilla S. Ridgeley	Drusilla S. Ridgeley	Drusilla S. Ridgeley
22.	Andrei I. Toumantzev	Andrei I. Tourmantzev	Andrei I. Toumantzov
23.	6-78912-e3e42	6-78912-3e3e42	6-78912-e3e42
24.	86529 Dunwoodie Drive	86529 Dunwoodie Drive	85629 Dunwoodie Drive
25.	1592514	1592574	1592574
26.	Ella Burk Newham	Ella Burk Newnham	Elena Burk Newnham
27.	5416R-1952TZ-op	5416R-1952TZ-op	5416R-1952TZ-op
28.	60646 West Touhy Avenue	60646 West Touhy Avenue	60646 West Touhey Avenue
29.	Mardikian & Moore, Inc.	Mardikian and Moore, Inc.	Mardikian & Moore, Inc.
30.	9670243	9670423	9670423
31.	Eduardo Ingles	Eduardo Inglese	Eduardo Inglese
32.	Roger T. DeAngelis	Roger T. D'Angelis	Roger T. DeAngeles
33.	7692138	7692138	7692138
34.	2695 East 3435 South	2695 East 3435 South	2695 East 3435 South
35.	63qs5-95YT3-001	63qs5-95YT3-001	63qs5-95YT3-001
36.	2789350	2789350	2798350
37.	Helmut V. Lochner	Helmut V. Lockner	Helmut W. Lochner
38.	2454803	2548403	2454803
39.	Lemberger, WA 28094-9182	Lemberger, VA 28094-9182	Lemberger, VA 28094-9182
40.	4168-GNP-78852	4168-GNP-78852	4168-GNP-78852
41.	Yoshihito Saito	Yoshihito Saito	Yoshihito Saito
42.	5927681	5927861	5927681
43.	O'Reilly Bay, LA 56212	O'Reillys Bay, LA 56212	O'Reilly Bay, LA 56212
44.	Francis Ransdell	Frances Ramsdell	Francis Ramsdell
45.	5634-OotV5a-16867	5634-Ootv5a-16867	5634-Ootv5a-16867
46.	Dolores Mollicone	Dolores Mollicone	Doloras Mollicone
47.	David C. Routzon	David E. Routzon	David C. Routzron
48.	8932 Shimabui Hwy.	8932 Shimabui Hwy.	8932 Shimabui Hwy.
49.	6177396	6177936	6177396
50.	A8987-B73245	A8987-B73245	A8987-B73245

END OF COMPARISONS QUESTIONS

Spelling

Time: 3 Minutes. 20 Questions.

Directions: Find the correct spelling of the word and darken the appropriate space on your answer sheet. If none of the spellings is correct, darken space D.

51. (A) anticipate
    (B) antisipate
    (C) anticapate
    (D) none of these

52. (A) similiar
    (B) simmilar
    (C) similar
    (D) none of these

53. (A) sufficiantly
    (B) suficeintly
    (C) sufficiently
    (D) none of these

54. (A) intelligence
    (B) inteligence
    (C) intellegence
    (D) none of these

55. (A) referance
    (B) referrence
    (C) referense
    (D) none of these

56. (A) conscious
    (B) consious
    (C) conscius
    (D) none of these

57. (A) paralell
    (B) parellel
    (C) parellell
    (D) none of these

58. (A) abundence
    (B) abundance
    (C) abundants
    (D) none of these

59. (A) corregated
    (B) corrigated
    (C) corrugated
    (D) none of these

60. (A) accumalation
    (B) accumulation
    (C) accumullation
    (D) none of these

61. (A) resonance
    (B) resonence
    (C) resonnance
    (D) none of these

62. (A) benaficial
    (B) benefitial
    (C) beneficial
    (D) none of these

63. (A) spesifically
    (B) specificially
    (C) specifically
    (D) none of these

64. (A) elemanate
    (B) elimenate
    (C) elliminate
    (D) none of these

65. (A) collosal
    (B) colosal
    (C) collossal
    (D) none of these

66. (A) auxillary
    (B) auxilliary
    (C) auxiliary
    (D) none of these

67. (A) inimitable
    (B) inimitible
    (C) inimatable
    (D) none of these

68. (A) disapearance
    (B) dissapearance
    (C) disappearence
    (D) none of these

69. (A) appelate
    (B) appellate
    (C) apellate
    (D) none of these

70. (A) esential
    (B) essential
    (C) essencial
    (D) none of these

END OF SPELLING QUESTIONS

Computations

Time: 8 Minutes. 15 Questions.

Directions: Perform the computation as indicated in the question and find the answer among the list of alternative responses. If the correct answer is not given among the choices, mark E.

71. 83
     −56
(A) 23
(B) 29
(C) 33
(D) 37
(E) none of these

72. 15
     +17
(A) 22
(B) 32
(C) 39
(D) 42
(E) none of these

73. 32
     × 7
(A) 224
(B) 234
(C) 324
(D) 334
(E) none of these

74. 39
     × 2
(A) 77
(B) 78
(C) 79
(D) 81
(E) none of these

75. 43
     −15
(A) 23
(B) 32
(C) 33
(D) 35
(E) none of these

76. 50
     +49
(A) 89
(B) 90
(C) 99
(D) 109
(E) none of these

77. 6)366
(A) 11
(B) 31
(C) 36
(D) 66
(E) none of these

78. 38   (A) 111
    × 3   (B) 113
             (C) 115
             (D) 117
             (E) none of these

79. 19   (A) 20
    +21   (B) 30
             (C) 40
             (D) 50
             (E) none of these

80. 13   (A) 5
    −6   (B) 7
             (C) 9
             (D) 11
             (E) none of these

81. 6)180   (A) 29
             (B) 31
             (C) 33
             (D) 39
             (E) none of these

82. 10   (A) 0
    × 1   (B) 1
             (C) 10
             (D) 100
             (E) none of these

83. 7)287   (A) 21
             (B) 27
             (C) 31
             (D) 37
             (E) none of these

84. 12   (A) 21
    +11   (B) 22
             (C) 23
             (D) 24
             (E) none of these

85. 85   (A) 19
    −64   (B) 21
             (C) 29
             (D) 31
             (E) none of these

END OF COMPUTATIONS QUESTIONS

END OF PART A

Part B—Verbal Ability

Sample Questions

There are four kinds of questions in Part B. Each kind of question has its own set of directions, but the portions containing the different kinds of questions are not separately timed. There are 55 questions in Part B, and candidates are allowed 50 minutes to complete the entire part. The four kinds of questions are:

Following Written Instructions	20 questions
Grammar/Punctuation	20 questions
Vocabulary Reading Comprehension	15 questions altogether

Directions for following written instructions: These questions test your ability to follow instructions. Each question directs you to mark a specific number and letter combination on your answer sheet. The questions require your total concentration because the answers that you are instructed to mark are, for the most part, NOT in numerical sequence (i.e., you would not use Number 1 on your answer sheet to answer Question 1; Number 2 for Question 2; etc.). Instead, you must mark the number and space specifically designated in each test question.

1. Look at the numbers below. Draw one line under the lowest number. Now, on your answer sheet, find that number and darken letter C for that number.

    4   2   3   6

2. Circle the middle letter in the line below. Now, on your answer sheet, find the number 3 and darken the space for the letter you just circled.

    F   A   D   B   E

3. Subtract 8 from 9 and write your answer on the line below. Now, on your answer sheet, darken space D for the space of the number you wrote.

    _____

The remaining questions are to be answered on the answer sheet in numerical sequence: Question 4 is to be answered in Space 4, Question 5 in Space 5, and so forth.

Directions for Grammar/Punctuation Questions: Each question consists of a sentence written in four different ways. Choose the sentence that is most appropriate with respect to grammar, usage, and punctuation, so as to be suitable for a business letter or report, and darken its letter on your answer sheet.

4. (A) Your pen is different from mine.
   (B) Your pen is different to mine.
   (C) Your pen is different than mine.
   (D) Your pen is different with mine.

Directions for Vocabulary Questions: Each question consists of a sentence containing a word in **boldface** type. Choose the best meaning for the word in **boldface** type and darken its letter on your answer sheet.

5. A passing grade on the special exam may **exempt** the applicant from the experience requirements for that job. **Exempt** most nearly means
   (A) prohibit
   (B) excuse
   (C) subject
   (D) specify

Directions for Reading Comprehension Questions: Read each paragraph and answer the question that follows it by darkening the letter of the correct answer on your answer sheet.

6. The work goals of an agency can best be reached if the employees understand and agree with these goals. One way to gain such understanding and agreement is for management to encourage and seriously consider suggestions from employees in the setting of agency goals.

   The paragraph best supports the statement that understanding and agreement with agency goals can be gained by

   (A) allowing the employees to set agency goals
   (B) reaching agency goals quickly
   (C) legislative review of agency operations
   (D) employee participation in setting agency goals

Sample Answer Sheet
1. Ⓐ Ⓑ Ⓒ Ⓓ Ⓔ   4. Ⓐ Ⓑ Ⓒ Ⓓ Ⓔ
2. Ⓐ Ⓑ Ⓒ Ⓓ Ⓔ   5. Ⓐ Ⓑ Ⓒ Ⓓ Ⓔ
3. Ⓐ Ⓑ Ⓒ Ⓓ Ⓔ   6. Ⓐ Ⓑ Ⓒ Ⓓ Ⓔ

Correct Answers to Sample Questions
1. Ⓐ Ⓑ Ⓒ ● Ⓔ   4. ● Ⓑ Ⓒ Ⓓ Ⓔ
2. Ⓐ Ⓑ ● Ⓓ Ⓔ   5. Ⓐ ● Ⓒ Ⓓ Ⓔ
3. Ⓐ Ⓑ Ⓒ ● Ⓔ   6. Ⓐ Ⓑ Ⓒ ● Ⓔ

U.S. Postal Service Clerk-Typist and Clerk-Stenographer Exam / 145

Part B

Time: 50 Minutes. 55 Questions.

Directions: Questions 1-20 test your ability to follow instructions. Each question directs you to mark a specific number and letter combination on your answer sheet. The questions require your total concentration because the answers that you are instructed to mark are, for the most part, NOT in numerical sequence (i.e., you would not use Number 1 on your answer sheet to answer Question 1; Number 2 for Question 2; etc.). Instead, you must mark the number and space specifically designated in each test question.

1. Look at the letters below. Draw a circle around the letter that comes first in the alphabet. Now, on your answer sheet, find Number 12 and darken the space for the letter you just circled.

    E   G   D   Z   B   F

2. Draw a line under the odd number below that is more than 5 but less than 10. Find this number on your answer sheet and darken space E.

    8   10   5   6   11   9

3. Divide the number 16 by 4 and write your answer on the line below. Now find this number on your answer sheet and darken space A.

    _____

4. Write the letter C on the line next to the left-hand number below. Now, on your answer sheet, darken the space for the number-letter combination you see.

    5 _____   19 _____   7 _____

5. If in any week Wednesday comes before Tuesday, write the number 15 on the line below. If not, write the number 18. Now, on your answer sheet, darken the letter A for the number you just wrote.

    _____

6. Count the number of Bs in the line below and write that number at the end of the line. Now, on your answer sheet, darken the letter D for the number you wrote.

    A D A E B D C A _____

7. Write the letter B on the line with the highest number. Now, on your answer sheet, darken the number-letter combination that appears on that line.

    16 _____   9 _____   20 _____   11 _____

8. If the product of 6 × 4 is greater than the product of 8 × 3, write the letter E on the line below. If not, write the letter C. Now, on your answer sheet find number 8 and darken the space for the letter you just wrote.

   _____

9. Write the number 2 in the largest circle below. Now, on your answer sheet, darken the space for the number-letter combination in that circle.

   (___A)   [___D]   (___C)   [___B]

10. Write the letter D on the line next to the number that is the sum of 7 + 4 + 4. Now, on your answer sheet, darken the space for that number-letter combination.

    13 _____   14 _____   15 _____   16 _____   17 _____

11. If 5 × 5 equals 25 and 5 + 5 equals 10, write the number 17 on the line below. If not, write the number 10. Now, on your answer sheet, darken space E for the number you just wrote.

    _____

12. Circle the second letter below. On the line beside that letter write the number that represents the number of days in a week. Now, on your answer sheet, darken the space for that number-letter combination.

    _____ C   _____ D   _____ B   _____ E

13. If a triangle has more angles than a rectangle, write the number 13 in the circle below. If not, write the number 14 in the square. Now, on your answer sheet, darken the space for the number-letter combination in the figure that you just wrote in.

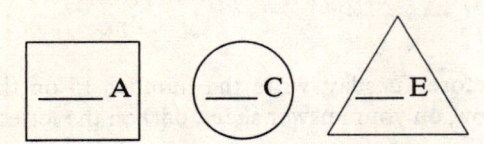

    [___A]   (___C)   △___E

14. Count the number of Bs below and write that number at the end of the line. Subtract 2 from that number. Now, on your answer sheet, darken space E for the number that represents 2 less than the number of Bs in the line.

    B E A D E C C B B B A E B D _____

15. The numbers below represent morning pick-up times from neighborhood letter boxes. Draw a line under the number that represents the latest pick-up time. Now, on your answer sheet, darken space D for the number that is the same as the "minutes" of the time that you underlined.

    9:19   10:16   10:10

16. If a person who is 6 feet tall is taller than a person who is 5 feet tall and if a pillow is softer than a rock, darken space 11A on your answer sheet. If not, darken space 6B.

17. Write the fourth letter of the alphabet on the line next to the third number below. Now, on your answer sheet, darken that number-letter combination.

    10 _____   19 _____   13 _____   4 _____

18. Write the letter B in the box containing the next to smallest number. On your answer sheet, darken the space for that number-letter combination.

    | 10____ | | 19____ | | 11____ | | 6____ |

19. Directly below you will see three boxes and three words. Write the third letter of the first word on the line in the second box. Now, on your answer sheet, darken the space for that number-letter combination.

    | 6____ | | 19____ | | 12____ | BAD DRAB ALE

20. Count the number of points on the figure below. If there are five or more points, darken the space for 6E on your answer sheet. If there are fewer than five points, darken 6A.

    ★

Directions: Each question from 21 through 40 consists of a sentence written in four different ways. Choose the sentence that is most appropriate with respect to grammar, usage, and punctuation, so as to be suitable for a business letter or report, and darken its letter on your answer sheet. Answer each question in the answer space with the corresponding number.

21. (A) Double parking is when you park your car alongside one that is already having been parked.
    (B) When one double parks, you park your car alongside one that is already parked.
    (C) Double parking is parking alongside a car already parked.
    (D) To double park is alongside a car already parked.

22. (A) This is entirely among you and he.
    (B) This is completely among him and you.
    (C) This is between you and him.
    (D) This is between he and you.

23. (A) As I said, "neither of them are guilty."
    (B) As I said, "neither of them are guilty".
    (C) As I said, "neither of them is guilty."
    (D) As I said, neither of them is guilty.

24. (A) I think that they will promote whoever has the best record.
    (B) The firm would have liked to have promoted all employees with good records.
    (C) Such of them that have the best records have excellent prospects of promotion.
    (D) I feel sure they will give the promotion to whomever has the best record.

25. (A) The receptionist must answer courteously the questions of all them callers.
    (B) The receptionist must answer courteously the questions what are asked by the callers.
    (C) There would have been no trouble if the receptionist had have always answered courteously.
    (D) The receptionist should answer courteously the questions of all callers.

26. (A) Since the report lacked the needed information, it was of no use to them.
    (B) This report was useless to them because there were no needed information in it.
    (C) Since the report did not contain the needed information, it was not real useful to them.
    (D) Being that the report lacked the needed information, they could not use it.

27. (A) The company had hardly declared the dividend till the notices were prepared for mailing.
    (B) They had no sooner declared the dividend when they sent the notices to the stockholders.
    (C) No sooner had the dividend been declared than the notices were prepared for mailing.
    (D) Scarcely had the dividend been declared than the notices were sent out.

28. (A) The supervisors reprimanded the typists, whom she believed had made careless errors.
    (B) The typists would have corrected the errors had they of known that the supervisor would see the report.
    (C) The errors in the typed reports were so numerous that they could hardly be overlooked.
    (D) Many errors were found in the reports which they typed and could not disregard them.

29. (A) "Are you absolutely certain, she asked, that you are right?"
    (B) "Are you absolutely certain," she asked, "that you are right?"
    (C) "Are you absolutely certain," she asked, "That you are right"?
    (D) "Are you absolutely certain", she asked, "That you are right?"

30. (A) He goes only to church on Christmas and Easter.
    (B) He only goes to church on Christmas and Easter.
    (C) He goes to only church on Christmas and Easter.
    (D) He goes to church only on Christmas and Easter.

31. (A) Most all these statements have been supported by persons who are reliable and can be depended upon.
    (B) The persons which have guaranteed these statements are reliable.
    (C) Reliable persons guarantee the facts with regards to the truth of these statements.
    (D) These statements can be depended on, for their truth has been guaranteed by reliable persons.

32. (A) The success of the book pleased both the publisher and authors.
    (B) Both the publisher and they was pleased with the success of the book.
    (C) Neither they or their publisher was disappointed with the success of the book.
    (D) Their publisher was as pleased as they with the success of the book.

33. (A) In reviewing the typists' work reports, the job analyst found records of unusual typing speeds.
    (B) It says in the job analyst's report that some employees type with great speed.
    (C) The job analyst found that, in reviewing the typists' work reports, that some unusual typing speeds had been made.
    (D) In the reports of typists' speeds, the job analyst found some records that are kind of unusual.

34. (A) Every carrier should always have something to throw; not something to throw at the dog but something what will divert its attention.
    (B) Every carrier should have something to throw—not something to throw at the dog but something to divert its attention.
    (C) Every carrier should always carry something to throw not something to throw at the dog but something that will divert it's attention.
    (D) Every carrier should always carry something to throw, not something to throw at the dog, but, something that will divert its' attention.

35. (A) Brown's & Company employees have recently received increases in salary.
    (B) Brown & Company recently increased the salaries of all its employees.
    (C) Recently Brown & Company has increased their employees' salaries.
    (D) Brown & Company have recently increased the salaries of all its employees.

36. (A) If properly addressed, the letter will reach my mother and I.
    (B) The letter had been addressed to myself and my mother.
    (C) I believe the letter was addressed to either my mother or I.
    (D) My mother's name, as well as mine, was on the letter.

37. (A) One of us have to make the reply before tomorrow.
    (B) Making the reply before tomorrow will have to be done by one of us.
    (C) One of us has to reply before tomorrow.
    (D) Anyone has to reply before tomorrow.

38. (A) You have got to get rid of some of these people if you expect to have the quality of the work improve.
    (B) The quality of the work would improve if they would leave fewer people do it.
    (C) I believe it would be desirable to have fewer persons doing this work.
    (D) If you had planned on employing fewer people than this to do the work, this situation would not have arose.

39. (A) The paper we use for this purpose must be light, glossy, and stand hard usage as well.
    (B) Only a light and a glossy, but durable, paper must be used for this purpose.
    (C) For this purpose, we want a paper that is light, glossy, but that will stand hard wear.
    (D) For this purpose, paper that is light, glossy, and durable is essential.

40. (A) This letter, together with the reports, are to be sent to the postmaster.
    (B) The reports, together with this letter, is to be sent to the postmaster.
    (C) The reports and this letter is to be sent to the postmaster.
    (D) This letter, together with the reports, is to be sent to the postmaster.

Directions: Each question from 41 through 48 consists of a sentence containing a word in **boldface** type. Choose the best meaning for the word in **boldface** type and darken its letter on your answer sheet. Answer each question in the answer space with the corresponding number.

41. Please consult your office **manual** to learn the proper operation of our copying machine. **Manual** means most nearly
    (A) labor
    (B) handbook
    (C) typewriter
    (D) handle

42. There is a specified punishment for each **infraction** of the rules. **Infraction** means most nearly
    (A) violation
    (B) use
    (C) interpretation
    (D) part

43. The order was **rescinded** within the week. **Rescinded** means most nearly
    (A) revised
    (B) canceled
    (C) misinterpreted
    (D) confirmed

44. If you have a question, please raise your hand to **summon** the test proctor. **Summon** means most nearly
    (A) ticket
    (B) fine
    (C) give
    (D) call

45. We dared not prosecute the terrorist for fear of **reprisal**. **Reprisal** means most nearly
    (A) retaliation
    (B) advantage
    (C) warning
    (D) denial

46. The increased use of dictation machines has severely **reduced** the need for office stenographers. **Reduced** means most nearly
    (A) enlarged
    (B) cut out
    (C) lessened
    (D) expanded

47. Frequent use of marijuana may **impair** your judgment. **Impair** means most nearly
    (A) weaken
    (B) conceal
    (C) improve
    (D) expose

48. It is altogether **fitting** that the parent discipline the child. **Fitting** means most nearly
 (A) illegal
 (B) bad practice
 (C) appropriate
 (D) required

Directions: For questions 49 through 55, read each paragraph and answer the question that follows it by darkening the letter of the correct answer on your answer sheet. Answer each question in the answer space with the corresponding number.

49. A survey to determine the subjects that have helped students most in their jobs shows that typewriting leads all other subjects in the business group. It also leads among the subjects college students consider most valuable and would take again if they were to return to high school.

The paragraph best supports the statement that

(A) the ability to type is an asset in business and in school
(B) students who return to night school take typing
(C) students with a knowledge of typing do superior work in college
(D) success in business is assured those who can type

50. Telegrams should be clear, concise, and brief. Omit all unnecessary words. The parts of speech most often used in telegrams are nouns, verbs, adjectives, and adverbs. If possible, do without pronouns, prepositions, articles, and copulative verbs. Use simple sentences, rather than complex and compound.

The paragraph best supports the statement that in writing telegrams one should always use

(A) common and simple words
(B) only nouns, verbs, adjectives, and adverbs
(C) incomplete sentences
(D) only words essential to the meaning

51. Since the government can spend only what it obtains from the people, and this amount is ultimately limited by their capacity and willingness to pay taxes, it is very important that the people be given full information about the work of the government.

The paragraph best supports the statement that

(A) governmental employees should be trained not only in their own work, but also in how to perform the duties of other employees in their agency
(B) taxation by the government rests upon the consent of the people
(C) the release of full information on the work of the government will increase the efficiency of governmental operations
(D) the work of the government, in recent years, has been restricted because of reduced tax collections

52. Both the high school and the college should take the responsibility for preparing the student to get a job. Since the ability to write a good application letter is one of the first steps toward this goal, every teacher should be willing to do what he can to help the student learn to write such letters.

The paragraph best supports the statement that

(A) inability to write a good letter often reduces one's job prospects
(B) the major responsibility of the school is to obtain jobs for its students

(C) success is largely a matter of the kind of work the student applies for first
(D) every teacher should teach a course in the writing of application letters

53. Direct lighting is the least satisfactory lighting arrangement. The desk or ceiling light with a reflector that diffuses all the rays downward is sure to cause a glare on the working surface.

The paragraph best supports the statement that direct lighting is least satisfactory as a method of lighting chiefly because

(A) the light is diffused, causing eye strain
(B) the shade on the individual desk lamp is not constructed along scientific lines
(C) the working surface is usually obscured by the glare
(D) direct lighting is injurious to the eyes

54. "White collar" is a term used to describe one of the largest groups of workers in American industry and trade. It distinguishes those who work with the pencil and the mind from those who depend on their hands and the machine. It suggests occupations in which physical exertion and handling of materials are not primary features of the job.

The paragraph best supports the statement that "white collar" workers are

(A) not so strong physically as those who work with their hands
(B) those who supervise workers handling materials
(C) all whose work is entirely indoors
(D) not likely to use machines as much as are other groups of workers

55. In large organizations some standardized, simple, inexpensive method of giving employees information about company policies and rules, as well as specific instructions regarding their duties, is practically essential. This is the purpose of all office manuals of whatever type.

The paragraph best supports the statement that office manuals

(A) are all about the same
(B) should be simple enough for the average employee to understand
(C) are necessary to large organizations
(D) act as constant reminders to the employee of his duties

END OF PART B

Part C—Stenography

Sample Dictation

Have someone dictate the sample passage below to you. It should take 3 minutes. Take notes on your own paper.

Directions to person dictating: This practice dictation should be dictated at the rate of 80 words a minute. Do not dictate the punctuation except for periods, but dictate with the expression the punctuation indicates. Use a watch with a second hand to enable you to read the exercises at the proper speed.

Exactly on a minute start dictating.

Finish reading each two lines at the number of seconds indicated below.

I realize that this practice dictation is not a part of the examination	
proper and is not to be scored. (Period)	10
The work of preventing and correcting	20
physical defects in children is becoming more effective as a result of change	30
in the attitude of many parents. (Period) In order to bring about this change,	40
parents have been invited to visit the schools when their children are being examined	50
and to discuss the treatment necessary for the correction of defects. (Period)	1 min.
There is a distinct value in having a parent see that his or her child is not the	10
only one who needs attention. (Period) Otherwise a few parents might feel that they	20
were being criticized by having the defects of their children singled out for medical	30
treatment. (Period) The special classes that have been set up have shown the value of	40
the scientific knowledge that has been applied in the treatment of children. (Period)	50
In these classes the children have been taught to exercise by a trained teacher	2 min.
under medical supervision. (Period) The hours of the school day have been divided	10
between school work and physical activity that helps not only to correct their defects	20
but also to improve their general physical condition. (Period) This method of treatment	30
has been found to be very effective except for those who have severe medical	40
defects. (Period) Most parents now see how desirable it is to have these classes	50
that have been set up in the regular school system to meet special needs. (Period)	3 min.

154 / **Clerical Exams Handbook**

After dictating the practice, pause for 15 seconds to permit the competitor to complete note-taking. Then continue in accordance with the directions. After the sample dictation transcript has been completed, dictate the test on page 157.

Sample Dictation Transcript Sheet

The transcript below is part of the material that was dictated to you for practice, except that many of the words have been left out. From your notes, you are to tell what the missing words are. Proceed as follows:

    Compare your notes with the transcript and, when you come to a blank in the transcript, decide what word (or words) belongs there. For example, you will find that the word "practice" belongs in blank number 1. Look at the word list to see whether you can find the same word there. Notice what letter (A, B, C, or D) is printed beside it, and write that letter in the blank. For example, the word "practice" is listed, followed by the letter B. We have already written B in blank number 1 to show you how you are to record your choice. Now decide what belongs in each of the other blanks. (You may also write the word or words, or the shorthand for them, if you wish.) The same word may belong in more than one blank. If the exact answer is not listed, write E in the blank.

ALPHABETIC WORD LIST

Write E if the answer is **not** listed.

about — B	paper — B
against — C	parents — B
attitude — A	part — C
being — D	physical — D
childhood — B	portion — D
children — A	practical — A
correcting — C	practice — B
doctors — B	preliminary — D
effective — D	preventing — B
efficient — A	procedure — A
examination — A	proper — C
examining — C	reason for — A
for — B	result — B
health — B	result of — C
mothers — C	schools — C
never — C	to be — C
not — D	to prevent — A

TRANSCRIPT

I realize that this $\underline{B}\atop 1$ dictation is $\underline{}\atop 2$ a $\underline{}\atop 3$ of the $\underline{}\atop 4$ $\underline{}\atop 5$ and is $\underline{}\atop 6$ $\underline{}\atop 7$ scored.

The work $\underline{}\atop 8$ and $\underline{}\atop 9$ $\underline{}\atop 10$ defects in $\underline{}\atop 11$ is becoming more $\underline{}\atop 12$ as a $\underline{}\atop 13$ a change in the $\underline{}\atop 14$ of many $\underline{}\atop 15$.

ALPHABETIC WORD LIST

Write E if the answer is **not** listed.

all — A	reducing — A
at — C	satisfied — D
bring — A	say — C
collection — B	see — B
correction — C	soon — C
discuss — C	their — D
during — D	to discover — A
friend — A	to discuss — D
indicated — C	to endorse — C
insisted — D	to visit — B
is — B	treatments — A
is not — A	understand — D
know — A	undertake — B
knows — D	virtue — D
needed — B	visit — A
promote — B	volume — B
recognizing — D	young — C

TRANSCRIPT (Continued)

In order to ___ ___ this change, parents
        16 17

have been invited ___ the schools when
                   18

___ children are being examined and ___
 19   20

the ___ necessary for the ___ of defects.
    21   22

There is a distinct ___ in having a parent
                    23

___ that his or her child ___ the only one
 24   25

who needs attention . . . . (The rest of the

sample dictation is not transcribed here.)

Answer Sheet for Sample Dictation

1. Ⓐ Ⓑ Ⓒ Ⓓ Ⓔ   8. Ⓐ Ⓑ Ⓒ Ⓓ Ⓔ   15. Ⓐ Ⓑ Ⓒ Ⓓ Ⓔ   22. Ⓐ Ⓑ Ⓒ Ⓓ Ⓔ
2. Ⓐ Ⓑ Ⓒ Ⓓ Ⓔ   9. Ⓐ Ⓑ Ⓒ Ⓓ Ⓔ   16. Ⓐ Ⓑ Ⓒ Ⓓ Ⓔ   23. Ⓐ Ⓑ Ⓒ Ⓓ Ⓔ
3. Ⓐ Ⓑ Ⓒ Ⓓ Ⓔ   10. Ⓐ Ⓑ Ⓒ Ⓓ Ⓔ   17. Ⓐ Ⓑ Ⓒ Ⓓ Ⓔ   24. Ⓐ Ⓑ Ⓒ Ⓓ Ⓔ
4. Ⓐ Ⓑ Ⓒ Ⓓ Ⓔ   11. Ⓐ Ⓑ Ⓒ Ⓓ Ⓔ   18. Ⓐ Ⓑ Ⓒ Ⓓ Ⓔ   25. Ⓐ Ⓑ Ⓒ Ⓓ Ⓔ
5. Ⓐ Ⓑ Ⓒ Ⓓ Ⓔ   12. Ⓐ Ⓑ Ⓒ Ⓓ Ⓔ   19. Ⓐ Ⓑ Ⓒ Ⓓ Ⓔ
6. Ⓐ Ⓑ Ⓒ Ⓓ Ⓔ   13. Ⓐ Ⓑ Ⓒ Ⓓ Ⓔ   20. Ⓐ Ⓑ Ⓒ Ⓓ Ⓔ
7. Ⓐ Ⓑ Ⓒ Ⓓ Ⓔ   14. Ⓐ Ⓑ Ⓒ Ⓓ Ⓔ   21. Ⓐ Ⓑ Ⓒ Ⓓ Ⓔ

The correct answers for the sample dictation are:

1. **B**	8. **B**	14. **A**	20. **D**
2. **D**	9. **C**	15. **B**	21. **E**
3. **C**	10. **D**	16. **A**	22. **C**
4. **A**	11. **A**	17. **E**	23. **E**
5. **C**	12. **D**	18. **B**	24. **B**
6. **D**	13. **C**	19. **D**	25. **A**
7. **C**			

Compare your answers with the correct ones. If one of your answers does not agree with the correct answer, again compare your notes with the samples and make certain you understand the instructions.

Your notes should show that the word "bring" goes in blank 16, and "about" in blank 17. But "about" is *not in the list;* so E should be your answer for question 17.

The two words, "to visit—B," are needed for 18, and the one word "visit—A," would be an incorrect answer.

For the actual test you will use a separate answer sheet. As scoring will be done by an electronic machine, it is important that you follow directions carefully. Use the special pencil if one is furnished by the examiner. If no pencil is furnished, use only a number 2 pencil, as directed. Make a heavy mark for each answer. If you have to change your mark for any question, be sure to erase the first mark completely (do not merely cross it out) before making another.

156 / Clerical Exams Handbook

CORRECTLY FILLED TRANSCRIPTS FOR SAMPLE DICTATION

Check your notes against the dictation; check your notes against the alphabetic list of words and the transcript sheet; check the transcript against your answer grid. Identify your errors.

I realize that this <u>B</u> dictation is <u>D</u> a <u>C</u> of
      1   2   3

the <u>A</u> <u>C</u> and is <u>D</u> <u>C</u> scored.
  4 5   6 7

 The work <u>B</u> the <u>C</u> <u>D</u> defects in <u>A</u> is
      8   9 10   11

becoming more <u>D</u> as a <u>C</u> a change in the
      12   13

<u>A</u> of many <u>B</u> .
14   15

 In order to <u>A</u> <u>E</u> this change, parents
     16 17

have been invited <u>B</u> the schools when <u>D</u>
       18   19

children are being examined and <u>D</u> the <u>E</u>
          20   21

necessary for the <u>C</u> of defects. There is a
      22

distinct <u>E</u> in having a parent <u>B</u> that his or
   23   24

her child <u>A</u> the only one who needs
   25

attention . . . . (The rest of the sample

dictation is not transcribed here.)

Part C

Dictation Time: 3 Minutes.

Exactly on a minute start dictating.

Finish reading each two lines at the number of seconds indicated below.

In recent years there has been a great increase in the need for capable stenographers,	10
not only in business offices but also in public service agencies, both	20
governmental and private. (Period) The high schools and business schools in many parts of	30
the country have tried to meet this need by offering complete commercial courses. (Period)	40
The increase in the number of persons who are enrolled in these courses shows that	50
students have become aware of the great demand for stenographers. (Period) A person	1 min.
who wishes to secure employment in this field must be able to take dictation	10
and to transcribe the notes with both speed and accuracy. (Period) The rate of	20
speed at which dictation is given in most offices is somewhat less than that of	30
ordinary speech. (Period) Thus, one who has had a thorough training in shorthand	40
should have little trouble in taking complete notes. (Period) Skill in taking dictation	50
at a rapid rate is of slight value if the stenographer cannot also type the notes	2 min.
in proper form. (Period) A manager sometimes dictates a rough draft of the ideas	10
he/she wishes to have included in a letter, and leaves to the stenographer the task	20
of putting them in good form. (Period) For this reason, knowledge of the essentials	30
of grammar and of composition is as important as the ability to take	40
dictation. (Period) In addition, a stenographer should be familiar with the sources of	50
general information that are most likely to be used in office work. (Period)	3 min.

158 / Clerical Exams Handbook

Dictation Transcript

Time: 30 Minutes. 125 Questions.

ALPHABETIC WORD LIST

Write E if the answer is **not** listed.

also — A	offering — C
also in — C	officials — D
business — C	one — C
busy — D	only — B
capable — A	parts — A
commerce — C	private — C
commercial — D	public — D
county — B	recent — B
culpable — D	recurrent — A
decrease — A	school — C
governing — D	schools — B
governmental — C	servant — D
had been — B	stenographers — D
has been — D	stenos — A
many — A	their — D
most — D	there — B
need — C	tied — A
needy — D	to beat — C
offending — A	tried — B

TRANSCRIPT

In __ years __ __ a great __ in the __
     1   2 3   4   5

for __ __, not __ in __ __ but __ in
    6   7   8   9 10   11

__ __ agencies, both __ and __. The
12 13   14   15

high __ and __ schools in __ __ of
      16   17   18 19

the __ have __ this __ by __
    20   21 22   23   24

complete __ courses.
        25

ALPHABETIC WORD LIST

Write E if the answer is **not** listed.

awake — C	in a — B
aware — B	in the — A
be able — A	increase — C
be able to — C	increment — A
became — B	notations — B
better — A	notes — C
both — D	number — C
courses — D	numbers — D
curses — C	people — A
demand — C	person — C
demean — A	seclude — C
dictation — B	secure — B
dictation notes — C	speech — C
employing — A	speed — B
employment — D	students — C
enrolled — B	studies — D
enroute — D	the — C
feel — A	this — A
felt — D	transcribe — C
grate — D	transcript — D
great — A	who desires — C

TRANSCRIPT (continued)

The __ __ __ of __ who are __
     26 27 28   29   30

in these __ shows __ __ have __
          31   32 33   34

__ of the __ __ for stenographers. A
35   36 37

__ __ to __ __ in __ __ must
38 39   40 41   42 43

__ to take __ and to __ the __ with
44   45   46   47

__ __ and __ .
48 49   50

Continue on the next page without waiting for a signal.

ALPHABETIC WORD LIST

Write E if the answer is **not** listed.

also — D	rampant — B
also can — B	rate — C
at a — A	ratio — D
at the — C	should — D
compete — B	should not — A
complete — D	sight — C
dictates — B	slight — B
dictation — D	somehow — D
firm — C	speech — A
form — D	speed — A
gained — A	stenographer — C
give — D	taking — C
has — C	that — D
have — B	thorough — C
less — B	through — B
less than — A	treble — D
many — A	trial — A
most — D	typed — D
note — C	typewriter — A
notes — B	valuate — A
offices — C	value — C
orderly — C	what — C
ordinary — D	which — B
proffer — C	who gets — A
proper — A	who had — C

Continue on the next page without waiting for a signal.

TRANSCRIPT (continued)

The ___ of ___ at ___ dictation is ___ in
     51   52   53   54

___ ___ is ___ ___ than ___ of ___
55 56   57 58   59   60

___ . Thus, one ___ had a ___ in ___
61   62   63   64

shorthand ___ ___ little ___ in ___ ___
            65 66   67   68 69

___ . Skill in ___ ___ ___ ___ ___ is
70   71 72 73 74 75

of ___ ___ if the ___ cannot ___ ___
   76 77   78   79 80

the ___ in ___ ___ .
     81   82 83

ALPHABETIC WORD LIST

Write E if the answer is **not** listed.

ability — B	letter — D
adding — C	like — A
addition — A	likely — C
are — D	manager — A
as — A	management — B
composing — A	of the — D
composition — C	of these — A
dictates — B	office — A
essence — B	official — B
essentials — C	put in — D
form — A	putting — C
familial — C	reasoning — B
familiar — A	rough — A
general — C	roughly — D
generous — A	sauces — A
good — C	shall — D
grammatical — D	should — B
great — A	some times — A
had — A	somethings — D
have — B	source — D
ideals — C	stenographic — A
ideas — A	take — D
included — C	task — D
inclusive — A	this — A
information — D	to — A
important — B	to be — B
impotent — A	used — C
knowledge — B	useful — A
knowledgeable — C	wished — D
leaves — B	wishes — A
lets — C	with the — D

TRANSCRIPT (continued)

A ___ ___ ___ a ___ ___ ___ ___
 84 85 86   87 88 89 90

s/he ___ to ___ ___ in a ___ , and ___
    91   92 93   94   95

to the ___ the ___ of ___ them in ___
      96   97   98   99

___ . For ___ ___ ___ ___ ___ ___
100   101 102 103 104 105

of ___ and of ___ is ___ ___ ___
  106   107   108 109 110

___ to ___ dictation. In ___ ___
111   112   113 114

stenographer ___ be ___ ___ ___
            115   116 117 118

of ___ ___ that ___ most ___
  119 120   121   122

___ ___ in ___ work.
123 124   125

You will now have ten minutes to transfer your answers to the Part C answer sheet.

END OF EXAM

Correct Answers for U.S. Postal Service Clerk-Typist and Clerk-Stenographer Exam

PART A — CLERICAL ABILITY

1. E	16. A	31. D	46. B	61. A	76. C
2. D	17. E	32. E	47. E	62. C	77. E
3. A	18. B	33. A	48. A	63. C	78. E
4. D	19. A	34. A	49. C	64. D	79. C
5. A	20. C	35. A	50. A	65. D	80. B
6. C	21. A	36. B	51. A	66. C	81. E
7. B	22. E	37. E	52. C	67. A	82. C
8. D	23. C	38. C	53. C	68. D	83. E
9. E	24. B	39. D	54. A	69. B	84. C
10. C	25. D	40. A	55. D	70. B	85. B
11. C	26. E	41. A	56. A	71. E	
12. D	27. A	42. C	57. D	72. B	
13. C	28. B	43. C	58. B	73. A	
14. D	29. C	44. E	59. C	74. B	
15. C	30. D	45. D	60. B	75. E	

EXPLANATIONS

1. (E) Ha<u>c</u>hettson; Hac<u>k</u>ett
2. (D) 5923<u>3</u>262; 5923<u>3</u>362
3. (A) <u>M</u>YP; <u>N</u>YP
4. (D) Olivi<u>a</u> H.; Oliv<u>ier</u> E.; <u>R</u>. Olivia
5. (A) 00<u>1</u>0; 00<u>1</u>2
6. (C) 6<u>001</u>; 6<u>100</u>; 6<u>101</u>
7. (B) Va<u>nov</u>er; Va<u>n</u>story; Va<u>nS</u>winderen
8. (D) Fitz<u>G</u>ibbon; Fitz<u>s</u>immons; Fitz<u>S</u>imons
9. (E) 01<u>016</u>060; 01<u>066</u>010
10. (C) A<u>AS</u>; A<u>AZ</u>; A<u>SA</u>
11. (C) Paw<u>e</u>lek; Paw<u>lowicz</u>; Paw<u>lowski</u>
12. (D) 7<u>710</u>; 7<u>834</u>; 7<u>868</u>
13. (C) 3627<u>0000</u>; 3627<u>0013</u>; 3627<u>0030</u>
14. (D) Freed<u>e</u>nberg; Freed<u>e</u>nburg; Freed<u>i</u>nberg
15. (C) Prou<u>tey</u>; Prouty, <u>M</u>artha; Prouty, <u>M</u>yra
16. (A) 580<u>06</u>021; 580<u>06</u>130
17. (E) EKK-14<u>03</u>; EKK-14<u>43</u>
18. (B) <u>Daly</u>; <u>D'Amato</u>; <u>D'Amboise</u>

162 / **Clerical Exams Handbook**

19. **(A)** Sch<u>ae</u>ffer; Sch<u>a</u>ffert		
20. **(C)** P<u>SP</u>; <u>SPP</u>; <u>SPS</u>		
21. **(A)** Drusilla S. Ridgeley	Drusilla S. Ridgeley	Drusilla S. Ridgeley
22. **(E)** Andrei I. Toumantzev	Andrei I. Tou<u>r</u>mantzev	Andrei I. Toumant<u>zov</u>
23. **(C)** 6-78912-e3e42	6-78912-<u>3e</u>3e42	6-78912-e3e42
24. **(B)** 86529 Dunwoodie Drive	86529 Dunwoodie Drive	85<u>6</u>29 Dunwoodie Drive
25. **(D)** 1592<u>514</u>	1592574	1592574
26. **(E)** Ella Burk N<u>ew</u>ham	Ella Burk Newnham	<u>Elena</u> Burk Newnham
27. **(A)** 5416R-1952TZ-op	5416R-1952TZ-op	5416R-1952TZ-op
28. **(B)** 60646 West Touhy Avenue	60646 West Touhy Avenue	60646 West Tou<u>hey</u> Avenue
29. **(C)** Mardikian & Moore, Inc.	Mardikian <u>and</u> Moore, Inc.	Mardikian & Moore, Inc.
30. **(D)** 9670<u>243</u>	9670423	9670423
31. **(D)** Eduardo Ingles_	Eduardo Inglese	Eduardo Inglese
32. **(E)** Roger T. DeAngelis	Roger T. <u>D'</u>Angelis	Roger T. DeAnge<u>le</u>s
33. **(A)** 7692138	7692138	7692138
34. **(A)** 2695 East 3435 South	2695 East 3435 South	2695 East 3435 South
35. **(A)** 63qs5-95YT3-001	63qs5-95YT3-001	63qs5-95YT3-001
36. **(B)** 2789350	2789350	27<u>98</u>350
37. **(E)** Helmut V. Lochner	Helmut V. Lo<u>ck</u>ner	Helmut <u>W.</u> Lochner
38. **(C)** 2454803	2<u>548</u>403	2454803
39. **(D)** Lemberger, <u>WA</u> 28094-9182	Lemberger, VA 28094-9182	Lemberger, VA 28094-9182
40. **(A)** 4168-GNP-78852	4168-GNP-78852	4168-GNP-78852
41. **(A)** Yoshihito Saito	Yoshihito Saito	Yoshihito Saito
42. **(C)** 5927681	592<u>786</u>1	5927681
43. **(C)** O'Reilly Bay, LA 56212	O'Reilly<u>s</u> Bay, LA 56212	O'Reilly Bay, LA 56212
44. **(E)** Francis Ra<u>ns</u>dell	Fran<u>ces</u> Ramsdell	Francis Ramsdell
45. **(D)** 5634-Oot<u>V5</u>a-16867	5634-Ootv5a-16867	5634-Ootv5a-16867
46. **(B)** Dolores Mollicone	Dolores Mollicone	Dolo<u>ras</u> Mollicone
47. **(E)** David C. Routzon	David <u>E.</u> Routzon	David C. Rout<u>z</u>ron
48. **(A)** 8932 Shimabui Hwy.	8932 Shimabui Hwy.	8932 Shimabui Hwy.
49. **(C)** 6177396	6177<u>93</u>6	6177396
50. **(A)** A8987-B73245	A8987-B73245	A8987-B73245
51. **(A)** anticipate		
52. **(C)** similar		
53. **(C)** sufficiently		
54. **(A)** intelligence		

55. (**D**) reference
56. (**A**) conscious
57. (**D**) parallel
58. (**B**) abundance
59. (**C**) corrugated
60. (**B**) accumulation
61. (**A**) resonance
62. (**C**) beneficial
63. (**C**) specifically
64. (**D**) eliminate
65. (**D**) colossal
66. (**C**) auxiliary
67. (**A**) inimitable
68. (**D**) disappearance
69. (**B**) appellate
70. (**B**) essential
71. (**E**) $\begin{array}{r} 83 \\ -56 \\ \hline 27 \end{array}$
72. (**B**) $\begin{array}{r} 15 \\ +17 \\ \hline 32 \end{array}$
73. (**A**) $\begin{array}{r} 32 \\ \times\ 7 \\ \hline 224 \end{array}$
74. (**B**) $\begin{array}{r} 39 \\ \times\ 2 \\ \hline 78 \end{array}$
75. (**E**) $\begin{array}{r} 43 \\ -15 \\ \hline 28 \end{array}$
76. (**C**) $\begin{array}{r} 50 \\ +49 \\ \hline 99 \end{array}$
77. (**E**) $6\overline{)366} = 61$
78. (**E**) $\begin{array}{r} 38 \\ \times\ 3 \\ \hline 114 \end{array}$

164 / Clerical Exams Handbook

79. **(C)**   19
      +21
      ―――
      40

80. **(B)**   13
      −6
      ――
       7

81. **(E)**   30
      6)180

82. **(C)**   10
      ×1
      ――
      10

83. **(E)**   41
      7)287

84. **(C)**   12
      +11
      ――
      23

85. **(B)**   85
      −64
      ――
      21

Part B — Verbal Ability

1. **D**	12. **B**	23. **D**	34. **B**	45. **A**
2. **C**	13. **D**	24. **A**	35. **B**	46. **C**
3. **E**	14. **A**	25. **D**	36. **D**	47. **A**
4. **A**	15. **D**	26. **A**	37. **C**	48. **C**
5. **C**	16. **D**	27. **C**	38. **C**	49. **A**
6. **E**	17. **E**	28. **C**	39. **D**	50. **D**
7. **D**	18. **A**	29. **B**	40. **D**	51. **B**
8. **C**	19. **D**	30. **D**	41. **B**	52. **A**
9. **E**	20. **B**	31. **D**	42. **A**	53. **C**
10. **B**	21. **C**	32. **D**	43. **B**	54. **D**
11. **A**	22. **C**	33. **A**	44. **D**	55. **C**

Explanations

Questions 1–20. If you made any errors in the Following Written Instructions portion, go back and reread those questions more carefully.

21. **(C)** Sentence (C) is the best expression of the idea. Sentence (A) has two grammatical errors: the use of *when* to introduce a definition and the unacceptable verb form *is already having been parked*. Sentence (B) incorrectly shifts subjects from *one* to *you*. Sentence (D) does not make sense.

22. **(C)** Choice (B) is incorrect because only two persons are involved in this statement. *Between* is used when there are only two, *among* is reserved for three or more. (A) makes a similar error. In addition, both (A) and (D) use the pronoun *he*. The object of a preposition, in this case *between*, must be in the objective case, hence *him*.

23. **(D)** Punctuation aside, both (A) and (B) incorrectly place the verb in the plural, *are*. *Neither* is a singular indefinite pronoun. It means *not one and not the other* and requires a singular verb. The choice between (C) and (D) is more difficult, but basically this is a simple statement and not a direct quote.

24. **(A)** *Whoever* is the subject of the phrase *whoever has the best record*. Hence (A) is the correct answer and (D) is wrong. Both (B) and (C) are wordy and awkward.

25. **(D)** All the other choices contain obvious errors.

26. **(A)** Choice (B) uses the plural verb *were* with the singular subject *report*. (C) and (D) are colloquial and incorrect even for informal speech. They have no place in business writing.

27. **(C)** Choices (A) and (B) use adverbs incorrectly; choice (D) is awkward and unidiomatic.

28. **(C)** Choices (B) and (D) are obviously incorrect. In (A), the pronoun *who* should be the subject of the phrase, *who had made careless errors*.

29. **(B)** Only the quoted material should appear enclosed by quotation marks, so (A) is incorrect. Only the first word of a sentence should begin with a capital letter, so both (C) and (D) are wrong. In addition, only the quoted material itself is a question; the entire sentence is a statement. Therefore, the question mark must be placed inside the quotes.

30. **(D)** Choices (A) and (B) imply that he stays in church all day on Christmas and Easter and goes nowhere else. Choice (C) makes the same implication and in addition splits the infinitive awkwardly. In (D) the modifier *only* is correctly placed to tell us that the only times he goes to church are on Christmas and Easter.

31. **(D)** Choice (A) might state either *most* or *all* but not both; choice (B) should read *persons who;* choice (C) should read *with regard to.* . . .

32. **(D)** Choice (A) is incorrect because *both* can refer to only two, but the publisher and authors implies at least three; choice (B) requires the plural verb *were*; choice (C) requires the correlative construction *neither . . . nor*.

33. **(A)** Choices (C) and (D) are glaringly poor. Choice (B) is not incorrect, but choice (A) is far better.

34. **(B)** Choice (A) incorrectly uses a semicolon to separate a complete clause from a sentence fragment. Additionally, (A) incorrectly uses *what* in place of *that*. Choice (C) is a run-on sentence that also misuses an apostrophe: *It's* is the contraction for *it is*, not the possessive of *it*. Choice (D) uses commas indiscriminately; it also misuses the apostrophe.

35. **(B)** In choice (A) the placement of the apostrophe is inappropriate; choices (C) and (D) use the plural, but there is only one company.

36. **(D)** Choices (A) and (C) are incorrect in use of the subject form *I* instead of the object of the preposition *me*. Choice (B) incorrectly uses the reflexive *myself*. Only I can address a letter to myself.

37. **(C)** Choice (A) incorrectly uses the plural verb form *have* with the singular subject *one*. (B) is awkward and wordy. (D) incorrectly changes the subject from *one of us* to *anyone*.

38. **(C)** (A) is wordy. In (B), the correct verb should be *have* in place of *leave*. In (D), the word *arose* should be *arisen*.

39. **(D)** The first three sentences lack parallel construction. All the words that modify *paper* must appear in the same form.

40. **(D)** The phrase, *together with* . . . , is extra information and not a part of the subject; therefore, both (A) and (B) represent similar errors of agreement. Choice (C) also presents disagreement in number between subject and verb, but in this case the compound subject, indicated by the use of the conjunction, *and,* requires a plural verb.

41. **(B)** Even if you do not recognize the root *manu* meaning *hand* and relating directly to *handbook,* you should have no trouble getting this question right. If you substitute each of the choices in the sentence, you will readily see that only one makes sense.

42. **(A)** Within the context of the sentence, the thought of a specified punishment for use, interpretation, or an edition of the rules does not make too much sense. *Fraction* gives a hint of *part*, but you must also contend with the negative prefix *in*. Since it is reasonable to expect punishment for negative behavior with relation to the rules, *violation,* which is the meaning of INFRACTION, is the proper answer.

43. **(B)** The prefix should help you narrow your choices. The prefix *re* meaning *back* or *again* narrows the choices to (A) or (B). To RESCIND is to *take back* or to *cancel*.

44. **(D)** First eliminate (C) since it does not make sense in the sentence. Your experience with the word *summons* may be with relation to *tickets* and *fines,* but tickets and fines have nothing to do with asking questions while taking a test. Even if you are unfamiliar with the word SUMMON, you should be able to choose *call* as the best synonym in this context.

45. **(A)** REPRISAL means injury done for injury received or *retaliation*.

46. **(C)** To REDUCE is to *make smaller* or to *lessen*.

47. **(A)** To IMPAIR is to *make worse,* to *injure,* or to *weaken*.

48. **(C)** FITTING in this context means *suitable* or *appropriate*.

49. **(A)** The survey showed that of all subjects typing has helped most in business. It was also considered valuable by college students in their schoolwork.

50. **(D)** See the second sentence.

51. **(B)** According to the paragraph, the government can spend only what it obtains from the people. The government obtains money from the people by taxation. If the people are unwilling to pay taxes, the government has no source of funds.

52. **(A)** Step one in the job application process is often the application letter. If the letter is not effective, the applicant will not move on to the next step and job prospects will be greatly lessened.

53. **(C)** The second sentence states that direct lighting causes glare on the working surface.

54. **(D)** While all the answer choices are likely to be true, the answer suggested by the paragraph is that "white collar" workers work with their pencils and their minds rather than with their hands and machines.

55. **(C)** All the paragraph says is that office manuals are a necessity in large organizations.

U.S. Postal Service Clerk-Typist and Clerk-Stenographer Exam / 167

PART C — STENOGRAPHY

1. B	26. C	51. C	76. B	101. A
2. B	27. A	52. A	77. C	102. E
3. D	28. C	53. B	78. C	103. B
4. E	29. E	54. E	79. D	104. D
5. C	30. B	55. D	80. E	105. C
6. A	31. D	56. C	81. B	106. E
7. D	32. E	57. E	82. A	107. C
8. B	33. C	58. B	83. D	108. A
9. C	34. E	59. D	84. A	109. B
10. E	35. B	60. D	85. E	110. E
11. A	36. A	61. A	86. B	111. B
12. D	37. C	62. E	87. A	112. D
13. E	38. C	63. C	88. E	113. A
14. C	39. E	64. E	89. D	114. E
15. C	40. B	65. D	90. A	115. B
16. B	41. D	66. B	91. A	116. A
17. C	42. A	67. E	92. B	117. D
18. A	43. E	68. C	93. C	118. E
19. A	44. A	69. D	94. D	119. C
20. E	45. B	70. B	95. B	120. D
21. E	46. C	71. C	96. E	121. D
22. E	47. C	72. D	97. D	122. C
23. C	48. D	73. A	98. C	123. B
24. C	49. B	74. E	99. C	124. C
25. D	50. E	75. C	100. A	125. A

CORRECTLY FILLED TRANSCRIPT

In <u>B</u> years <u>B</u> <u>D</u> a great <u>E</u> in the <u>C</u> for
    1   2 3   4   5

<u>A</u> <u>D</u>, not <u>B</u> in <u>C</u> <u>E</u> but <u>A</u> in <u>D</u> <u>E</u>
6 7   8   9 10   11   12 13

agencies, both <u>C</u> and <u>C</u>. The high <u>B</u> and
               14   15   16

<u>C</u> schools in <u>A</u> <u>A</u> of the <u>E</u> have <u>E</u>
17   18 19   20   21

<u>E</u> this <u>C</u> by <u>C</u> complete <u>D</u> courses. The
22   23   24   25

<u>C</u> <u>A</u> <u>C</u> of <u>E</u> who are <u>B</u> in these <u>D</u>
26 27 28   29   30   31

shows <u>E</u> <u>C</u> have <u>E</u> <u>B</u> of the <u>A</u> <u>C</u>
      32 33   34 35   36 37

for stenographers. <u>A</u> <u>C</u> <u>E</u> to <u>B</u> <u>D</u> in
                38 39   40 41

<u>A</u> <u>E</u> must <u>A</u> to take <u>B</u> and to <u>C</u> the
42 43   44   45   46

<u>C</u> with <u>D</u> <u>B</u> and <u>E</u>.
47   48 49   50

168 / Clerical Exams Handbook

The C of A at B dictation is E in
    51   52   53   54
D C is E B than D of D A . Thus,
55 56 57 58   59   60 61
one E had a C E in shorthand D B
    62   63 64   65 66
little E in C D B . Skill in C D A
     67   68 69 70   71 72 73
E C is of B C if the C cannot D
74 75   76 77   78   79
E the B in A D .
80   81   82 83
  A A E B a A E D A s/he A
    84 85 86 87 88 89 90   91
to B C in a D , and B to the E the
  92 93   94   95   96
D of C them in C A . For A E
97   98   99 100   101 102
B D C of E and of C is A
103 104 105 106   107 108
B E B to D dictation. In A ,
109 110 111 112   113
E stenographer B be A D E of
114   115   116 117 118
C D that D most C B C in
119 120   121   122 123 124
A work.
125

Arco's *Practice for Clerical, Typing, and Stenographic Tests* offers techniques, strategies, and tips for taking dictation and answering stenography questions, along with lots of practice.

SCORE SHEET

Your score on Part A and Part B of the examination for Clerk-Typist and Clerk-Stenographer is based only on the number of correct answers. Wrong answers have no effect on the score. Part A and Part B are timed and administered as two separate units, but they are not scored separately. There is no Clerical Ability score and no Verbal Ability score; there is only a single Exam 710 score.

To determine your raw score on this exam, count up all of your correct answers on the full exam.

$$\frac{\text{Number Right}}{\rule{2cm}{0.4pt}} = \frac{\text{Raw Score}}{\rule{2cm}{0.4pt}}$$

Since there is only a single Exam 710 score, your performance on any single question type does not matter. In order to earn a high score, however, you must do well on all parts of the exam. Enter your scores below to chart your performance on each question type. Then concentrate your efforts toward improvement in the areas with which you had the most difficulty.

PART A

Sequencing, Questions 1-20. Number right _____ out of 20.
Comparisons, Questions 21-50. Number right _____ out of 30.
Spelling, Questions 51-70. Number right _____ out of 20.
Computations, Questions 71-85. Number right _____ out of 15.

PART B

Following Written Instructions, Questions 1-20. Number right _____ out of 20.
Grammar/Punctuation, Questions 21-40. Number right _____ out of 20.
Vocabulary/Reading Comprehension, Questions 41-55. Number right _____ out of 15.

Now use the self evaluation chart below to see where your total score falls on a scale from Poor to Excellent.

SELF EVALUATION CHART

	Excellent	Good	Average	Fair	Poor
Exam 710	125-140	109-124	91-108	61-90	0-6

PART C

Your score on Part C, the stenography test, is based on your number of correct answers minus one fourth of your wrong answers. To determine your score, divide the number of answers you got wrong by 4 and subtract that number from the number of answers you got right.

Number Right   −   Number Wrong ÷ 4   =   Raw Score

_____   −   _____   =   _____

Evaluate your performance on the stenography test by darkening the space in which your raw score falls in the chart below.

SELF EVALUATION CHART

Part C	Excellent	Good	Average	Fair	Poor
Stenography	111-125	96-110	81-95	51-80	0-50

THE TYPING TEST

A mastery of good typing skills is a basic prerequisite for all three postal positions that require typing: clerk-typist, clerk-stenographer, and mark-up clerk (automated). A high score on the written exam is not enough. While the score on the written exam determines your position on the list, your name cannot find its way onto the list at all unless you first demonstrate that your typing proficiency satisfies the speed and accuracy requirements mandated for the work position involved.

Assuming that you already know how to type, the best preparation for the Clerk-Typist and Clerk-Stenographer Typing Test, or indeed for any typing test, is typing. You may choose any material at all and practice copying it line for line, exactly as you see it. As on the actual typing test, spell, capitalize, punctuate, and begin and end lines exactly as they appear on the page being copied. The actual basic speed required on typing tests varies from 35 wpm to 50 wpm depending on the job itself. Once the minimum speed is met, accuracy counts even more than speed. Try to balance yourself so as to meet speed requirements while maintaining a very high level of accuracy.

If you are taking a typing exam in hopes of becoming a clerk-typist or clerk-stenographer with the U.S. Postal Service, you will take your test on a computer. If your typing test is being administered by a federal, state, county, or municipal entity or by a private employer, it may be administered on a computer or on a standard typewriter. Sometimes you are given the option of using a manual or electronic typewriter; you may even be permitted to bring your own typewriter if you wish. If you feel especially comfortable with your own typewriter and if it is easily portable, ask about this possibility. If you are taking your typing test on a typewriter that is being supplied, you will get a chance to turn the typewriter on and off and to check the preset margins and tabs to be sure they are accurate. You should not need to make any adjustments on a typewriter that is supplied.

The proctor will then distribute a practice exercise. For a postal position, the practice exercise should look very familiar. It is exactly the same exercise that appears on the sample question sheet that came with the yellow card telling you of your testing appointment. You should have already had lots of practice typing that paragraph. At any rate, in any typing test situation, the proctor will give you five minutes to practice copying a paragraph. This is a chance to limber up your fingers and to gain familiarity with the testing keyboard. This practice exercise will **not** count. If you have been practicing on a standard typewriter, the proctor will collect the papers and throw them into the wastebasket.

The following is a typical test exercise, though NOT the actual test exercise that you will be given. Follow instructions exactly, and practice, practice, practice. Words-per-minute points are marked on the test exercise for your guidance. Try to keep your typing error-free; if you make errors, try to increase your speed. Use an accurate signal timer or have a friend or relative time you.

Space, paragraph, spell, punctuate, capitalize, and begin and end each line precisely as shown in the exercise.

You will have exactly five minutes in which to make repeated copies of the test exercise itself on the paper that will be given to you. Each time you complete the exercise, simply double-space once and begin again. If you fill up one side of the paper, turn it over and continue typing on the other side. Keep on typing until told to stop.

Keep in mind that you must meet minimum standards in both speed and accuracy and that, above these standards, accuracy is twice as important as speed.

Test Exercise

	1st typing of exercise	2d typing of exercise
Because they have often learned to know types of archi-	___	52 wpm
tecture by decoration, casual observers sometimes fail to	___	54
realize that the significant part of a structure is not the	___	56
ornamentation but the body itself. Architecture, because	___	59
of its close contact with human lives, is peculiarly and	___	61
intimately governed by climate. For instance, a home built	___	64
for comfort in the cold and snow of the northern areas of	___	66
this country would be unbearably warm in a country with	___	68
weather such as that of Cuba. A Cuban house, with its open	___	71
court, would prove impossible to heat in a northern winter.	___	73
Since the purpose of architecture is the construction of	___	76
shelters in which human beings may carry on their numerous	___	78
activities, the designer must consider not only climatic con-	___	80
ditions, but also the function of a building. Thus, although	___	___
the climate of a certain locality requires that an auditorium	___	___
and a hospital have several features in common, the purposes	___	___
for which they will be used demand some difference in struc-	40 wpm	
ture. For centuries builders have first complied with these	42	
two requirements and later added whatever ornamentation they	44	___
wished. Logically, we should see as mere additions, not as	47	___
basic parts, the details by which we identify architecture.	49	___

EACH TIME YOU REACH THIS POINT, DOUBLE-SPACE ONCE AND BEGIN AGAIN.

The typing test for mark-up clerk applicants is quite different. You will take this test by private appointment, and all interaction will be between you and a personal computer. Do not be frightened. Even if you have had no experience whatsoever with computers, this is not an intimidating test. The computer is user-friendly and is very specific in spelling out directions. And, unless you are a typing whiz, the typing test itself is probably easier than the plain-paper copying test.

As the exam begins, the computer screen explains to you which buttons you will be using and what each does. You need to use very few buttons—letters, numbers, "return," "delete," and "lock caps." You will get a chance to use these and to become familiar with their operation as you fill in basic name and Social Security number types of information. A test administrator remains in the room to answer questions.

The computer then explains the typing task of the exam itself. A letter-number code appears on the upper right screen; you are to copy it. Then press the return button to bring the next code to the screen. That's it. The codes all consist of four letters and three numbers, such as TYH0346 or BZIP801. The faster you type, the more codes you have an opportunity to copy. In the explanation phase of the exam, you will have 15 seconds in which to copy five codes. The computer will tell you how many you copied correctly.

After the explanation phase comes a practice session. You will be allowed five minutes to correctly copy as many codes as you can, again one at a time. The five-minute practice session does not count. This is your chance to experiment with looking at your fingers or at the screen; with memorizing each code to be typed or with staring at the code while typing; with typing as fast as you can, not even looking at the screen to see if you are typing correctly; or with checking to make sure you are copying correctly and repairing errors before continuing.

The computer-administered alpha-numeric typing test differs from the plain-copy typing test in one very significant way. An error which has been corrected is not counted as an error. Since accuracy is so important and since correction is so easy on the computer, it is worthwhile to correct errors. Unless you are extremely inaccurate, you will not lose much time correcting errors and will gain valuable points through accuracy.

Here is a suggested approach:

1. Look at the code and quickly memorize it; four letters and three numbers should pose no problem for such a short-term task.

2. Type in the code, looking at the center of the screen where the letters and numbers that you are typing appear.

3. Delete and retype if you spot an error.

4. Hit the return button and repeat this process.

The five-minute practice period should allow you to establish a rhythm for this process. When the five minutes are up, your score will flash on the screen. A score of 14 is required for passing. If you have scored 14 or higher, approach the actual test with confidence. If your score is lower than 14, be reassured that it will not be counted. Remember that you used the first few minutes of the practice period to perfect your system. You now have five minutes to use the system with which you have become comfortable. Your second score, the score that does count, will likely be higher.

The actual test session is exactly like the practice session, but with different codes, of course. At the end of the five-minute test, your final score will appear on the screen. You will know instantly whether you have passed or failed; whether you are eligible or ineligible. If you are eligible, you can expect to be called for an employment interview sometime in the near future.

Since the computer typing test is so different from the plain-paper typing test, it requires preparation of a different kind. If you have access to a computer on which to practice, that is ideal. Program an exam like the one just described if you know how. If not, make a list of codes to be copied, leaving lots of space between codes so that you don't have to expend energy keeping your place, and copy codes into the computer. If you must practice on a typewriter, correction is more difficult, but the practice will be useful anyway. The important thing is to let your fingers get used to hitting the correct letters and numbers in rapid succession.

The practice exercise that follows provides a sample of the Mark-up Clerk typing test. You can use it as a model to prepare more exercises for your own use.

Practice Exercise

RJKF566	BVEI155	GKZP876
YTMN068	FUQS478	EDBJ582
FULD727	JMGE610	OLDE751
TTHU950	SQWP010	LEAP274
NORT707	BDEY851	PHYX593
FLIO015	CZDT874	BLDV592
OYJX055	FTTD123	KHTP805
GYKN094	RHVZ417	IFWK173
WEST301	TGIF629	YCWI142
DRHK967	PDQD157	OLZT809
AVNB893	EAST383	VMHW649
RKBY775	GSAP013	HTCQ858
LGBU919	UQFP180	JFTA862

Answer Sheet for Senior Office Typist Exam (Court System)

TEAR HERE

1. Ⓐ Ⓑ Ⓒ Ⓓ Ⓔ
2. Ⓐ Ⓑ Ⓒ Ⓓ Ⓔ
3. Ⓐ Ⓑ Ⓒ Ⓓ Ⓔ
4. Ⓐ Ⓑ Ⓒ Ⓓ Ⓔ
5. Ⓐ Ⓑ Ⓒ Ⓓ Ⓔ
6. Ⓐ Ⓑ Ⓒ Ⓓ Ⓔ
7. Ⓐ Ⓑ Ⓒ Ⓓ Ⓔ
8. Ⓐ Ⓑ Ⓒ Ⓓ Ⓔ
9. Ⓐ Ⓑ Ⓒ Ⓓ Ⓔ
10. Ⓐ Ⓑ Ⓒ Ⓓ Ⓔ
11. Ⓐ Ⓑ Ⓒ Ⓓ Ⓔ
12. Ⓐ Ⓑ Ⓒ Ⓓ Ⓔ
13. Ⓐ Ⓑ Ⓒ Ⓓ Ⓔ
14. Ⓐ Ⓑ Ⓒ Ⓓ Ⓔ
15. Ⓐ Ⓑ Ⓒ Ⓓ Ⓔ
16. Ⓐ Ⓑ Ⓒ Ⓓ Ⓔ
17. Ⓐ Ⓑ Ⓒ Ⓓ Ⓔ
18. Ⓐ Ⓑ Ⓒ Ⓓ Ⓔ
19. Ⓐ Ⓑ Ⓒ Ⓓ Ⓔ
20. Ⓐ Ⓑ Ⓒ Ⓓ Ⓔ
21. Ⓐ Ⓑ Ⓒ Ⓓ Ⓔ
22. Ⓐ Ⓑ Ⓒ Ⓓ Ⓔ
23. Ⓐ Ⓑ Ⓒ Ⓓ Ⓔ
24. Ⓐ Ⓑ Ⓒ Ⓓ Ⓔ
25. Ⓐ Ⓑ Ⓒ Ⓓ Ⓔ
26. Ⓐ Ⓑ Ⓒ Ⓓ Ⓔ
27. Ⓐ Ⓑ Ⓒ Ⓓ Ⓔ
28. Ⓐ Ⓑ Ⓒ Ⓓ Ⓔ
29. Ⓐ Ⓑ Ⓒ Ⓓ Ⓔ
30. Ⓐ Ⓑ Ⓒ Ⓓ Ⓔ
31. Ⓐ Ⓑ Ⓒ Ⓓ Ⓔ
32. Ⓐ Ⓑ Ⓒ Ⓓ Ⓔ
33. Ⓐ Ⓑ Ⓒ Ⓓ Ⓔ
34. Ⓐ Ⓑ Ⓒ Ⓓ Ⓔ
35. Ⓐ Ⓑ Ⓒ Ⓓ Ⓔ
36. Ⓐ Ⓑ Ⓒ Ⓓ Ⓔ
37. Ⓐ Ⓑ Ⓒ Ⓓ Ⓔ
38. Ⓐ Ⓑ Ⓒ Ⓓ Ⓔ
39. Ⓐ Ⓑ Ⓒ Ⓓ Ⓔ
40. Ⓐ Ⓑ Ⓒ Ⓓ Ⓔ
41. Ⓐ Ⓑ Ⓒ Ⓓ Ⓔ
42. Ⓐ Ⓑ Ⓒ Ⓓ Ⓔ
43. Ⓐ Ⓑ Ⓒ Ⓓ Ⓔ
44. Ⓐ Ⓑ Ⓒ Ⓓ Ⓔ
45. Ⓐ Ⓑ Ⓒ Ⓓ Ⓔ
46. Ⓐ Ⓑ Ⓒ Ⓓ Ⓔ
47. Ⓐ Ⓑ Ⓒ Ⓓ Ⓔ
48. Ⓐ Ⓑ Ⓒ Ⓓ Ⓔ
49. Ⓐ Ⓑ Ⓒ Ⓓ Ⓔ
50. Ⓐ Ⓑ Ⓒ Ⓓ Ⓔ
51. Ⓐ Ⓑ Ⓒ Ⓓ Ⓔ
52. Ⓐ Ⓑ Ⓒ Ⓓ Ⓔ
53. Ⓐ Ⓑ Ⓒ Ⓓ Ⓔ
54. Ⓐ Ⓑ Ⓒ Ⓓ Ⓔ
55. Ⓐ Ⓑ Ⓒ Ⓓ Ⓔ
56. Ⓐ Ⓑ Ⓒ Ⓓ Ⓔ
57. Ⓐ Ⓑ Ⓒ Ⓓ Ⓔ
58. Ⓐ Ⓑ Ⓒ Ⓓ Ⓔ
59. Ⓐ Ⓑ Ⓒ Ⓓ Ⓔ
60. Ⓐ Ⓑ Ⓒ Ⓓ Ⓔ
61. Ⓐ Ⓑ Ⓒ Ⓓ Ⓔ
62. Ⓐ Ⓑ Ⓒ Ⓓ Ⓔ
63. Ⓐ Ⓑ Ⓒ Ⓓ Ⓔ
64. Ⓐ Ⓑ Ⓒ Ⓓ Ⓔ
65. Ⓐ Ⓑ Ⓒ Ⓓ Ⓔ
66. Ⓐ Ⓑ Ⓒ Ⓓ Ⓔ
67. Ⓐ Ⓑ Ⓒ Ⓓ Ⓔ
68. Ⓐ Ⓑ Ⓒ Ⓓ Ⓔ
69. Ⓐ Ⓑ Ⓒ Ⓓ Ⓔ
70. Ⓐ Ⓑ Ⓒ Ⓓ Ⓔ
71. Ⓐ Ⓑ Ⓒ Ⓓ Ⓔ
72. Ⓐ Ⓑ Ⓒ Ⓓ Ⓔ
73. Ⓐ Ⓑ Ⓒ Ⓓ Ⓔ
74. Ⓐ Ⓑ Ⓒ Ⓓ Ⓔ
75. Ⓐ Ⓑ Ⓒ Ⓓ Ⓔ
76. Ⓐ Ⓑ Ⓒ Ⓓ Ⓔ
77. Ⓐ Ⓑ Ⓒ Ⓓ Ⓔ
78. Ⓐ Ⓑ Ⓒ Ⓓ Ⓔ
79. Ⓐ Ⓑ Ⓒ Ⓓ Ⓔ
80. Ⓐ Ⓑ Ⓒ Ⓓ Ⓔ
81. Ⓐ Ⓑ Ⓒ Ⓓ Ⓔ
82. Ⓐ Ⓑ Ⓒ Ⓓ Ⓔ
83. Ⓐ Ⓑ Ⓒ Ⓓ Ⓔ
84. Ⓐ Ⓑ Ⓒ Ⓓ Ⓔ
85. Ⓐ Ⓑ Ⓒ Ⓓ Ⓔ
86. Ⓐ Ⓑ Ⓒ Ⓓ Ⓔ
87. Ⓐ Ⓑ Ⓒ Ⓓ Ⓔ
88. Ⓐ Ⓑ Ⓒ Ⓓ Ⓔ
89. Ⓐ Ⓑ Ⓒ Ⓓ Ⓔ
90. Ⓐ Ⓑ Ⓒ Ⓓ Ⓔ
91. Ⓐ Ⓑ Ⓒ Ⓓ Ⓔ
92. Ⓐ Ⓑ Ⓒ Ⓓ Ⓔ
93. Ⓐ Ⓑ Ⓒ Ⓓ Ⓔ
94. Ⓐ Ⓑ Ⓒ Ⓓ Ⓔ
95. Ⓐ Ⓑ Ⓒ Ⓓ Ⓔ
96. Ⓐ Ⓑ Ⓒ Ⓓ Ⓔ
97. Ⓐ Ⓑ Ⓒ Ⓓ Ⓔ
98. Ⓐ Ⓑ Ⓒ Ⓓ Ⓔ
99. Ⓐ Ⓑ Ⓒ Ⓓ Ⓔ
100. Ⓐ Ⓑ Ⓒ Ⓓ Ⓔ

SENIOR OFFICE TYPIST EXAM (COURT SYSTEM)

3 Hours—95 Questions

Section One: Spelling

Directions: Choose the word that is correctly spelled and mark its letter on your answer sheet.

1. (A) apellate
   (B) appelate
   (C) appeallate
   (D) appellate

2. (A) presumption
   (B) presoumption
   (C) presumsion
   (D) presumptsion

3. (A) litigiant
   (B) litigent
   (C) litigant
   (D) litigint

4. (A) committment
   (B) commitment
   (C) comittment
   (D) comitment

5. (A) affidavid
   (B) afidavis
   (C) affidavit
   (D) afidavit

6. (A) arraign
   (B) arrain
   (C) arreign
   (D) areign

7. (A) cumalative
   (B) cummuletive
   (C) cummalative
   (D) cumulative

8. (A) severance
   (B) severance
   (C) severence
   (D) severants

9. (A) adjurment
   (B) adjuornment
   (C) ajournment
   (D) adjournment

10. (A) comenced
    (B) commentced
    (C) commenced
    (D) commensced

Directions: Each question consists of three sentences with one underlined word. One of the underlined words might be spelled incorrectly. On your answer sheet, mark the letter of the sentence which contains the incorrectly spelled word. If no sentence contains a misspelled word, mark (D).

11. (A) Punishment must be a planned part of a <u>comprehensive</u> program of treating delinquency.
    (B) It is easier to spot inexperienced check <u>forjers</u> than other criminals.
    (C) Even young vandals and <u>hooligans</u> can be reformed if given adequate attention.
    (D) No error.

177

12. (A) The court officer does not have authority to make exceptions.
    (B) Usually the violations are the result of illegal and dangerous driving behavior.
    (C) The safety division is required to investigate if the dispatcher files a complaint.
    (D) No error.

13. (A) Comic books that glorify the criminal have a distinct influence in producing young criminals.
    (B) Some of the people behind bars are innocent people who have been put there by mistake.
    (C) Educational achievment is closely associated with delinquency.
    (D) No error.

14. (A) Disciplinary action is most effective when it is taken promptly.
    (B) Release on "personal recognizance" refers to release without bail.
    (C) Parole violators forfeit their freedom.
    (D) No error.

15. (A) Some responsibilities take precedence over preservation of evidence.
    (B) Objects should not be touched unless there is some compelling reason.
    (C) The detension system works unfairly against people who are single and unemployed.
    (D) No error.

16. (A) Evidence is inmaterial if it does not prove the truth of a fact at issue.
    (B) Without qualms, the offender will lie and manipulate others.
    (C) If spectators become disorderly, the court officer may threaten to cite them for contempt of court.
    (D) No error.

17. (A) Under certain conditions, circumstantial evidence may be admissible.
    (B) Just because evidence is circumstantial does not mean that it is irrelevant.
    (C) An aggressive offender may appear to be very hostile.
    (D) No error.

18. (A) A victim of assault may want to take revenge.
    (B) The result of the trial was put in doubt when the prosecuter produced a surprise witness.
    (C) The court officer must maintain order and decorum in the courtroom.
    (D) No error.

19. (A) A person whose accident record can be explained by a correctable physical defect cannot be called "accident-prone."
    (B) A litigant should not be permitted to invoke the aid of technical rules.
    (C) Refusal to waive immunity automatically terminates employment.
    (D) No error.

20. (A) Court employees may be fired for malfeasance.
    (B) A common tactic used by defense lawyers is embarrassment of the witness.
    (C) The criminal justice system may be called an "adversary system."
    (D) No error.

Section Two: Grammar

Directions: Choose the sentence that is grammatically **incorrect** and mark its letter on your answer sheet.

21. (A) One of us has to reply before tomorrow.
    (B) All employees who had served from 40 to 51 years were retired.
    (C) The personnel office takes care of employment, dismissals, and etc.
    (D) We often come across people with whom we disagree.

22. (A) The jurors have been instructed to deliver a sealed verdict.
    (B) The court may direct the convict to be imprisoned in a county penitentiary instead of a state prison.
    (C) Conveying self-confidence is displaying assurance.
    (D) He devotes as much, if not more, time to his work than the rest of the employees.

23. (A) In comparison with that kind of pen, this kind is more preferable.
    (B) The jurors may go to dinner only with the permission of the judge.
    (C) There was neither any intention to commit a crime nor any injury incurred.
    (D) It is the sociological view that all weight should be given to the history and development of the individual.

24. (A) The supervisor makes the suggestions for improvement, not the employee.
    (B) Violations of traffic laws and illegal and dangerous driving behavior constitutes bad driving.
    (C) Cynics take the position that the criminal is rarely or never reformed.
    (D) The ultimate solution to the housing problem of the hardcore slum does not lie in code enforcement.

25. (A) No crime can occur unless there is a written law forbidding the act or omission in question.
    (B) If one wants to prevent crime, we must deal with the possible criminals before they reach the prison.
    (C) One could reasonably say that the same type of correctional institution is not desirable for the custody of all prisoners.
    (D) When you have completed the report, you may give it to me or directly to the judge.

26. (A) The structure of an organization should be considered in determining the organization's goals.
    (B) Complaints are welcomed because they frequently bring into the open conditions and faults in service that should be corrected.
    (C) The defendant had a very unique alibi, so the judge dismissed the case.
    (D) Court officers must direct witnesses to seats when the latter present themselves in court to testify.

27. (A) The clerk promptly notified the judge of the fire for which he was highly praised.
    (B) There is justice among thieves; the three thieves divided the goods equally among themselves.
    (C) If he had been notified promptly, he might have been here on time.
    (D) Though doubt may exist about the mailability of some matter, the sender is fully liable for law violation if such matter should be nonmailable.

Directions: Choose the sentence that is grammatically **correct** and mark its letter on your answer sheet.

28. (A) In high-visibility crimes, it is apparent to all concerned that they are criminal acts at the time when they are committed.
    (B) Statistics tell us that more people are killed by guns than by any kind of weapon.
    (C) Reliable persons guarantee the facts with regards to the truth of these statements.
    (D) The errors in the typed report were so numerous that they could hardly be overlooked.

29. (A) She suspects that the service is not so satisfactory as it should be.
    (B) The court officer goes to the exhibit table and discovered that Exhibit B is an entirely different document.
    (C) The jurors and alternates comprise a truly diverse group.
    (D) Our aim should be not merely to reform law breakers but striking at the roots of crime.

30. (A) Close examination of traffic accident statistics reveal that traffic accidents are frequently the result of violations of traffic laws.
    (B) If you had planned on employing fewer people than this to do the work, this situation would not have arose.
    (C) As far as good looks and polite manners are concerned, they are both alike.
    (D) If a murder has been committed with a bow and arrow, it is irrelevant to show that the defendant was well acquainted with firearms.

31. (A) An individual engages in criminal behavior if the number of criminal patterns which he or she has acquired exceeds the number of noncriminal patterns.
    (B) Every person must be informed of the reason for their arrest unless arrested in the actual commission of a crime.
    (C) The one of the following motorists to which it would be most desirable to issue a summons is the one which was late for an important business appointment.
    (D) The officer should glance around quickly but with care to determine whether his entering the area will damage any evidence.

32. (A) The typist would of corrected the errors had she realized that the supervisor would see the report.
    (B) If the budget allows, we are likely to reemploy anyone whose training fits them to do the work.
    (C) Since the report lacked the needed information, it was of no value to me.
    (D) There would have been no trouble if the receptionist would have always answered courteously.

33. (A) Due to the age of the defendant, the trial will be heard in Juvenile Court and the record will be sealed.
    (B) Calculate the average amount stolen per incident by dividing the total value by the amount of offenses.
    (C) The combination to the office safe is known only to the chief clerk and myself.
    (D) Hearsay is evidence based on repeating the words told by another and not based on personal observation or knowledge.

34. (A) A court officer needs specific qualifications that are different than those required of police officers.
    (B) Understanding how one's own work contributes to the effort of the entire agency indicates an appreciation for the importance of that job.
    (C) If only one guard was assigned to the jury room, the chances of wrongdoing would be heightened.
    (D) One should not use an improved method for performing a a task until you have obtained approval of the supervisor.

Section Three: Clerical Checking

Directions: For each question, compare the name/address/number listings in all three columns. Then mark:

A if the listings in ALL THREE columns are exactly ALIKE
B if only the listings in COLUMNS 1 and 3 are exactly ALIKE
C if only the listings in COLUMNS 1 and 2 are exactly ALIKE
D if the listings in ALL THREE columns are DIFFERENT

Column 1	Column 2	Column 3
35. John H. Smith 238 N. Monroe Street Phila., PA 19147 176-54-326 5578-98765-33	John H. Smith 238 N. Monroe Street Phila., PA 19147 176-54-326 5578-98765-33	John H. Smith 238 N. Monroe Street Phila., PA 19147 176-54-326 5578-98765-33
36. Evan A. McKinley 2872 Broadway East Amherst, NY 14051 212-883-5184 9803-115-6848	Evan A. McKinley 2872 Broadway East Amherst, NY 14051 212-883-5184 9083-115-6848	Evan A. McKinley 2872 Broadway East Amherst, NV 14051 212-883-5184 9083-115-6848
37. Luigi Antonio Cruz, Jr. 2695 East 3435 South Salt Lake City, UT 84109 801-485-1563, x.233 013-5589734-9	Luigi Antonio Cruz, Jr. 2695 East 3435 South Salt Lake City, UT 84109 801-485-1563, x.233 013-5589734-9	Luigi Antonio Cruz, Jr. 2695 East 3435 South Salt Lake City, UT 84109 801-485-1563, x.233 013-5589734-9
38. Educational Records Inst. P.O. Box 44268a Atlanta, Georgia 30337 18624-40-9128 63qs5-95YT3-001	Educational Records Inst. P.O. Box 44268a Atlanta, Georgia 30337 18624-40-9128 63qs5-95YT3-001	Educational Records Inst. P.O. Box 44286a Atlanta, Georgia 30337 18624-40-9128 63qs5-95YT3-001
39. Sr. Consultant, Labor Rel. Benner Mgmt. Group 86408 W. 3rd Ave. Trowbridge, MA 02178 617-980-1136	Sr. Consultant, Labor Rel. Banner Mgmt. Group 86408 W. 3rd Ave. Trowbridge, MA 02178 617-980-1136	Sr. Consultant, Labor Rel. Benner Mgmt. Group 84608 W. 3rd Ave. Trowbridge, MA 02178 617-980-1136

	Column 1	Column 2	Column 3
40.	Marina Angelika Salvis P.O.B. 11283 Gracie Sta. Newtown, PA 18940-0998 215-382-0628 4168-GNP-78852	Marina Angelika Salvis P.O.B. 11283 Gracie Sta. Newtown, PA 18940-0998 215-382-0628 4168-GNP-78852	Marina Angelika Salvis P.O.B. 11283 Gracie Sta. Newtown, PA 18940-0998 215-382-0628 4168-GNP-78852
41.	Durham Reichard, III 8298 Antigua Terrace Gaithersburg, MD 20879 301-176-9887-8 0-671-843576-X	Durham Reichard, III 8298 Antigua Terrace Gaithersburg, MD 20879 301-176-9887-8 0-671-843576-X	Durham Reichard, III 8298 Antigua Terrace Gaithersberg, MD 20879 301-176-9887-8 0-671-843576-X
42.	L. Chamberlain Smythe Mardikian & Moore, Inc. Cor. Mott Street at Pell San Francisco, Calif. 58312-398401-25	L. Chamberlain Smythe Mardikian and Moore, Inc. Cor. Mott Street at Pell San Francisco, Calif. 58312-398401-25	L. Chamberlain Smythe Mardikian & Moore, Inc. Cor. Mott Street at Pell San Francisco, Calif. 58312-398401-25
43.	Ramona Fleischer-Chris 60646 West Touhy Avenue Sebastopol, CA 95472 707-998-0104 0-06-408632-0	Ramona Fleisher-Chris 60646 West Touhy Avenue Sebastopol, CA 95472 707-998-0104 0-06-408632-0	Ramona Fleischer-Chris 60646 West Touhey Avenue Sebastopol, CA 95472 707-998-0104 0-06-408632-0
44.	George Sebastian Barnes Noble/Encore/Dalton 43216 M Street, NE Washington, DC 20036 202-222-1272	George Sebastian Barnes Noble/Encore/Dalton 43216 M. Street, NE Washington, DC 20036 202-222-1272	George Sebastian Barnes Noble/Encore/Dalton 43216 M Street, NE Washington, DC 20036 202-222-1272
45.	Baldwin Algonquin, III 2503 Bartholemew Way Lemberger, VA 28094-9182 9-1-303-558-8536 683-64-0828	Baldwin Algonquin, III 2503 Bartholemew Way Lemberger, VA 28094-9182 9-1-303-558-8536 683-64-0828	Baldwin Algonquin, III 2503 Bartholomew Way Lemberger, VA 28094-9182 9-1-303-558-8536 683-64-0828
46.	Huang Ho Cheung 612 Gallopade Gallery, E. Seattle, WA 98101-2614 001-206-283-7722 5416R-1952TZ-op	Huang Ho Cheung 612 Gallopade Gallery, E. Seattle, WA 98101-2614 001-206-283-7722 5416R-1952TZ-op	Huang Ho Cheung 612 Gallopade Gallery, E. Seattle, WA 98101-2614 001-206-283-7722 5416R-1952TZ-op
47.	Hilliard H. Hyacinth 86529 Dunwoodie Drive Kanakao, HI 91132 808-880-8080 6-78912-e3e42	Hilliard H. Hyacinth 86529 Dunwoodie Drive Kanakao, HI 91132 808-880-8080 6-78912-3e3e42	Hilliard H. Hyacinth 85629 Dunwoodie Drive Kanakao, HI 91132 808-880-8080 6-78912-e3e42

	Column 1	Column 2	Column 3
48.	Anoko Kawamoto 8932 Shimabui Hwy. O'Reilly Bay, LA 56212 713-864-7253-4984 5634-Ootv5a-16867	Anoko Kawamoto 8932 Shimabui Hwy. O'Reillys Bay, LA 56212 713-864-7253-4984 5634-Ootv5a-16867	Anoko Kawamoto 8932 Shimabui Hwy. O'Reilly Bay, LA 56212 713-864-7253-4984 5634-Ootv5a-16867
49.	Michael Chrzanowski 312 Colonia del Valle 4132 ES, Mexico DF 001-45-67265 A8987-B73245	Michael Chrzanowski 312 Colonia del Valle 4132 ES, Mexico DF 001-45-67265 A8987-B73245	Michael Chrzanowski 312 Colonia del Valle 4132 ES, Mexico D.F. 001-45-67265 A8987-B73245
50.	Leonard Wilson-Wood 6892 Grand Boulevard, W. St. Georges South, DE 302-333-4273 0-122365-3987	Leonard Wilson-Wood 6892 Grand Boulevard, W. St. Georges South, DE 302-333-4273 0-122365-3987	Leonard Wilson-Wood 6892 Grand Boulevard, W. St. Georges South, DE 302-333-4273 0-122365-3987

Section Four: Office Record Keeping

Directions: Study the information given in the tables and combine the information as indicated. Answer the multiple-choice questions in accordance with the information on the tables. You are NOT permitted to use a calculator to arrive at totals.

DAILY LOG OF CASES

Monday				
Judge	*Date Filed*	*Sum at Issue*	*Disposition*	*Award*
Baron	6/5/91	$ 9,500	adjourned	X
Lee	4/2/92	20,000	dismissed	X
Conlon	12/8/90	12,000	settled	X
Ramos	3/31/92	5,500	settled	X
Lee	10/8/91	10,000	dismissed	X
Jones	1/5/92	14,000	found for plaintiff	$15,000
Baron	5/1/93	7,600	adjourned	X

Tuesday				
Judge	*Date Filed*	*Sum at Issue*	*Disposition*	*Award*
Ramos	2/2/92	$ 3,000	found for plaintiff	$ 3,375
Amati	8/6/92	8,000	dismissed	X
Moro	4/8/91	11,500	found for plaintiff	9,000
Jones	11/17/90	12,000	adjourned	X
Conlon	12/4/90	4,500	adjourned	X
Amati	6/12/91	2,000	settled	X

DAILY LOG OF CASES

Wednesday

Judge	Date Filed	Sum at Issue	Disposition	Award
Conlon	1/7/93	$10,000	dismissed	X
Baron	5/3/92	5,000	adjourned	X
Ramos	6/22/91	7,500	found for plaintiff	$ 6,000
Moro	2/15/93	22,000	settled	X
Lee	9/7/92	8,000	settled	X
Conlon	11/30/90	16,000	found for plaintiff	17,250
Amati	7/10/92	10,000	found for plaintiff	10,850

Thursday

Judge	Date Filed	Sum at Issue	Disposition	Award
Jones	5/18/92	$ 7,500	found for plaintiff	$ 6,000
Amati	3/6/91	9,250	settled	X
Conlon	3/31/92	6,000	adjourned	X
Moro	8/28/91	12,000	adjourned	X
Conlon	10/30/90	4,600	found for plaintiff	5,000

Friday

Judge	Date Filed	Sum at Issue	Disposition	Award
Lee	4/12/92	$ 6,000	adjourned	X
Baron	1/28/93	9,500	dismissed	X
Ramos	7/17/92	28,000	found for plaintiff	$20,000
Amati	12/2/91	15,000	settled	X
Lee	2/21/92	8,000	found for plaintiff	8,625
Moro	5/9/91	22,000	settled	X
Baron	8/25/91	11,000	dismissed	X
Jones	11/4/90	5,500	settled	X

DAILY BREAKDOWN OF CASES

	Mon.	Tue.	Wed.	Thurs.	Fri.	Total
Case Status						
Dismissed	2	1	1	0	2	6
Adjourned						
Settled						
Found for Plaintiff						
Total Cases						
Cases Filed by Year	Mon. 1	Tue. 2	Wed. 1	Thurs. 1	Fri. 1	Total 6
1990						
1991						
1992						
1993						
Total Cases						

| SUMMARY OF CASES ||||||
Judge	Dismissed	Adjourned	Settled	Found for Plaintiff	Total
Amati	1		3	1	5
Baron					
Conlon					
Jones					
Lee					
Moro					
Ramos					

51. The judge scheduled to hear the greatest number of cases in this week was

    (A) Amati
    (B) Lee
    (C) Conlon
    (D) Ramos

52. The judge who determined no cash awards in this week was

    (A) Moro
    (B) Jones
    (C) Baron
    (D) Lee

53. How many judges were assigned to hear more than one case in one day?

    (A) 1
    (B) 2
    (C) 3
    (D) 4

54. In how many cases was the sum finally awarded lower than the sum at issue?

    (A) 2
    (B) 3
    (C) 4
    (D) 5

55. How many of the cases filed in 1990 were dismissed?

    (A) 0
    (B) 1
    (C) 2
    (D) 3

56. Of the cases adjourned, the greatest number were filed in

    (A) 1990
    (B) 1991
    (C) 1992
    (D) 1993

57. Which two judges were scheduled to sit on only three days?

    (A) Jones and Baron
    (B) Baron and Lee
    (C) Lee and Moro
    (D) Ramos and Jones

186 / Clerical Exams Handbook

58. In which month was the greatest number of cases filed?

(A) February
(B) May
(C) August
(D) November

59. The total amount of money awarded on Wednesday was

(A) $33,500
(B) $34,100
(C) $35,300
(D) $45,000

60. The total amount of money awarded by Jones was

(A) $39,000
(B) $21,500
(C) $21,000
(D) $17,500

61. The amount at issue in the cases that were adjourned on Thursday was

(A) $12,100
(B) $18,000
(C) $21,350
(D) $29,250

62. When the amount of an award is greater than the sum at issue, the higher award represents an additional sum meant to cover plaintiff's costs in the suit. The total amount awarded this week to cover costs was

(A) $ 4,500
(B) $ 4,850
(C) $ 9,000
(D) $13,500

63. If all the plaintiffs who filed cases in 1993 were awarded exactly the sums for which they sued, they would have received a total of

(A) $41,500
(B) $45,100
(C) $48,600
(D) $49,100

64. The total amount awarded to plaintiffs who filed their cases in 1990 was

(A) $ 1,650
(B) $20,600
(C) $22,250
(D) $22,650

65. Comparing cases filed in 1991 with cases filed in 1992,

(A) four more of the 1991 cases were settled than 1992 cases
(B) two fewer 1992 cases were settled than 1991 cases
(C) an equal number of cases was settled from the two years
(D) three more of the 1991 cases were settled than 1992 cases

Section Five: Reading, Understanding, & Interpreting Written Material

Directions: Each passage below contains 15 numbered blanks. Read the passage once quickly to get the overall idea. Below each passage are listed sets of words numbered to match the blanks. Read the passage through a second time, more slowly, and choose the word from each set which makes the most sense both in the sentence and the total paragraph. Mark the letter of that word on your answer sheet.

A large proportion of people __66__ bars are __67__ convicted criminals, __68__ people who have been arrested and are being __69__ until __70__ trial in __71__. Experts have often pointed out that this __72__ system does not operate fairly. For instance, a person who can afford to pay bail usually will not get locked up. The theory of the bail system is that the person will make sure to show up in court when he or she is supposed to; __73__, bail will be forfeited—the person will __74__ the __75__ that was put up. Sometimes a person __76__ can show that he or she is a stable __77__ with a job and a family will be released on "personal recognizance" (without bail). The result is that the well-to-do, the __78__, and the family men can often __79__ the detention system. The people who do wind up in detention tend to __80__ the poor, the unemployed, the single, and the young.

66. (A) under
    (B) at
    (C) tending
    (D) behind

67. (A) always
    (B) not
    (C) hardened
    (D) very

68. (A) but
    (B) and
    (C) also
    (D) although

69. (A) hanged
    (B) freed
    (C) held
    (D) judged

70. (A) your
    (B) his
    (C) daily
    (D) their

71. (A) jail
    (B) court
    (C) fire
    (D) judgment

72. (A) school
    (B) court
    (C) detention
    (D) election

73. (A) otherwise
    (B) therefore
    (C) because
    (D) then

74. (A) save
    (B) spend
    (C) lose
    (D) count

75. (A) wall
    (B) money
    (C) front
    (D) pretense

76. (A) whom
    (B) which
    (C) what
    (D) who

77. (A) citizen
    (B) horse
    (C) cleaner
    (D) clown

78. (A) handsome
    (B) athletic
    (C) employed
    (D) alcoholic

79. (A) survive
    (B) avoid
    (C) provide
    (D) institute

80. (A) become
    (B) help
    (C) be
    (D) harm

___81___ acts are classified according to ___82___ standards. One is whether the ___83___ is major or minor. A major offense, such as murder, would be ___84___ a felony, ___85___ a minor offense, such as reckless driving, would be considered a misdemeanor. ___86___ standard of classification is the specific kind of crime committed. Examples are burglary and robbery, which are ___87___ often used incorrectly by individuals who are ___88___ aware of the actual ___89___ as defined by law. A person who breaks ___90___ a building to commit a ___91___ or other major crime is ___92___ of burglary, while robbery is the felonious taking of an individual's ___93___ from his person or ___94___ his immediate ___95___ by the use of violence or threat.

81. (A) People's
    (B) Criminal
    (C) Felonious
    (D) Numerous

82. (A) decent
    (B) published
    (C) community
    (D) several

83. (A) crime
    (B) act
    (C) offender
    (D) standard

84. (A) labeled
    (B) convicted
    (C) executed
    (D) tried

85. (A) moreover
    (B) because
    (C) whereas
    (D) hence

86. (A) Gold
    (B) Juried
    (C) Another
    (D) My

87. (A) crimes
    (B) terms
    (C) verdicts
    (D) sentences

88. (A) sometimes
    (B) very
    (C) not
    (D) angrily

89. (A) difference
    (B) definitions
    (C) crimes
    (D) victims

90. (A) down
    (B) into
    (C) apart
    (D) from

91. (A) felony
    (B) burglary
    (C) robbery
    (D) theft

92. (A) accused
    (B) convicted
    (C) freed
    (D) guilty

93. (A) life
    (B) liberty
    (C) property
    (D) weapon

94. (A) throughout
    (B) in
    (C) by
    (D) for

95. (A) lifetime
    (B) home
    (C) presence
    (D) concern

190 / Clerical Exams Handbook

Correct Answers for Senior Office Typist Exam

1. D	21. C	41. C	61. B	81. B
2. A	22. D	42. B	62. A	82. D
3. C	23. A	43. D	63. D	83. A
4. B	24. B	44. B	64. C	84. A
5. C	25. B	45. C	65. B	85. C
6. A	26. C	46. A	66. D	86. C
7. D	27. A	47. D	67. B	87. B
8. B	28. D	48. B	68. A	88. C
9. D	29. C	49. C	69. C	89. A
10. C	30. D	50. A	70. D	90. B
11. B	31. A	51. C	71. B	91. D
12. D	32. C	52. C	72. C	92. D
13. C	33. D	53. D	73. A	93. C
14. D	34. B	54. C	74. C	94. B
15. C	35. B	55. A	75. B	95. C
16. A	36. D	56. C	76. D	
17. D	37. A	57. B	77. A	
18. B	38. C	58. B	78. C	
19. A	39. D	59. B	79. B	
20. D	40. A	60. C	80. C	

EXPLANATIONS

1. **(D)** appellate

2. **(A)** presumption

3. **(C)** litigant

4. **(B)** commitment

5. **(C)** affidavit

6. **(A)** arraign

7. **(D)** cumulative

8. **(B)** severance

9. **(D)** adjournment

10. **(C)** commenced

11. **(B)** forgers

12. **(D)** no error

13. **(C)** achievement

14. **(D)** no error

15. **(C)** detention

16. **(A)** immaterial

17. **(D)** no error

18. **(B)** prosecutor

19. **(A)** correctible

20. **(D)** no error

21. **(C)** There should be no "and" before the "etc." at the end of a series of words.

22. **(D)** This is an incomplete comparison. It should read: "He devotes as much *as*, if not more, time to his work than the rest of the employees."

23. **(A)** "More preferable" is a redundancy. "Preferable" alone is quite adequate.

24. **(B)** The compound subject requires the plural form of the verb—constitute.

25. **(B)** This sentence shifts point of view midstream. It could read either "If one wants to prevent crime, one must deal…" or "If we want to prevent crime, we must deal…"

26. **(C)** "Unique" means that there is only one; therefore the word can take no qualifier.

27. **(A)** This is an ambiguous statement. Was the judge praised for the fire? Was the clerk praised for the fire? It would be better to say, "The clerk was highly praised for promptly notifying the judge of the fire."

28. **(D)** is correct. (A) reads as if all concerned are criminal acts. Since guns are a kind of weapon, (B) would have to read, "…than any *other* kind of weapon." In (C), "regards" is the wrong word. The word required is "regard."

29. **(C)** is correct. In (A) the idiomatic form is "*as* satisfactory." (B) confuses two tenses in the same sentence. It would be correct to say the the court officer *went* and discovered. (D) requires a parallel construction, either "reforming and striking" or "to reform and to strike."

30. **(D)** is correct. In (A) "examination" being singular requires the singular verb, "reveals." In (B) we need "would not have *arisen*." As for (C), the word "alike" obviously includes "both," so the word "both" is redundant.

31. **(A)** is correct. In (B) every person is singular and therefore must be informed for the reason for *his* (or *her*) arrest. In (C), a motorist is a person, not a thing, so use *who* and *to whom* rather than *which*. In (D) we need the parallelism of "quickly but carefully."

32. **(C)** is correct. In (A) we need the auxiliary verb have in place of the incorrect of. In (B) "anyone" is singular so the referrent pronoun must also be singular. In (D), the construction is awkward. "...if the receptionist had always answered..." is sufficient and accurate.

33. **(D)** is correct. (A) is incorrect because it is poor form to begin a sentence with "due to." In (B) what is meant is the *number* of offenses. In (C) we need a simple objective case pronoun, "...is known only to the chief clerk and *me*."

34. **(B)** is correct. In (A) the correct idiomatic form is "different *from*." (C) requires a subjunctive form because the statement is contrary to fact. "If only one guard *were* . . . ." (D) shifts point of view. For consistency the pronoun throughout may be either "one" or "you."

35. **(B)** In Column 2, Phila, PA 19147 differs from Phila., PA 19147.

36. **(D)** In Column 3, East Amherst, NV 14051 differs from East Amherst, NY 14051. In Column 2, 9083-115-6848 differs from 9803-115-6848.

37. **(A)** All columns are alike.

38. **(C)** In Column 3, P.O. Box 44286a differs from P.O. Box 44268a.

39. **(D)** In Column 2, Banner differs from Benner. In Column 3, 84608 differs from 86408.

40. **(A)** All columns are alike.

41. **(C)** In Column 3, Gaithersberg differs from Gaithersburg.

42. **(B)** In Column 2, the word *and* is spelled out; in Column 1, the same effect is gained with &.

43. **(D)** In Column 2, Fleisher differs from Fleischer. In Column 3, Touhey differs from Touhy.

44. **(B)** In Column 2, 43216 M. Street, NE differs from 43216 M Street, NE.

45. **(C)** In Column 3, Bartholomew differs from Bartholemew.

46. **(A)** All columns are alike.

47. **(D)** In Column 3, 85629 Dunwoodie Drive differs from 86529 Dunwoodie Drive. In Column 2, 6-78912-3e3e42 differs from 6-78912-e3e42.

48. **(B)** In Column 2, O'Reillys Bay differs from O'Reilly Bay.

49. **(C)** In Column 3, Mexico D.F. differs from Mexico DF.

50. **(A)** All columns are alike.

51. **(C)** Conlon was scheduled to hear six cases, Amati and Lee were scheduled for five apiece, and Ramos was scheduled for four.

52. **(C)** Of the cases Baron was scheduled to hear, three were adjourned and two were dismissed. Jones gave cash awards in two cases, and Moro and Lee gave cash awards in one each.

53. **(D)** Lee and Baron were both scheduled for two trials on Monday and Friday, Amati was scheduled for two on Tuesday, and Conlon was scheduled for two on Wednesday and Thursday.

54. **(C)** On Tuesday, Moro awarded $9,000 in a suit for $11,500; on Wednesday, Ramos awarded $6,000 in a suit for $7,500; on Thursday, Jones awarded $6,000 in a suit for $7,500; and on Friday, Ramos awarded $20,000 in a suit for $28,000.

55. **(A)** Of the six cases filed in 1990, two were settled, two were adjourned, and two were adjudicated. None was dismissed.

56. **(C)** Three of the 1992 cases were adjourned, one 1993 case was adjourned, and two each of 1990 and 1991 cases were adjourned.

57. **(B)** Lee and Baron each sat on Monday, Wednesday, and Friday. Jones sat on Monday, Tuesday, Thursday, and Friday. Moro sat on Tuesday, Wednesday, Thursday, and Friday. Ramos sat on Monday, Tuesday, Wednesday, and Friday.

58. **(B)** Four cases were filed in May. Three cases were filed in each of February, August, and November.

59. **(B)** $6,000 + $17,250 + $10,850 = $34,100

60. **(C)** $15,000 + $6,000 = $21,000

61. **(B)** $6,000 + $12,000 = $18,000

62. **(A)**

$15,000 − $14,000 =	$1,000	(Jones on Monday)
$3,375 − $3,000 =	$375	(Ramos on Tuesday)
$17,250 − $16,000 =	$1,250	(Conlon on Wednesday)
$10,850 − $10,000 =	$850	(Amati on Wednesday)
$5,000 − $4,600 =	$400	(Conlon on Thursday)
$8,625 − $8,000 =	$625	(Lee on Friday)
	$4,500	

63. **(D)**

5/1/93	$ 7,600
1/7/93	10,000
2/15/93	22,000
+1/28/93	9,500
	$49,100

64. **(C)** On Wednesday, Conlon awarded $17,250 in a 11/30/90 case.
    On Thursday, Conlon awarded 5,000 in a 10/30/90 case.
    $22,250

194 / Clerical Exams Handbook

65. **(B)** Four 1991 cases were settled; only two 1992 cases were settled.

66 through 80 completed paragraph:

A large proportion of people <u>behind</u> bars are <u>not</u> convicted criminals, <u>but</u> people who
                                            66   67   68
have been arrested and are being <u>held</u> until <u>their</u> trial in <u>court</u>. Experts have often pointed
                             69   70   71
out that this <u>detention</u> system does not operate fairly. For instance, a person who can afford
              72
to pay bail usually will not get locked up. The theory of the bail system is that the person will make sure to show up in court when he or she is supposed to; <u>otherwise</u>, bail will be
                                                                                       73
forfeited—the person will <u>lose</u> the <u>money</u> that was put up. Sometimes a person <u>who</u> can
                             74   75   76
show that he or she is a stable <u>citizen</u> with a job and a family will be released on "personal
                                77
recognizance" (without bail). The result is that the well-to-do, the <u>employed</u>, and the family
                                                                                                   78
men can often <u>avoid</u> the detention system. The people who do wind up in detention tend
                 79
to <u>be</u> the poor, the unemployed, the single, and the young.
   80

81 through 95 completed paragraph:

<u>Criminal</u> acts are classified according to <u>several</u> standards. One is whether the <u>crime</u> is
 81   82   83
major or minor. A major offense, such as murder, would be <u>labeled</u> a felony, <u>whereas</u> a
                                                                                    84   85
minor offense, such as reckless driving, would be considered a misdemeanor. <u>Another</u>
                                                                                                                      86
standard of classification is the specific kind of crime committed. Examples are burglary and robbery, which are <u>terms</u> often used incorrectly by individuals who are <u>not</u> aware of
                                     87   88
the actual <u>difference</u> as defined by law. A person who breaks <u>into</u> a building to commit a
              89   90
<u>theft</u> or other major crime is <u>guilty</u> of burglary, while robbery is the felonious taking of an
 91   92
individual's <u>property</u> from his person or <u>in</u> his immediate <u>presence</u> by the use of violence
             93   94   95
or threat.

Answer Sheet for Municipal Office Aide Exam

1. Ⓐ Ⓑ Ⓒ Ⓓ	21. Ⓐ Ⓑ Ⓒ Ⓓ	41. Ⓐ Ⓑ Ⓒ Ⓓ	61. Ⓐ Ⓑ Ⓒ Ⓓ
2. Ⓐ Ⓑ Ⓒ Ⓓ	22. Ⓐ Ⓑ Ⓒ Ⓓ	42. Ⓐ Ⓑ Ⓒ Ⓓ	62. Ⓐ Ⓑ Ⓒ Ⓓ
3. Ⓐ Ⓑ Ⓒ Ⓓ	23. Ⓐ Ⓑ Ⓒ Ⓓ	43. Ⓐ Ⓑ Ⓒ Ⓓ	63. Ⓐ Ⓑ Ⓒ Ⓓ
4. Ⓐ Ⓑ Ⓒ Ⓓ	24. Ⓐ Ⓑ Ⓒ Ⓓ	44. Ⓐ Ⓑ Ⓒ Ⓓ	64. Ⓐ Ⓑ Ⓒ Ⓓ
5. Ⓐ Ⓑ Ⓒ Ⓓ	25. Ⓐ Ⓑ Ⓒ Ⓓ	45. Ⓐ Ⓑ Ⓒ Ⓓ	65. Ⓐ Ⓑ Ⓒ Ⓓ
6. Ⓐ Ⓑ Ⓒ Ⓓ	26. Ⓐ Ⓑ Ⓒ Ⓓ	46. Ⓐ Ⓑ Ⓒ Ⓓ	66. Ⓐ Ⓑ Ⓒ Ⓓ
7. Ⓐ Ⓑ Ⓒ Ⓓ	27. Ⓐ Ⓑ Ⓒ Ⓓ	47. Ⓐ Ⓑ Ⓒ Ⓓ	67. Ⓐ Ⓑ Ⓒ Ⓓ
8. Ⓐ Ⓑ Ⓒ Ⓓ	28. Ⓐ Ⓑ Ⓒ Ⓓ	48. Ⓐ Ⓑ Ⓒ Ⓓ	68. Ⓐ Ⓑ Ⓒ Ⓓ
9. Ⓐ Ⓑ Ⓒ Ⓓ	29. Ⓐ Ⓑ Ⓒ Ⓓ	49. Ⓐ Ⓑ Ⓒ Ⓓ	69. Ⓐ Ⓑ Ⓒ Ⓓ
10. Ⓐ Ⓑ Ⓒ Ⓓ	30. Ⓐ Ⓑ Ⓒ Ⓓ	50. Ⓐ Ⓑ Ⓒ Ⓓ	70. Ⓐ Ⓑ Ⓒ Ⓓ
11. Ⓐ Ⓑ Ⓒ Ⓓ	31. Ⓐ Ⓑ Ⓒ Ⓓ	51. Ⓐ Ⓑ Ⓒ Ⓓ	71. Ⓐ Ⓑ Ⓒ Ⓓ
12. Ⓐ Ⓑ Ⓒ Ⓓ	32. Ⓐ Ⓑ Ⓒ Ⓓ	52. Ⓐ Ⓑ Ⓒ Ⓓ	72. Ⓐ Ⓑ Ⓒ Ⓓ
13. Ⓐ Ⓑ Ⓒ Ⓓ	33. Ⓐ Ⓑ Ⓒ Ⓓ	53. Ⓐ Ⓑ Ⓒ Ⓓ	73. Ⓐ Ⓑ Ⓒ Ⓓ
14. Ⓐ Ⓑ Ⓒ Ⓓ	34. Ⓐ Ⓑ Ⓒ Ⓓ	54. Ⓐ Ⓑ Ⓒ Ⓓ	74. Ⓐ Ⓑ Ⓒ Ⓓ
15. Ⓐ Ⓑ Ⓒ Ⓓ	35. Ⓐ Ⓑ Ⓒ Ⓓ	55. Ⓐ Ⓑ Ⓒ Ⓓ	75. Ⓐ Ⓑ Ⓒ Ⓓ
16. Ⓐ Ⓑ Ⓒ Ⓓ	36. Ⓐ Ⓑ Ⓒ Ⓓ	56. Ⓐ Ⓑ Ⓒ Ⓓ	76. Ⓐ Ⓑ Ⓒ Ⓓ
17. Ⓐ Ⓑ Ⓒ Ⓓ	37. Ⓐ Ⓑ Ⓒ Ⓓ	57. Ⓐ Ⓑ Ⓒ Ⓓ	77. Ⓐ Ⓑ Ⓒ Ⓓ
18. Ⓐ Ⓑ Ⓒ Ⓓ	38. Ⓐ Ⓑ Ⓒ Ⓓ	58. Ⓐ Ⓑ Ⓒ Ⓓ	78. Ⓐ Ⓑ Ⓒ Ⓓ
19. Ⓐ Ⓑ Ⓒ Ⓓ	39. Ⓐ Ⓑ Ⓒ Ⓓ	59. Ⓐ Ⓑ Ⓒ Ⓓ	79. Ⓐ Ⓑ Ⓒ Ⓓ
20. Ⓐ Ⓑ Ⓒ Ⓓ	40. Ⓐ Ⓑ Ⓒ Ⓓ	60. Ⓐ Ⓑ Ⓒ Ⓓ	80. Ⓐ Ⓑ Ⓒ Ⓓ

Raw score = number right _____

TEAR HERE

MUNICIPAL OFFICE AIDE EXAM

3½ Hours—80 Questions, all of equal weight

Directions: Choose the best answer to each question and mark its letter on the answer sheet. Correct answers are on page 212.

1. Assume that a few co-workers meet near your desk and talk about personal matters during working hours. Lately, this practice has interfered with your work. In order to stop this practice, the best action for you to take *first* is to

    (A) ask your supervisor to put a stop to the co-workers' meeting near your desk
    (B) discontinue any friendship with this group
    (C) ask your co-workers not to meet near your desk
    (D) request that your desk be moved to another location

2. In order to maintain office coverage during working hours, your supervisor has scheduled your lunch hour from 1 P.M. to 2 P.M. and your co-worker's lunch hour from 12 P.M. to 1 P.M. Lately, your co-worker has been returning late from lunch each day. As a result you don't get a full hour, since you must return to the office by 2 P.M. Of the following, the best action for you to take *first* is to

    (A) explain to your co-worker in a courteous manner that his or her lateness is interfering with your right to a full hour for lunch
    (B) tell your co-worker that his lateness must stop or you will report him to your supervisor
    (C) report your co-worker's lateness to your supervisor
    (D) leave at 1 P.M. for lunch, whether your co-worker has returned or not

3. Assume that, as an office worker, one of your jobs is to open mail sent to your unit, read the mail for content, and send the mail to the appropriate person for handling. You accidentally open and begin to read a letter marked "personal" addressed to a co-worker. Of the following, the best action for you to take is to

    (A) report to your supervisor that your co-worker is receiving personal mail at the office
    (B) destroy the letter so that your co-worker doesn't know you saw it
    (C) reseal the letter and place it on the co-worker's desk without saying anything
    (D) bring the letter to your co-worker and explain that you opened it by accident

4. Suppose that in evaluating your work your supervisor gives you an overall good rating, but states that you sometimes turn in work with careless errors. The best action for you to take would be to

    (A) ask a co-worker who is good at details to proofread your work
    (B) take time to do a careful job, paying more attention to detail
    (C) continue working as usual since occasional errors are to be expected
    (D) ask your supervisor if he or she would mind correcting your errors

198 / Clerical Exams Handbook

5. Assume that you are taking a telephone message for a co-worker who is not in the office at the time. Of the following, the *least* important item to write on the message is the

   (A) length of the call
   (B) name of the caller
   (C) time of the call
   (D) telephone number of the caller

Each of questions 6 through 13 consists of a sentence which may or may not be an example of good English. The underlined parts of each sentence may be correct or incorrect. Examine each sentence considering grammar, punctuation, spelling, and capitalization. If the English usage in the underlined parts of the sentence given is better than any of the changes in the underlined words suggested in option B, C, or D, choose option A. If the changes in the underlined words suggested in option B, C, or D would make the sentence correct, choose the correct option. Do not choose an option that will change the meaning of the sentence.

6. This Fall the office will be closed on Columbus Day, October 9th.

   (A) Correct as is
   (B) fall...Columbus Day, October
   (C) Fall...columbus day, October
   (D) fall...Columbus Day, october

7. This manual discribes the duties performed by an office aide.

   (A) Correct as is
   (B) describe the duties performed
   (C) discribe the duties performed
   (D) describes the duties performed

8. There weren't no paper in the supply closet.

   (A) Correct as is
   (B) weren't any
   (C) wasn't any
   (D) wasn't no

9. The new employees left there office to attend a meeting.

   (A) Correct as is
   (B) they're
   (C) their
   (D) thier

10. The office worker started working at 8;30 A.M.

    (A) Correct as is
    (B) 8:30 A.M.
    (C) 8;30 A,M.
    (D) 8:30 AM.

11. The alphabet, or A to Z sequence are the basis of most filing systems.

    (A) Correct as is
    (B) alphabet, or A to Z sequence, is
    (C) alphabet, or A to Z, sequence are
    (D) alphabet, or A too Z sequence, is

12. Those file cabinets are five feet tall.

    (A) Correct as is
    (B) Them. . .feet
    (C) Those. . .foot
    (D) Them. . .foot

13. The office aide checked the register and finding the date of the meeting.

    (A) Correct as is
    (B) regaster and finding
    (C) register and found
    (D) regaster and found

Each of questions 14 through 21 has two lists of numbers. Each list contains three sets of numbers. Check each of the three sets in the list on the right to see if they are the same as the corresponding set in the list on the left. Mark your answers

A if NONE of the sets in the right list are the SAME as those in the left list
B if ONLY ONE of the sets in the right list is the SAME as those in the left list
C if ONLY TWO of the sets in the right list are the SAME as those in the left list
D if ALL THREE sets in the right list are the SAME as those in the left list

14. 7354183476   7354983476
    4474747744   4474747774
    57914302311   57914302311

15. 7143592185   7143892185
    8344517699   8344518699
    9178531263   9178531263

16. 2572114731   257214731
    8806835476   8806835476
    8255831246   8255831246

17. 331476853821   331476858621
    6976658532996   6976655832996
    3766042113715   3766042113745

18. 8806663315   8806663315
    74477138449   74477138449
    211756663666   211756663666

19. 990006966996   99000696996
    53022219743   53022219843
    4171171117717   4171171177717

20. 24400222433004   24400222433004
    5300030055000355 5300030055500355
    20000075532002022 20000075532002022

21. 6111666406600011116   61116664066001116
    7111300117001100733   7111300117001100733
    26666446664476518   26666446664476518

200 / *Clerical Exams Handbook*

Each of questions 22 through 25 has two lists of names and addresses. Each list contains three sets of names and addresses. Check each of the three sets in the list on the right to see if they are the same as the corresponding set in the list on the left. Mark your answers

A if NONE of the sets in the right list are the SAME as those in the left list
B if ONLY ONE of the sets in the right list is the SAME as those in the left list
C if ONLY TWO of the sets in the right list are the SAME as those in the left list
D if ALL THREE sets in the right list are the SAME as those in the left list

22. Mary T. Berlinger
2351 Hampton St.
Monsey, N.Y. 20117

Eduardo Benes
473 Kingston Avenue
Central Islip, N.Y. 11734

Alan Carrington Fuchs
17 Gnarled Hollow Road
Los Angeles, California 91635

Mary T. Berlinger
2351 Hampton St.
Monsey, N.Y. 20117

Eduardo Benes
473 Kingston Avenue
Central Islip, N.Y. 11734

Alan Carrington Fuchs
17 Gnarled Hollow Road
Los Angeles, California 91685

23. David John Jacobson
178 35 St. Apt. 4C
New York, N.Y. 00927

Ann-Marie Calonella
7243 South Ridge Blvd.
Bakersfield, California 96714

Pauline M. Thompson
872 Linden Ave.
Houston, Texas 70321

David John Jacobson
178 53 St. Apt. 4C
New York, N.Y. 00927

Ann-Marie Calonella
7243 South Ridge Blvd.
Bakersfield, California 96714

Pauline M. Thomson
872 Linden Ave.
Houston, Texas 70321

24. Chester LeRoy Masterton
152 Lacy Rd.
Kankakee, Ill. 54532

William Maloney
S. LaCrosse Pla.
Wausau, Wisconsin 52146

Cynthia V. Barnes
16 Pines Rd.
Greenpoint, Mississippi 20376

Chester LeRoy Masterson
152 Lacy Rd.
Kankakee, Ill. 54532

William Maloney
S. LaCross Pla.
Wausau, Wisconsin 52146

Cynthia V. Barnes
16 Pines Rd.
Greenpoint, Mississippi 20376

25. Marcel Jean Frontenac
6 Burton On The Water
Calender, Me. 01471

J. Scott Marsden
174 S. Tipton St.
Cleveland, Ohio

Lawrence T. Haney
171 McDonough St.
Decatur, Ga. 31304

Marcel Jean Frontenac
6 Burton On The Water
Calender, Me. 01471

J. Scott Marsden
174 Tipton St.
Cleveland, Ohio

Lawrence T. Haney
171 McDonough St.
Decatur, Ga. 31304

You are to answer questions 26 through 31 *solely* on the basis of the information contained in the following passage:

Duplicating is the process of making a number of identical copies of letters, documents, etc., from an original. Some duplicating processes make copies directly from the original document. Other duplicating processes require the preparation of a special master, and copies are then made from the master. Four of the most common duplicating processes are stencil, fluid, offset, and Xerox.

In the stencil process, the typewriter is used to cut the words into a master, called a stencil. Drawings, charts, or graphs can be cut into the stencil using a stylus. As many as 3,500 good-quality copies can be reproduced from one stencil. Various grades of finished paper from inexpensive mimeograph to expensive bond can be used.

The fluid process is a good method of copying from 50 to 125 good-quality copies from a master which is prepared with a special dye. The master is placed on the duplicator, and special paper with a hard finish is moistened and then passed through the duplicator. Some of the dye on the master is dissolved, creating an impression on the paper. The impression becomes lighter as more copies are made, and once the dye on the master is used up, a new master must be made.

The offset process is the most adaptable office duplicating process because this process can be used for making a few copies or many copies. Masters can be made on paper or plastic for a few hundred copies or on metal plates for as many as 75,000 copies. By using a special technique called photo-offset, charts, photographs, illustrations, or graphs can be reproduced on the master plate. The offset process is capable of producing large quantities of fine, top-quality copies on all types of finished paper.

The Xerox process reproduces an exact duplicate from an original. It is the fastest duplicating method because the original material is placed directly on the duplicator, eliminating the need to make a special master. Any kind of paper can be used. The Xerox process is the most expensive duplicating process; however, it is the best method of reproducing small quantities of good-quality copies of reports, letters, official documents, memos, or contracts.

26. Of the following, the most efficient method of reproducing 5,000 copies of a graph is

   (A) stencil
   (B) fluid
   (C) offset
   (D) Xerox

27. The offset process is the most adaptable office duplicating process because

   (A) it is the quickest duplicating method
   (B) it is the least expensive duplicating method
   (C) it can produce a small number or large number of copies
   (D) a softer master can be used over and over again

28. Which one of the following duplicating processes uses moistened paper?

   (A) Stencil
   (B) Fluid
   (C) Offset
   (D) Xerox

29. The fluid process would be the best process to use for reproducing

    (A) five copies of a school transcript
    (B) 50 copies of a memo
    (C) 500 copies of a form letter
    (D) 5,000 copies of a chart

30. Which one of the following duplicating processes does *not* require a special master?

    (A) Fluid
    (B) Xerox
    (C) Offset
    (D) Stencil

31. Xerox is not used for all duplicating jobs because

    (A) it produces poor-quality copies
    (B) the process is too expensive
    (C) preparing the master is too time-consuming
    (D) it cannot produce written reports

For questions 32 through 35, select the choice that is closest in meaning to the underlined word.

Sample

This division reviews the fiscal reports of the agency. In this sentence the word fiscal means most nearly

(A) financial
(B) critical
(C) basic
(D) personnel

The correct answer is **(A)** "financial," because "financial" is closest to "fiscal."

32. A central file eliminates the need to retain duplicate material. The word retain means most nearly

    (A) keep
    (B) change
    (C) locate
    (D) process

33. Filing is a routine office task. Routine means most nearly

    (A) proper
    (B) regular
    (C) simple
    (D) difficult

34. Sometimes a word, phrase, or sentence must be deleted to correct an error. Deleted means most nearly

    (A) removed
    (B) added
    (C) expanded
    (D) improved

35. Your supervisor will evaluate your work. Evaluate means most nearly

(A) judge
(B) list
(C) assign
(D) explain

Code Table

T	M	V	D	S	P	R	G	B	H
1	2	3	4	5	6	7	8	9	0

The code table above shows 10 letters with matching numbers. For each question 36 through 43, there are three sets of letters. Each set of letters is followed by a set of numbers which *may or may not* match their correct letter according to the code table. For each question, check all three sets of letters and numbers and mark your answer

A if NO PAIRS are CORRECTLY MATCHED
B if only ONE PAIR is CORRECTLY MATCHED
C if only TWO PAIRS are CORRECTLY MATCHED
D if ALL THREE PAIRS are CORRECTLY MATCHED

Sample question:

TMVDSP - 123456
RGBHTM - 789011
DSPRGB - 256789

In the sample question above, the first set of numbers correctly matches its set of letters. But the second and third pairs contain mistakes. In the second pair, M is incorrectly matched with number 1. According to the code table, the letter M should be correctly matched with number 2. In the third pair, the letter D is incorrectly matched with number 2. According to the code table, the letter D should be correctly matched with number 4. Since only one of the pairs is correctly matched, the answer to this sample question is B.

36. RSBMRM - 759262
    GDSRVH - 845730
    VDBRTM - 349713

37. TGVSDR - 183247
    SMHRDP - 520647
    TRMHSR - 172057

38. DSPRGM - 456782
    MVDBHT - 234902
    HPMDBT - 062491

39. BVPTRD - 936184
    GDPHMB - 807029
    GMRHMV - 827032

40. MGVRSH - 283750
    TRDMBS - 174295
    SPRMGV - 567283

41. SGBSDM - 489542
    MGHPTM - 290612
    MPBMHT - 269301

42. TDPBHM - 146902
    VPBMRS - 369275
    GDMBHM - 842902

43. MVPTBV - 236194
    PDRTMB - 647128
    BGTMSM - 981232

In each of the questions 44 through 49, the names of four people are given. For each question, choose as your answer the one of the four names given which should be filed *first* according to the usual system of alphabetical filing of names, as described in the paragraph below.

In filing names, you must start with the last name. Names are filed in order of the first letter of the last name, then the second letter, etc. Therefore BAILY would be filed before BROWN, which would be filed before COLT. A name with fewer letters of the same type comes first, i.e., Smith before Smithe. If the last names are the same, the names are filed alphabetically by the first name. If the first name is an initial, a name with an initial would come before a first name that starts with the same letter as the initial. Therefore, I. BROWN would come before IRA BROWN. Finally, if both last name and first name are the same, the name would be filed alphabetically by the middle name, once again an initial coming before a middle name that starts with the same letter as the initial. If there is no middle name at all, the name would come before those with middle initials or names.

Sample Question:

(A) Lester Daniels
(B) William Dancer
(C) Nathan Danzig
(D) Dan Lester

The last names beginning with D are filed before the last name beginning with L. Since DANIELS, DANCER, and DANZIG all begin with the same three letters, you must look at the fourth letter of the last name to determine which name should be filed first. C comes before I or Z in the alphabet, so DANCER is filed before DANIELS or DANZIG. Therefore, the answer to the above sample question is B.

44. (A) Scott Biala
    (B) Mary Byala
    (C) Martin Baylor
    (D) Francis Bauer

45. (A) Howard J. Black
    (B) Howard Black
    (C) J. Howard Black
    (D) John H. Black

46. (A) Theodora Garth Kingston
    (B) Theadore Barth Kingston
    (C) Thomas Kingston
    (D) Thomas T. Kingston

47. (A) Paulette Mary Huerta
    (B) Paul M. Huerta
    (C) Paulette L. Huerta
    (D) Peter A. Huerta

48. (A) Martha Hunt Morgan
    (B) Martin Hunt Morgan
    (C) Mary H. Morgan
    (D) Martine H. Morgan

49. (A) James T. Meerschaum
    (B) James M. Mershum
    (C) James F. Mearshaum
    (D) James N. Meshum

50. Which one of the following statements about proper telephone usage is *not* always correct? When answering the telephone, you should

    (A) know who you are speaking to
    (B) give the caller your undivided attention
    (C) identify yourself to the caller
    (D) obtain the information the caller wishes before you do your other work

51. Assume that, as a member of a Worker's Safety Committee in your agency, you are responsible for encouraging other employees to follow correct safety practices. While you are working on your regular assignment, you observe an employee violating a safety rule. Of the following, the best action for you to take *first* is to

    (A) speak to the employee about safety practices and order him or her to stop violating the safety rule
    (B) speak to the employee about safety practices and point out the safety rule he or she is violating
    (C) bring the matter up in the next committee meeting
    (D) report this violation of the safety rule to the employee's supervisor

52. Assume that you have been temporarily assigned by your supervisor to do a job which you do not want to do. The best action for you to take is to

    (A) discuss the job with your supervisor explaining why you don't want to do it
    (B) discuss the job with your supervisor and tell him or her that you will not do it
    (C) ask a co-worker to take your place on this job
    (D) do some other job that you like; your supervisor may give the job you don't like to someone else

53. Assume that you keep the confidential personnel files of employees in your unit. A friend asks you to obtain some information from the file of one of your co-workers. The best action to take is to

    (A) ask the co-worker if you can give the information to your friend
    (B) ask your supervisor if you can give the information to your friend
    (C) give the information to your friend
    (D) refuse to give the information to your friend

You are to answer questions 54 through 57 *solely* on the basis of the information contained in the following passage:

> The city government is committed to providing a safe and healthy work environment for all city employees. An effective agency safety program reduces accidents by educating employees about the types of careless acts that can cause accidents. Even in an office, accidents can happen. If each employee is aware of possible safety hazards, the number of accidents on the job can be reduced.
>
> Careless use of office equipment can cause accidents and injuries. For example, file cabinet drawers which are filled with papers can be so heavy that the entire cabinet could tip over from the weight of one open drawer.
>
> The bottom drawers of desks and file cabinets should never be left open, since employees could easily trip over open drawers and injure themselves.
>
> When reaching for objects on a high shelf, an employee should use a strong, sturdy object such as a stepstool to stand on. Makeshift platforms made out of books, papers, or boxes can easily collapse. Even chairs can slide out from underfoot, causing serious injury.
>
> Even at an employee's desk, safety hazards can occur. Frayed or cut wires should be repaired or replaced immediately. Typewriters which are not firmly anchored to the desk or table could fall, causing injury.
>
> Smoking is one of the major causes of fires in the office. A lighted match or improperly extinguished cigarette thrown into a wastebasket filled with paper could cause a major fire with possible loss of life. Where smoking is permitted, ashtrays should be used. Smoking is particularly dangerous in offices where flammable chemicals are used.

54. The goal of an effective safety program is to

(A) reduce office accidents
(B) stop employees from smoking on the job
(C) encourage employees to continue their education
(D) eliminate high shelves in offices

55. Desks and file cabinets can become safety hazards when

(A) their drawers are left open
(B) they are used as wastebaskets
(C) they are makeshift
(D) they are not anchored securely to the floor

56. Smoking is especially hazardous when it occurs

(A) near exposed wires
(B) in a crowded office
(C) in an area where flammable chemicals are used
(D) where books and papers are stored

57. Accidents are likely to occur when

(A) employees' desks are cluttered with books and papers
(B) employees are not aware of safety hazards
(C) employees close desk drawers
(D) stepstools are used to reach high objects

58. Assume that part of your job as a worker in the accounting division of a city agency is to answer the telephone. When you first answer the telephone, it is *least* important to tell the caller

    (A) your title
    (B) your name
    (C) the name of your unit
    (D) the name of your agency

59. Assume that you are assigned to work as a receptionist and your duties are to answer phones, greet visitors, and do other general office work. You are busy with a routine job when several visitors approach your desk. The best action to take is to

    (A) ask the visitors to have a seat and assist them after your work is completed
    (B) tell the visitors that you are busy and they should return at a more convenient time
    (C) stop working long enough to assist the visitors
    (D) continue working and wait for the visitors to ask you for assistance

60. Assume that your supervisor has chosen you to take a special course during working hours to learn a new payroll procedure. Although you know that you were chosen because of your good work record, a co-worker, who feels that he or she should have been chosen, has been telling everyone in your unit that the choice was unfair. Of the following, the best way to handle this situation *first* is to

    (A) suggest to the co-worker that everything in life is unfair
    (B) contact your union representative in case your co-worker presents a formal grievance
    (C) tell your supervisor about your co-worker's complaints and let him or her handle the situation
    (D) tell the co-worker that you were chosen because of your superior work record

61. Assume that while you are working on an assignment that must be completed quickly, a supervisor from another unit asks you to obtain information for her. Of the following, the best way to respond to her request is to

    (A) tell her to return in an hour, since you are busy
    (B) give her the names of some people in her own unit who could help her
    (C) tell her you are busy and refer her to a co-worker
    (D) tell her that you are busy, and ask her if she could wait until you finish your assignment

62. A co-worker in your unit is often off from work because of illness. Your supervisor assigns the co-worker's work to you when she is not there. Lately, doing her work has interfered with your own job. The best action for you to take *first* is to

    (A) discuss the problem with your supervisor
    (B) complete your own work before starting your co-worker's work
    (C) ask other workers in your unit to assist you
    (D) work late in order to get the jobs done

63. During the month of June, 40,587 people attended a city-owned swimming pool. In July, 13,014 more people attended the swimming pool than the number that had attended in June. In August, 39,655 people attended the swimming pool. The total number of people who attended the swimming pool during the months of June, July, and August was

    (A) 80,242   (C) 133,843
    (B) 93,256   (D) 210,382

64. Assume a city agency has 775 office workers. If 2 out of 25 office workers were absent on a particular day, how many office workers reported to work on that day?

(A) 713
(B) 744
(C) 750
(D) 773

Questions 65 through 72 test how well you understand what you read. It will be necessary for you to read carefully because your answers to these questions must be based *only* on the information in the following paragraphs.

The telephone directory is made up of two books. The first book consists of the introductory section and the alphabetical listing of names section. The second book is the classified directory (also known as the Yellow Pages). Many people who are familiar with one book do not realize how useful the other can be. The efficient office worker should become familiar with both books in order to make the best use of this important source of information.

The introductory section gives general instructions for finding numbers in the alphabetical listing and classified directory. This section also explains how to use the telephone company's many services, including the operator and information services; gives examples of charges for local and long-distance calls; and lists area codes for the entire country. In addition, this section provides a useful postal ZIP code map.

The alphabetical listing of names section lists the names, addresses, and telephone numbers of subscribers in an area. Guide names, or "telltales," are on the top corner of each page. These guide names indicate the first and last name to be found on that page. "Telltales" help locate any particular name quickly. A cross-reference spelling is also given to help locate names which are spelled several different ways.

City, State, and Federal Government agencies are listed in the blue pages of the alphabetical book under the major government heading. For example, an agency of the Federal Government would be listed under "United States Government."

The classified directory, or Yellow Pages, is a separate book. In this section are advertising services, public transportation line maps, shopping guides, and listings of businesses arranged by the type of product or services they offer. This book is most useful when looking for the name or phone number of a business when all that is known is the type of product offered and the address, or when trying to locate a particular type of business in an area. Businesses listed in the classified directory can usually be found in the alphabetical listing of names section. When the name of the business is known, you will find the address or phone number more quickly in the alphabetical listing of names section.

65. The introductory section provides

(A) shopping guides
(B) government listings
(C) business listings
(D) information services

66. Advertising services would be found in the

   (A) introductory section
   (B) alphabetical listing of names section
   (C) classified directory
   (D) information services

67. According to the information in the passage for locating government agencies, the Information Office of the Department of Consumer Affairs of New York City government would be alphabetically listed *first* under

   (A) "I" for Information Office
   (B) "D" for Department of Consumer Affairs
   (C) "N" for New York City
   (D) "G" for government

68. When the name of a business is known, the quickest way to find the phone number is to look in the

   (A) classified directory
   (B) introductory section
   (C) alphabetical listing of names section
   (D) advertising service section

69. The quickest way to find the phone number of a business when the type of service a business offers and its address is known, is to look in the

   (A) classified directory
   (B) alphabetical listing of names section
   (C) introductory section
   (D) information service

70. What is a "telltale"?

   (A) An alphabetical listing
   (B) A guide name
   (C) A map
   (D) A cross-reference listing

71. The best way to find a postal ZIP code is to look in the

   (A) classified directory
   (B) introductory section
   (C) alphabetical listing of names section
   (D) government heading

72. To help find names that have several different spellings, the telephone directory provides

   (A) cross-reference spelling
   (B) "telltales"
   (C) spelling guides
   (D) advertising services

73. Assume that your agency has been given $2,025 to purchase file cabinets. If each file cabinet costs $135, how many file cabinets can your agency purchase?

   (A) 8
   (B) 10
   (C) 15
   (D) 16

74. Assume that your unit ordered 14 staplers at a total cost of $30.20 and each stapler costs the same amount. The cost of one stapler was most nearly

(A) $1.02
(B) $1.61
(C) $2.16
(D) $2.26

75. Assume that you are responsible for counting and recording licensing fees collected by your department. On a particular day your department collected in fees 40 checks in the amount of $6 each; 80 checks in the amount of $4 each; 45 $20 bills; 30 $10 bills; 42 $5 bills; and 186 $1 bills. The total amount in fees collected on that day was

(A) $1,406
(B) $1,706
(C) $2,156
(D) $2,356

76. Assume that you are responsible for your agency's petty cash fund. During the month of February you pay out 7 subway fares at $1.25 each and one taxi fare for $7.30; you pay out nothing else from the fund. At the end of February, you count the money left in the fund and find 3 $1 bills, 4 quarters, 5 dimes, and 4 nickels. The amount of money you had available in the petty cash fund at the *beginning* of February was

(A) $4.70
(B) $11.35
(C) $16.05
(D) $20.75

77. You overhear your supervisor criticize a co-worker for handling equipment in an unsafe way. You feel that the criticism may be unfair. Of the following, it would be best for you to

(A) take your co-worker aside and tell him or her how you feel about your supervisor's comments
(B) interrupt the discussion and defend your co-worker to your supervisor
(C) continue working as if you had not overheard the discussion
(D) make a list of other workers who have violated safety rules and give it to your supervisor

78. Assume that you have been assigned to work on a long-term project with an employee who is known for being uncooperative. In beginning to work with this employee, it would be *least* desirable for you to

(A) understand why the person is uncooperative
(B) act in a calm manner rather than an emotional manner
(C) be appreciative of the co-worker's work
(D) report the co-worker's lack of cooperation to your supervisor

79. Assume that you are assigned to sell tickets at a city-owned ice skating rink. An adult ticket costs $3.75 and a children's ticket costs $2.00. At the end of a day, you find that you have sold 36 adult tickets and 80 children's tickets. The total amount of money you collected for that day was

(A) $285.50
(B) $295.00
(C) $298.75
(D) $301.00

80. If each office worker files 487 index cards in one hour, how many cards can 26 office workers file in one hour?

    (A) 10,662
    (B) 12,175
    (C) 12,662
    (D) 14,266

Correct Answers for Municipal Office Aide Exam

1. C	11. B	21. C	31. B	41. A	51. B	61. D	71. B
2. A	12. A	22. C	32. A	42. D	52. A	62. A	72. A
3. D	13. C	23. B	33. B	43. A	53. D	63. C	73. C
4. B	14. B	24. B	34. A	44. D	54. A	64. A	74. C
5. A	15. B	25. C	35. A	45. B	55. A	65. D	75. C
6. B	16. C	26. C	36. B	46. B	56. C	66. C	76. D
7. D	17. A	27. C	37. B	47. B	57. B	67. C	77. C
8. C	18. D	28. B	38. C	48. A	58. A	68. C	78. D
9. C	19. A	29. B	39. A	49. C	59. C	69. A	79. B
10. B	20. C	30. B	40. D	50. D	60. C	70. B	80. C

Explanations

Questions 1 through 5 rely on your common sense and good judgment in interpersonal relations.

6. **(B)** The seasons are not capitalized, but names of holidays and months are.

7. **(D)** The subject of the sentence, the manual, is singular, so the verb must be singular as well. The correct spelling is *describes*.

8. **(C)** "Paper" is a singular noun taking the singular verb "was." The construction "...n't no" constitutes an unacceptable double negative.

9. **(C)** "Their" is the possessive. "They're" is the contraction for "they are." "There" refers to a place. Choice (D) is a misspelling.

10. **(B)** The correct way to express time is 8:30 A.M.

11. **(B)** The "alphabet," singular, "is." The phrase "or A to Z sequence" is extra information about the alphabet, so it is enclosed by commas. "Too" means "also" or "excessive" and is the incorrect spelling of *to*.

12. **(A)** "Five" is plural, so use the plural "feet."

13. **(C)** "Checked and found"—both verbs must be in the past tense. The correct spelling is *register*.

For questions 14 through 25, we have circled the areas of difference.

14. **(B)** The numbers are alike in only one set.

```
7354①83476          7354⑨83476
44747477④4          44747477⑦4
57914302311         57914302311
```

15. **(B)** The numbers are alike in only one set.

7143592185	7143892185
8344517699	8344518699
9178531263	9178531263

16. **(C)** The numbers are alike in two sets.

2572114731	257214731
8806835476	8806835476
8255831246	8255831246

17. **(A)** None of the sets are alike.

331476853821	331476858621
6976658532996	6976655832996
3966042113715	3766042113745

18. **(D)** All of the sets are exactly alike.

19. **(A)** None of the sets are alike

990006966996	99000696996
53022219743	53022219843
4171171117717	4171171177717

20. **(C)** The numbers are alike in two sets.

24400222433004	24400222433004
5300030055000355	5300030055500355
20000075532002022	20000075532002022

21. **(C)** The numbers are alike in two sets.

611166640660001116	61116664066001116
7111300117001100733	7111300117001100733
26666446664476518	266664466644766518

22. **(C)** The names and addresses are exactly alike in two sets.

Mary T. Berlinger 2351 Hampton St. Monsey, N.Y. 20117	Mary T. Berlinger 2351 Hampton St. Monsey, N.Y. 20117
Eduardo Benes 473 Kingston Avenue Central Islip, N.Y. 11734	Eduardo Benes 473 Kingston Avenue Central Islip, N.Y. 11734
Alan Carrington Fuchs 17 Gnarled Hollow Road Los Angeles, California 91635	Alan Carrington Fuchs 17 Gnarled Hollow Road Los Angeles, California 91685

23. **(B)** The names and addresses are alike in only one set.

David John Jacobson 178 35 St. Apt. 4C New York, N.Y. 00927	David John Jacobson 178 53 St. Apt. 4C New York, N.Y. 00927

214 / *Clerical Exams Handbook*

    Ann-Marie Calonella   Ann-Marie Calonella
    7243 South Ridge Blvd.   7243 South Ridge Blvd.
    Bakersfield, California 96714   Bakersfield, California 96714

    Pauline M. Tho(mps)on   Pauline M. Tho(ms)on
    872 Linden Ave.   872 Linden Ave.
    Houston, Texas 70321   Houston, Texas 70321

24. **(B)** The names and addresses are alike in only one set.

    Chester LeRoy Master(t)on   Chester LeRoy Master(s)on
    152 Lacy Rd.   152 Lacy Rd.
    Kankakee, Ill. 54532   Kankakee, Ill. 54532

    William Maloney   William Maloney
    S. LaCros(se) Pla.   S. LaCros(s) Pla.
    Wausau, Wisconsin 52146   Wausau, Wisconsin 52146

    Cynthia V. Barnes   Cynthia V. Barnes
    16 Pines Rd.   16 Pines Rd.
    Greenpoint, Mississippi 20376   Greenpoint, Mississippi 20376

25. **(C)** The names and addresses are exactly alike in two sets.

    Marcel Jean Frontenac   Marcel Jean Frontenac
    6 Burton On The Water   6 Burton On The Water
    Calender, Me. 01471   Calender, Me. 01471

    J. Scott Marsden   J. Scott Marsden
    174 (S.) Tipton St.   174 ( ) Tipton St.
    Cleveland, Ohio   Cleveland, Ohio

    Lawrence T. Haney   Lawrence T. Haney
    171 McDonough St.   171 McDonough St.
    Decatur, Ga. 31304   Decatur, Ga. 31304

26. **(C)** The offset process can produce up to 75,000 good copies. Stencil is good for up to 3,500 and fluid process for only up to 125. Xerox is very expensive for that many copies.

27. **(C)** See the first sentence of the fourth paragraph.

28. **(B)** See the second sentence of the third paragraph.

29. **(B)** In (C) and (D) the numbers are too high for the fluid process. Five copies would be most efficiently reproduced by the Xerox process without preparing a master.

30. **(B)** See the last paragraph.

31. **(B)** Again, refer to the last paragraph.

If you made errors in questions 32 through 35, consult a dictionary. For questions 36 through 43, the areas of miscoding are marked.

36. **(B)** Only one set is correctly coded.

    RSBM(R)M - 7592(6)2
    GDSRVH   - 845730
    VDBRT(M) - 34971(3)

37. **(B)** Only one set is correctly coded.
    TGV(S)DR   - 183(2)47
    SMH(R)D(P) - 520(6)4(7)
    TRMHSR   - 172057

38. **(C)** Two sets are correctly coded.
    DSPRGM   - 456782
    MVDBH(T)   - 23490(2)
    HPMDBT   - 062491

39. **(A)** No sets are correctly coded.
    BVPT(R)D   - 9361(8)4
    G(DP)HMB   - 8(07)029
    GMRH(MV)   - 8270(32)

40. **(D)** All three sets are correctly coded.

41. **(A)** No sets are correctly coded.
    (S)GBSDM   - (4)89542
    M(G)HPTM   - 2(9)0612
    MPB(M)HT   - 269(3)01

42. **(D)** All three sets are correctly coded.

43. **(A)** No sets are correctly coded.
    MVPTB (V)   - 23619(4)
    PDRTM (B)   - 64712(8)
    BGTM(S) M   - 9812(3)2

44. **(D)** Bauer—Baylor—Biala—Byala

45. **(B)** Howard—Howard J.—J. Howard—John H.

46. **(B)** Theadore—Theodora—Thomas—Thomas T.

47. **(B)** Paul M.—Paulette L.—Paulette Mary—Peter A.

48. **(A)** Martha—Martin—Martine—Mary

49. **(C)** Mearshaum—Meerschaum—Mershum—Meshum

50. **(D)** You must always identify yourself, find out to whom you are speaking, and be courteous to the caller, but sometimes a return call could give information at a later hour or date.

216 / *Clerical Exams Handbook*

51. **(B)** The first thing to do is speak to the employee who may not even be aware of the rule.

52. **(A)** Be "up front" with your supervisor. Refusing to do a distasteful task or trying to hand it off to someone else is not proper business procedure.

53. **(D)** Confidential means "private."

54. **(A)** See the first paragraph.

55. **(A)** See the third paragraph.

56. **(C)** See the last paragraph.

57. **(B)** See the first paragraph.

58. **(A)** Think of what the caller needs to know. He or she needs to know what agency has been reached and to whom he or she is speaking. Your title is irrelevant.

59. **(C)** A receptionist receives visitors.

60. **(C)** No matter how you approach the co-worker, you are likely to create ill-feeling. Let your supervisor handle this tricky office morale problem.

61. **(D)** Your own work comes first, but you do want to be helpful. Tactfully offer to help out when your own work is completed, and let the supervisor ask for a referral if she needs the information more quickly.

62. **(A)** The supervisor does the assigning and is responsible for having the work done. Let the supervisor know what the problem is.

63. **(C)**
    June   40,587
    July   40,587 + 13,014 = 53,601
 + August   39,655
        Total   133,842

64. **(A)** 775 ÷ 25 = 31 groups of 25 workers in the agency.
       31 × 2 = 62 absent that day (2 from each group of 25)
       775 − 62 = 713 present

65. **(D)** See the second paragraph.

66. **(C)** See the last paragraph.

67. **(C)** See the fourth paragraph.

68. **(C)** See the third paragraph.

69. **(A)** See the last paragraph.

70. **(B)** See the second sentence of the third paragraph.

71. **(B)** See the second paragraph.

72. **(A)** See the last sentence of the third paragraph.

73. **(C)** $2,025 ÷ $135 = $15

74. **(C)** $30.20 ÷ 14 = $2.157 = $2.16

75. **(C)**
    40 checks   @ $6   = $240
    80 checks   @ 4   =   320
    45 bills   @ 20   =   900
    30 bills   @ 10   =   300
    42 bills   @ 5   =   210
  + 186 bills   @ 1   =   186
                      Total   = $2,156

76. **(D)**
    7 fares   @ $1.25 = $ 8.75
  + 1 fare   @ 7.30 =   7.30
          Total spent   = $16.05

    3 dollar bills   = $3.00
    4 quarters   =   1.00
    5 dimes   =   .50
  + 4 nickels   =   .20
    Amount left   = $4.70

    Amount spent   = $16.05
  + Amount left   =   4.70
    Amount to begin = $20.75

77. **(C)** The remarks were not meant for your ears. Do your own work and mind your own business.

78. **(D)** You've just begun to work, and the co-worker has not had a chance to prove cooperative or uncooperative. There is nothing to report.

79. **(B)**
    36 adults   @ $3.75 = $135
  + 80 children   @ 2.00 =   160
                Total   = $295

80. **(C)** 487 × 26 = 12,662

TYPICAL PRIVATE SECTOR CLERICAL EXAMINATION

Section A—Filing

Directions: Arrange the names in each question in proper alphabetical order for filing. Correct answers are on pages 227–228.

1. Adam Dunn
   E. Dunn
   A. Duncan
   Edward Robert Dunn

2. Paul Moore
   William Moore
   Paul A. Moore
   William Allen Moore

3. William Carver
   Howard Cambell
   Arthur Chambers
   Charles Banner

4. George Peters
   Eric Petersen
   G. Peters
   E. Petersen

5. Edward Hallam
   Jos. Frank Hamilton
   Edward A. Hallam
   Joseph F. Hamilton

6. William O'Hara
   Arthur Gordon
   James DeGraff
   Anne von Glatin

7. Theodore Madison
   Timothy McGill
   Thomas MacLane
   Thomas A. Madison

1. _____
   _____
   _____
   _____

2. _____
   _____
   _____
   _____

3. _____
   _____
   _____
   _____

4. _____
   _____
   _____
   _____

5. _____
   _____
   _____
   _____

6. _____
   _____
   _____
   _____

7. _____
   _____
   _____
   _____

8. Dr. Chas. D. Peterson
   Miss Irene F. Petersen
   Lawrence E. Peterson
   Prof. N. A. Petersen

9. Edward La Gabriel
   Marie Doris Gabriel
   Marjorie N. Gabriel
   Mrs. Marian Gabriel

10. Herbert Restman
    H. Restman
    Harry Restmore
    H. Restmore

11. Timothy Macalan
    Fred McAlden
    Thomas MacAllister
    Mrs. Frank McAllen

12. Peter La Vance
    George Van Meer
    Wallace De Vance
    Leonard Vance

13. Devine, Sarah
    Devine, S.
    Devine, Sara H.
    Devin, Sarah

14. Bennet, C.
    Benett, Chuck
    Bennet, Chas.
    Bennett, Charles

15. Rivera, Ilena
    Riviera, Ilene
    Rivere, I.
    Riviera Ilana

16. Corral, Dr. Robert
    Carrale, Prof. Robert
    Corren, R.
    Corret, Ron

17. Chas. A. Levine
    Kurt Levene
    Charles Levine
    Kurt E. Levene

8. _____
   _____
   _____
   _____

9. _____
   _____
   _____
   _____

10. _____
    _____
    _____
    _____

11. _____
    _____
    _____
    _____

12. _____
    _____
    _____
    _____

13. _____
    _____
    _____
    _____

14. _____
    _____
    _____
    _____

15. _____
    _____
    _____
    _____

16. _____
    _____
    _____
    _____

17. _____
    _____
    _____
    _____

18. Prof. Geo. Kinkaid
    Mr. Alan Kinkaid
    Dr. Albert A. Kinkade
    Kincade, Lillian

19. Charles Green
    Chas. T. Greene
    Charles Thomas Greene
    Wm. A. Greene

20. Doris MacAllister
    D. McAllen
    Lewis T. MacBride
    Lewis McBride

21. Robert B. Pierce
    R. Bruce Pierce
    Ronald Pierce
    Robert Bruce Pierce

22. Charlotte Stair
    C. B. Stare
    Charles B. Stare
    Elaine La Stella

23. James Borenstein
    Frieda Albrecht
    Samuel Brown
    George Appelman

24. James McCormack
    Ruth MacNamara
    Kathryn McGillicuddy
    Frances Mason

25. A. S. Martinson
    Albert Martinson
    Albert S. Martinson
    M. Martanson

18. _____

19. _____

20. _____

21. _____

22. _____

23. _____

24. _____

25. _____

Section B—Spelling

Directions: In the following list, some words are spelled correctly and some words are misspelled. On the line to the right, write the correct spelling of each misspelled word. If a word is spelled correctly, write the letter "C."

1. professor   1. _____
2. sabbatical   2. _____
3. associate   3. _____
4. dictater   4. _____
5. accidently   5. _____
6. bureau   6. _____
7. auxilary   7. _____
8. synthesis   8. _____
9. receiveable   9. _____
10. facsimile   10. _____
11. proxey   11. _____
12. negotiable   12. _____
13. confidential   13. _____
14. pertainent   14. _____
15. corrective   15. _____
16. satisfactorally   16. _____
17. accomplishment   17. _____
18. bookeeping   18. _____
19. beforhand   19. _____
20. supervisor   20. _____
21. manifest   21. _____
22. machinary   22. _____
23. harassment   23. _____
24. bankrupcy   24. _____
25. requisition   25. _____
26. pollish   26. _____
27. acknowledgment   27. _____
28. typograpfical   28. _____
29. codify   29. _____
30. performance   30. _____
31. weight   31. _____
32. occasionally   32. _____
33. carefuly   33. _____
34. deceit   34. _____
35. efficiently   35. _____
36. scheduling   36. _____
37. distorsion   37. _____
38. exemplify   38. _____
39. chronological   39. _____
40. liability   40. _____
41. courtesy   41. _____
42. notarary   42. _____
43. memmoranda   43. _____
44. ellimination   44. _____
45. clogging   45. _____
46. refered   46. _____
47. aggressive   47. _____
48. shelfs   48. _____
49. personnel   49. _____
50. initiative   50. _____
51. occurance   51. _____
52. guage   52. _____
53. resources   53. _____
54. appearence   54. _____
55. rehearsal   55. _____
56. departmental   56. _____
57. sacrilegious   57. _____
58. subdivision   58. _____
59. self-evident   59. _____

60. over-charge   60. _____
61. primery   61. _____
62. cessation   62. _____
63. obediance   63. _____
64. employees   64. _____
65. conspicuous   65. _____
66. assinement   66. _____
67. thier   67. _____
68. effectual   68. _____
69. acreage   69. _____
70. frequently   70. _____
71. commisioner   71. _____
72. alien   72. _____
73. embarassment   73. _____
74. conference   74. _____
75. have'nt   75. _____
76. admissible   76. _____

77. allowance   77. _____
78. wellcome   78. _____
79. salarys   79. _____
80. proffitable   80. _____
81. engineerred   81. _____
82. interview   82. _____
83. procedure   83. _____
84. nineth   84. _____
85. simultanous   85. _____
86. handicaped   86. _____
87. foriegner   87. _____
88. italicize   88. _____
89. overhear   89. _____
90. evaluation   90. _____

Section C—Grammar, Punctuation, and Capitalization

Directions: Some of the following sentences are correct as written. Others contain an error of grammar, punctuation, or capitalization. On the lines beside each sentence, rewrite the sentence correctly. If the sentence contains no error, write "Correct as written."

1. He was not informed, that he would have to work overtime. 1. _____

2. The wind blew several papers off of his desk. 2. _____

3. Charles Dole, who is a member of the committee, was asked to confer with commissioner Wilson. 3. _____

4. Miss Bell will issue a copy to whomever asks for one. 4. _____

5. Most employees, and he is no exception do not like to work overtime. 5. _____

6. This is the man whom you interviewed last week. 6. _____

7. Of the two cities visited, White Plains is the cleanest. 7. _____

8. Although he was willing to work on other holidays, he refused to work on labor day. 8. _____

9. If an employee wishes to attend the conference, he should fill out the necessary forms. 9. _____

10. The division chief reports that an engineer and an inspector is needed for this special survey. 10. _____

11. The work was assigned to Miss Green and me. 11. _____

12. The staff regulations state that an employee, who is frequently tardy, may receive a negative evaluation. 12. _____

13. He is the kind of person who is always willing to undertake difficult assignments. 13. _____

Typical Private Sector Clerical Examination / 223

14. Mr. Wright's request cannot be granted under no conditions.

15. George Colt a new employee was asked to deliver the report to the Domestic Relations Court.

16. The supervisor entered the room and said, "The work must be completed today."

17. The employees were given their assignments and, they were asked to begin work immediately.

18. The letter will be sent to the United States senate this week.

19. When the supervisor entered the room, he noticed that the book was laying on the desk.

20. All the clerks, including those who have been appointed recently are required to work on the new assignment.

21. One of our clerks were promoted yesterday.

22. Between you and me, I would prefer not going there.

23. The National alliance of Businessmen is trying to persuade private businesses to hire youth in the summertime.

24. The supervisor who is on vacation, is in charge of processing vouchers.

25. The activity of the committee at its conferences is always stimulating.

26. After checking the addresses again, the letters went to the mailroom.

27. The director, as well as the employees, are interested in sharing the dividends.

28. Mrs. Black the supervisor of the unit, has many important duties.

29. We spoke to the man whom you saw yesterday.

30. When a holiday falls on sunday, it is officially celebrated on monday.   30. _____

31. Neither Mr. Smith nor Mr. Jones was able to finish his assignment on time.   31. _____

32. The task of filing these cards is to be divided equally between you and he.   32. _____

33. He is an employee whom we consider to be efficient.   33. _____

34. I believe that the new employees are not as punctual as us.   34. _____

35. The employees, working in this office, are to be congratulated for their work.   35. _____

Section D—Proofreading

Directions: The letter which follows contains far more errors than you are likely to encounter in anything which you must proofread. Read through the letter and make your corrections directly on the page, between the lines and in the margins. Then type the letter, incorporating all of your corrections. The correctly typed letter appears on page 216. Each corrected error is underlined and numbered. Following the corrected letter, you will find an explanation for each correction.

january 24th, 1993

Mr Steven p Anderson
Alacon Manufacturin Comp. Inc
387 Bramson Bullevard
Waltham, MA., 02154

Re: Red worsted wool
Die lot no 68423

My Dear Mr. Andreson,

My knitting store Wooly crafts of 12 Myrtle Ln., Beloit, Wisconsin, tole me to right to you to tell you, about my disappointtion with you're wool. I bought sevin skeins of wool to make a sweater in decembr of 1991. After a few month's i put the work a side. last week i buyed another skien of the same die lot 64823 to finnish the the sweater. The red does'nt match, it is not the same.

Mrs Browne the store Manager said that "The yarn is two old. That may be so, but i read on the rapper that you offer a garantee. The garante says this wool will not fade." Be sure to match die lots. satisfaction is garanteed."

The hole sweater is know good. I am non satisfied. You could:

1) send me a refund for all nine skeins of wool
b) send me new wool

I am wait for you'r reply as to how you plan to handel my complain?

Very Truly Yours:

Mollie Jones Customer

Correct Answers

Section A—Filing

Correct alphabetical filing is made much easier when all names are placed in reverse order, that is, with last name first.

1. Duncan, A.
   Dunn, Adam
   Dunn, E.
   Dunn, Edward Robert

2. Moore, Paul
   Moore, Paul A.
   Moore, William
   Moore, William Allen

3. Banner, Charles
   Cambell, Howard
   Carver, William
   Chambers, Arthur

4. Peters, G.
   Peters, George
   Petersen, E.
   Petersen, Eric

5. Hallam, Edward
   Hallam, Edward A.
   Hamilton, Joseph F.
   Hamilton, Jos. Frank

6. DeGraff, James
   Gordon, Arthur
   O'Hara, William
   von Glatin, Anne

7. MacLane, Thomas
   Madison, Theodore
   Madison, Thomas A.
   McGill, Timothy

8. Petersen, Irene F., Miss
   Petersen, N. A., Prof.
   Peterson, Chas. D., Dr.
   Peterson, Lawrence E.

9. Gabriel, Marian, Mrs.
   Gabriel, Marie Doris
   Gabriel, Marjorie N.
   La Gabriel, Edward

10. Restman, H.
    Restman, Herbert
    Restmore, H.
    Restmore, Harry

11. Macalan, Timothy
    MacAllister, Thomas
    McAlden, Fred
    McAllen, Frank, Mrs.

12. De Vance, Wallace
    La Vance, Peter
    Vance, Leonard
    Van Meer, George

13. Devin, Sarah
    Devine, S.
    Devine, Sara H.
    Devine, Sarah

14. Benett, Chuck
    Bennet, C.
    Bennet, Chas.
    Bennett, Charles

15. Rivera, Ilena
    Rivere, I.
    Riviera, Ilana
    Riviera, Ilene

16. Carrale, Robert, Prof.
    Corral, Robert, Dr.
    Corren, R.
    Corret, Ron

17. Levene, Kurt
    Levene, Kurt E.
    Levine, Charles
    Levine, Chas. A.

18. Kincade, Lillian
    Kinkade, Albert A., Dr.
    Kinkaid, Alan, Mr.
    Kinkaid, Geo., Prof.

19. Green, Charles
    Greene, Chas. T.
    Greene, Charles Thomas
    Greene, Wm. A.

20. MacAllister, Doris
    MacBride, Lewis T.
    McAllen, D.
    McBride, Lewis

21. Pierce, R. Bruce
    Pierce, Robert B.
    Pierce, Robert Bruce
    Pierce, Ronald

22. La Stella, Elaine
    Stair, Charlotte
    Stare, C. B.
    Stare, Charles B.

23. Albrecht, Frieda
    Appelman, George
    Borenstein, James
    Brown, Samuel

24. MacNamara, Ruth
    Mason, Frances
    McCormack, James
    McGillicudy, Kathryn

25. Martanson, M.
    Martinson, A. S.
    Martinson, Albert
    Martinson, Albert S.

Section B—Spelling

1. C
2. C
3. C
4. dictator
5. accidentally
6. C
7. auxiliary
8. C
9. receivable
10. C
11. proxy
12. C
13. C
14. pertinent
15. C
16. satisfactorily
17. C
18. bookkeeping
19. beforehand
20. C
21. C
22. machinery
23. C
24. bankruptcy
25. C
26. polish
27. C
28. typographical
29. C
30. performance
31. C
32. C
33. carefully
34. C
35. C
36. C
37. distortion
38. C
39. C
40. C
41. C
42. notary
43. memoranda
44. elimination
45. C
46. referred
47. C
48. shelves
49. C
50. C

51. occurrence
52. gauge
53. C
54. appearance
55. C
56. C
57. C
58. C
59. C
60. overcharge
61. primary
62. C
63. obedience
64. C
65. C
66. assignment
67. their
68. C
69. C
70. C
71. commissioner
72. C

73. embarrassment
74. C
75. haven't
76. C
77. C
78. welcome
79. salaries
80. profitable
81. engineered
82. C
83. C
84. ninth
85. simultaneous
86. handicapped
87. foreigner
88. C
89. C
90. C

SECTION C—GRAMMAR, PUNCTUATION, AND CAPITALIZATION

1. He was not informed <u>that</u> he would have to work overtime. There is no reason for a comma between the verb and its object.

2. The wind blew several papers <u>off his</u> desk. *Off of* is unacceptable usage.

3. Charles Dole, who is a member of the committee, was asked to confer with Commis-sioner Wilson. *Commissioner Wilson* is a specific commissioner, so the <u>C</u> must be capitalized.

4. Miss Bell will issue a copy to <u>whoever</u> asks for one. *Whoever* is the subject of the verb *asks*.

5. Most employees, and he is no exceptio<u>n,</u> do not like to work overtime. A parenthetical expression must *always* be enclosed by commas.

230 / Clerical Exams Handbook

6. This sentence is correct.

7. Of the two cities visited, White Plains is the <u>cleaner</u>. The comparative *er* is used when only two items are being compared. *Est* requires three or more items.

8. Although he was willing to work on other holidays, he refused to work on <u>L</u>abor <u>D</u>ay. *Labor Day* is a proper name; it must have initial caps.

9. This sentence is correct.

10. The division chief reports that an engineer and an inspector <u>are</u> needed for this special survey. A plural subject requires a plural verb.

11. This sentence is correct.

12. The staff regulations state that an employ<u>ee who</u> is frequently tard<u>y may</u> receive a negative evaluation. A restrictive clause, that is, a clause that is vital to the meaning of a sentence, should not be set off by commas.

13. This sentence is correct.

14. Mr. Wright's request cannot be granted under <u>any</u> conditions. Use of a double negative is not permitted.

15. George Colt<u>, a</u> new employee<u>,</u> was asked to deliver the report to the Domestic Relations Court. "*A new employee*" is an appositive and must be set off by commas.

16. This sentence is correct.

17. The employees were given their assignments<u>,</u> and they were asked to begin work immediately. Two independent clauses connected by *and* must be separated by a comma placed before the *and*.

18. The letter will be sent to the United States <u>S</u>enate this week. This very specific *Senate* must begin with a capital letter.

19. When the supervisor entered the room, he noticed that the book was <u>lying</u> on the desk. The verb *to lay* should be used only when it could be replaced with the verb *to put*. At all other times use a form of the verb *to lie*.

20. All the clerks, including those who have been appointed recently<u>,</u> are required to work on the new assignment. Omitting the clause "*including those who have been appointed recently*" does not change the meaning of the remaining words. Therefore, this is a nonrestrictive clause and should be set off by commas.

21. One of our clerks <u>was</u> promoted yesterday. The subject of the sentence is *one*, which takes a singular verb.

22. This sentence is correct.

23. The National Alliance of Businessmen is trying to persuade private businesses to hire youth in the summertime. Each important word in the name of the organization must begin with a capital letter.

24. The supervisor, who is on vacation, is in charge of processing vouchers, OR The supervisor who is on vacation is in charge of processing vouchers. The first version indicates that there is only one supervisor and that supervisor happens to be on vacation. In this case, "who is on vacation" is a nonrestrictive clause and is set off by commas. The second version indicates that there are several supervisors, but the one in charge of processing vouchers is on vacation. In this case, "who is on vacation" is a restrictive clause and should not be set off by commas. The sentence is correct with either two commas or with no commas, depending on the meaning intended, but one comma is definitely wrong.

25. This sentence is correct.

26. After the addresses were checked again, the letters went to the mailroom. As the sentence was originally written, the letters did the checking of the addresses.

27. The director, as well as the employees, is interested in sharing the dividends. The *director* is the subject of the sentence and requires a singular verb.

28. Mrs. Black, the supervisor of the unit, has many important duties. *The supervisor of the unit* is an appositive and must be set off by commas.

29. This sentence is correct.

30. When a holiday falls on Sunday, it is officially celebrated on Monday. Days of the week must be capitalized.

31. This sentence is correct.

32. The task of filing these cards is to be divided equally between you and him. *Him* is an object of the preposition *between*.

33. This sentence is correct.

34. I believe that the new employees are not as punctual as we. *As* is an adverb and so does not take an object. You can check your answer in such an instance by silently finishing off the sentence "...*as we are.*"

35. The employees working in this office are to be congratulated for their work. *Working in this office* is a restrictive clause so must not be set off by commas.

232 / *Clerical Exams Handbook*

SECTION D—PROOFREADING—CORRECTLY TYPED LETTER

January 24, 1993
$\overline{1}$ $\overline{2}$

Mr. Steven P. Anderson
$\overline{3}$ $\overline{4}\overline{5}$

Alacon Manufacturing Co. Inc.
$\overline{6}\overline{7}\overline{8}$

387 Bramson Boulevard
$\overline{9}$

Waltham, MA 02154
$\overline{}$
$\overline{10,11}$

              Re: Red worsted wool
              Dye lot no. 68423
              $\overline{12}$ $\overline{13}$

My dear Mr. Anderson:
$\overline{14}\overline{15}\overline{16}$

    My knitting store, Wooly Crafts, of 12 Myrtle Lane, Beloit, Wisconsin, told me to
$\overline{17}\overline{18}\overline{19}\overline{20}\overline{21}$
write to you to tell you about my disappointment with your wool.
$\overline{22}\overline{23}\overline{24}\overline{25}$

    I bought seven skeins of wool to make a sweater in December of 1991. After a few
$\overline{26}\overline{27}\overline{28}$
months I put the work aside. Last week I bought another skein of the same dye lot 68423
$\overline{29}\overline{30}\overline{31}\overline{32}\overline{33}\overline{34}\overline{35}\overline{36}\overline{37}$
to finish the sweater. The red doesn't match; it is not the same.
$\overline{38}\overline{39}\overline{40}\overline{41}$

    Mrs. Browne, the store manager, said that the yarn is too old. That may be so, but I
$\overline{42}\overline{43}\overline{44}\overline{45}\overline{46}\overline{47}\overline{48}$
read on the wrapper that you offer a guarantee. The guarantee says, "This wool will not
$\overline{49}\overline{50}\overline{51}\overline{52}\overline{53}\overline{54}$
fade. Be sure to match dye lots. Satisfaction is guaranteed."
$\overline{55}\overline{56}\overline{57}\overline{58}\overline{59}$

    The whole sweater is no good. I am not satisfied. You could:
$\overline{60}\overline{61}\overline{62}$

1) send me a refund for all eight skeins of wool
$\overline{63}$

2) send me new wool
$\overline{64}$

I am waiting for your reply as to how you plan to handle my complaint.
$\overline{65}\overline{66}\overline{67}\overline{68}\overline{69}$

                      Very truly yours,
                        $\overline{70}\overline{71}\overline{72}$

Mollie Jones, Customer
$\overline{73}$

EXPLANATIONS

1. Capitalize days of the week, months of the year, and holidays.

2. When typing a full date, do not use *th* or *rd*.

3. Use a period after an abbreviation.

4. Capitalize all proper names. The initial stands for the name.

5. Use a period after the initial in a person's name.

6. Spelling error.

7. The abbreviation of *Company* is *Co*. There may or may not be a comma between *Co.* and *Inc.*, depending upon the actual company name. An error cannot be assumed.

8. Use a period after an abbreviation.

9. Spelling error.

10. Do not use a period after official Postal Service two-letter state name designations.

11. Do not use a comma between Postal Service two-letter state name designation and ZIP code.

12. Incorrect word choice. The word referring to color is "dye."

13. Use a period after an abbreviation.

14. Capitalize only first and last words, titles, and proper names in the salutation.

15. Spelling error. See inside address, above.

16. Use a colon after the salutation in a business letter.

17. An appositive must be set off by commas.

18. Capitalize all proper names, including, but not limited to, names of people.

19. An appositive must be set off by commas. (See #17)

20. Abbreviate *street*, *road*, *lane*, etc., only on the envelope and the inside address.

21. Spelling error.

22. Wrong word choice.

23. Comma is not needed here.

234 / Clerical Exams Handbook

24. The word, as written, does not exist.

25. *You're* is the contraction for *you are*. The correct possessive of *you* is *your*.

26. Begin a new paragraph for a new thought.

27. Spelling error.

28. Capitalize days of the week and months of the year. Also spelling error here.

29. This should not be a possessive. The plural of *month* is *months*.

30. Capitalize the letter *I* when it stands alone.

31. One word.

32. Capitalize the first word of a complete sentence.

33. Capitalize the letter *I* when it stands alone.

34. The past tense of *buy* is *bought*.

35. Spelling error.

36. Incorrect word choice. (See #12)

37. Typographical error. Check against dye lot number in reference line.

38. Spelling error.

39. Repeated word.

40. In a contraction, insert an apostrophe in place of the omitted letter or letters. Here, does + not = doesn't.

41. A semicolon may be used to join two short, related independent clauses. As originally written, this is a comma splice.

42. Use a period after an abbreviation.

43. An appositive must be set off by commas.

44. A nonspecific title should not be capitalized.

45. An appositive must be set off by commas. (See #43)

46. The word "that" introduces an indirect quote. An indirect quote must not be enclosed by quotation marks.

47. Wrong word choice. The word meaning "excessively" is *too*.

48. Capitalize the letter *I* when it stands alone.

49. Spelling error.

50. Spelling error.

51. Spelling error.

52. A comma separates a short direct quotation from the speaker.

53. All directly quoted material must be enclosed by quotation marks.

54. Capitalize the first word of a complete sentence.

55. The quotation does not end here.

56. Word choice. (See #12 and #36)

57. Capitalize the first word of a complete sentence.

58. Spelling error.

59. A period *always* goes inside the quotation marks, whether the quotation marks are used to denote quoted material, to set off titles, or to isolate words used in a special sense.

60. Wrong word choice. The word meaning "entire" is *whole*.

61. Wrong word choice. The negative is *no*.

62. Spelling error.

63. Look back at the letter to be sure all facts are accurate and internally consistent. $7 + 1 = 8$.

64. Internal style must be consistent too. The figure *1)* must be followed by *2)*; *a)* and *b)* would be equally acceptable.

65. Word ending omitted.

66. The correct possessive form of *you* is *your*.

67. Spelling error.

68. Spelling error.

69. Do not use a question mark after an indirect question; use a period.

70. Capitalize only the first word in a complimentary closing.

71. Capitalize only the first word in a complimentary closing.

72. The complimentary close of a letter is followed by a comma.

73. Use a comma to separate a name from a title.